Comprehension Assessment

Solving Problems in the Teaching of Literacy

Cathy Collins Block, Series Editor

Recent Volumes

Comprehension Assessment

A Classroom Guide

JoAnne Schudt Caldwell

THE GUILFORD PRESS
New York   London

© 2008 The Guilford Press
A Division of Guilford Publications, Inc.
72 Spring Street, New York, NY 10012
www.guilford.com

Printed in the United States of America

This book is printed on acid-free paper.

Last digit is print number: 9   8   7   6   5   4   3   2   1

Library of Congress Cataloging-in-Publication Data

Caldwell, JoAnne (JoAnne Schudt)
    Comprehension assessment : a classroom guide / by JoAnne Schudt Caldwell.
        p.   cm. — (Solving problems in the teaching of literacy)
    Includes bibliographical references and index.
    ISBN 978-1-59385-707-3 (pbk. : alk. paper) — ISBN 978-1-59385-708-0
(hardcover : alk. paper)
    1. Reading comprehension—Ability testing.   2. Reading—Ability testing.
I. Title.
    LB1050.45.C335 2008
    372.48—dc22
                                                   2008002156

About the Author

JoAnne Schudt Caldwell, PhD, is a Professor at Cardinal Stritch University in Milwaukee, Wisconsin. She is presently the Associate Dean of the College of Education and Leadership. Dr. Caldwell is the author of *Reading Assessment* (2nd ed.); coauthor, with Lauren Leslie, of *Qualitative Reading Inventory—4* and *Intervention Strategies to Follow Informal Reading Inventory Assessment: So What Do I Do Now?*; and coauthor, with Joyce Holt Jennings and Janet W. Lerner, of *Reading Problems: Assessment and Teaching Strategies.*

Preface

Teachers are incredibly busy individuals. Elementary teachers teach a variety of subjects. Middle school and high school teachers teach a variety of students and may meet as many as six different groups over the course of the school day. Like all professionals, teachers continually want to update their skills. However, they are part of a system that makes it extremely difficult to do so. Although schools and districts schedule regular professional development opportunities that offer teachers opportunities to learn about best practices, districts seldom include the time or opportunity for application or ongoing discussion. Teachers have little time to interact with their peers, and prep periods are seldom scheduled so that they can engage in professional dialogue and team planning. As a result, teachers often find it difficult to translate new learning into effective action. Teachers are also on the proverbial firing line. No Child Left Behind legislation has forced accountability on our nation's schools in the form of standardized test scores, and if test scores are low, it is usually the teachers who are blamed.

This book is based on three principles. First, comprehension assessment in the classroom can and should improve. Few teachers would disagree with that statement. Students cannot learn unless they comprehend, and it is the role of the teacher to foster and assess their comprehension. How to best assess comprehension is a topic that spontaneously and often comes up in discussions with both elementary and secondary teachers. Second, comprehension assessment can improve only to the extent that teachers are able, within the confines of their professional and personal obligations, to make reasonable changes. A massive and instant transformation of classroom practice is not going to occur, but under the right conditions small steps can gradually lead to big ones. Change is difficult and occurs only if approached in small increments and with appropriate support. Third, the relative isolation of classroom teachers is not conducive to change of any kind. It needs to be broken, and teachers should have an opportunity to collaborate with their peers in improving classroom practice.

This book is for all teachers—primary, elementary, middle school, and secondary—because although there are many variations in classrooms at different levels, there is one constant: Students cannot learn unless they comprehend, and it is the role of the teacher to foster and assess their comprehension.

If I could mandate how this book would be used, it would be as a means of informing and enhancing classroom comprehension instruction and assessment. This is primarily a book for individual teachers to read and apply in small steps to their classroom practice. It is not a book for researchers, although it is based on research. It is a book for busy practitioners who know there are better ways to assess comprehension and want some suggestions for doing so. Most chapters list possible guidelines for teachers to implement, not all at once, but over a period of time and according to their individual classroom needs.

A school or district director of instruction or a principal could use this book as a guide for implementing change over the course of several years. This would not be a quick fix (seldom are such fixes very effective or lasting). Teachers and administrators could form a learning community, read the book, discuss its contents and work together over time to put new policies and practices into operation. Why would this be a good idea? If comprehension assessment improves and becomes more fine-tuned, educators will know much more about their students—what they can do and what they still need to learn. Such knowledge can lead to more focused instruction and, if instruction improves, the comprehension and learning of students can similarly increase. And who knows? Those standardized test scores may increase as well!

I have made every attempt to construct a readable book, one that can be easily comprehended. Allied to this is my attempt to craft a pragmatic book, one with suggestions that can be carried out by an individual educator according to the needs of his or her classroom. The book begins with a definition of that complex entity we call comprehension and moves to a discussion of the assessment process. After a discussion of basic principles of comprehension assessment, it addresses several methods for assessing comprehension: questions, open-ended assessments, student dialogue, word learning, and comprehension assessment proxies. The final chapters address classroom grading and standardized testing and include a modest proposal for using classroom comprehension assessment as a complement or counterpart to standardized testing.

Teachers in our schools are doing a great job, but most would say they could be doing better. This book is for those teachers.

Contents

CHAPTER 1

Defining Comprehension

A Difficult Task

Overview

Comprehension assessment is usually thought of in relation to reading. Students read standardized test passages and indicate their comprehension by answering questions. They read stories, novels, and textbooks, and teachers assess their understanding of the content in a variety of ways. However, we also assess students' comprehension after listening and viewing. Students participate in class discussions, and they listen to their teachers. They have access to multimedia/ hypermedia. They watch demonstrations and pay attention to explanations. They contribute to class projects and conduct experiments. Educators need to know what students have comprehended as a result of these varied activities.

We read, listen, watch, and participate in a variety of experiences for two basic reasons: to learn and to enjoy. Sometimes these two purposes converge, as when an avid gardener reads a book or watches a televised garden show on how to grow orchids. Although the gardener's primary purpose is to increase knowledge, the process of reading or watching a show about a favorite subject is also a pleasurable one. At other times, learning may not be as enjoyable. Consider how we feel as we read income tax instructions and mortgage agreements, or listen to an insurance agent explain why our policy does not cover an accident or illness. Our knowledge increases, but we would hardly consider the process a pleasant one. However, whether we are involved in learning or enjoyment, the center of the experience is our successful comprehension. We cannot learn if we do not understand, and something that is meaningless gives little pleasure and has less purpose.

This is a book about comprehension assessment, so it must begin by defining comprehension. This is not an easy task. In fact, some would consider it an impossible one. Comprehension is an unobservable mental process. It is also an extremely complicated and multifaceted entity, and despite decades of research we do not completely understand it. As educators, we must learn as much as possible about the comprehension process, but we must also accept the fact that our understanding of it will never be complete.

Comprehension after Reading, Listening, or Viewing

Reading and Listening Comprehension

Is comprehension after reading the same as comprehension after listening? Oral and written language basically share the same vocabulary and the same grammar. *Dog* has the same meaning whether we read the three-letter word or hear its spoken counterpart. For the most part, word order and tense are the same. For example, nouns usually precede verbs, and adjectives usually precede nouns. The affix *ing* indicates something is happening in the present, and *ed* signals a past event. "Reading seems to depend on a set of language processes that are common to both reading and listening" (Daneman, 1991, p. 526), as suggested by the fact that good readers tend to be good listeners and poor readers tend to be poor listeners. In addition, at all age levels there are very strong correlations between reading comprehension and listening comprehension, which has led to the conclusion that "reading comprehension ability is indistinguishable from listening comprehension ability" (Palmer, MacCleod, Hunt, & Davidson, as cited in Daneman, 1991, p. 526).

Of course, there are differences. In reading we do not have access to the context of the listening situation, the body language of the speaker, and the speaker's tone of voice. Listeners use these to interpret meaning. Depending on prior conversation, tone of voice, and the attitude of the speaker, a listener can interpret "Shut up!" as an expression of extreme surprise or as an angry warning to stop talking. In reading, we can go back to the text and review what was read, something impossible to do when listening unless the dialogue is taped or transcribed in some way. A more obvious difference is input, oral versus written. In listening, the brain must decode a series of sounds and attach meaning to them. In reading, the brain must decode a series of letters and letter patterns, match them to recognizable patterns of sounds, and then attach meaning.

The existence of a close relationship between listening and reading comprehension is based on several premises. One involves reading potential (Sticht & James, 1984). Oral language develops to a high degree before written language, and a "person's oral language comprehension level establishes a goal or potential for what can be comprehended through reading" (p. 294). There are strong correlations between oral language skills measured in preschool and kindergarten and later reading ability, with language skills being as the most important predictor of reading achievement (Paris, Carpenter, Paris, & Hamilton, 2005). Do our brains do different things when we read a story versus listen to the same story on a CD? Research strongly suggests that comprehension of the same text following listening or reading generates the same meaning structures, as indicated by ideas recalled and inferences made, thus supporting the suggestion that "internally, reading and auding are the same language" (Sticht & James, 1984, p. 303).

Viewing Comprehension

What about comprehension of visual stimuli such as demonstrations, videos, and other multimedia? Some theorists suggest that visual material and verbal material are processed differently (Paivio, 1986, cited in Kamil, Intrator, & Kim, 2000). This dual coding theory explains comprehension in terms of a verbal system and a nonverbal, or visual, system. The visual system handles graphics and text; the auditory system handles sound and speech. The two systems can function independently or in an integrated fashion. The nonverbal system, often referred to as the imagery system, also handles representation of affect or emotional response to stimuli. It is suggested that information processed in two modalities may be more easily remembered than information stored in a single code (Sadowski, Goetz, & Fritz, 1993). In contrast to the dual coding theory, Van den Broek et al. (2005) suggest that children who are good comprehenders following listening are also good comprehenders of televised segments. They propose that "comprehension skills are not specific to a particular medium but generalize across comprehension contexts" (p. 123).

The dual coding theory has been applied to comprehension of multimedia (Mayer & Moreno, 1998; Moreno & Mayer, 2000). Multimedia is defined as a medium that consists of multiple information sources such as printed words, spoken words, pictures, diagrams, animation, and forms of simulation. Verbal information such as printed and spoken words enter the verbal system. Pictures, animation, and simulation enter the visual system. The learner selects relevant aspects of each and organizes the information in each system into a meaningful interpretation. Finally, the learner builds connections between the information present in the two systems. Chun and Plass (1977) describe the learner as actively selecting significant images and words from a multimedia experience. The learner then "organizes these words and images into coherent mental representations and integrates the newly constructed verbal and visual representations with one another" (p. 66).

One might suppose that such a complex process would affect comprehension negatively; however, this is not the case. Dual coding of information actually enhances comprehension under certain conditions. Although comprehension and learning may be enhanced by multimedia, there are no suggestions that comprehension resulting from multimedia experiences differs in any qualitative way from comprehension following reading or listening. Factors such as expertise, motivation, and type of material affect comprehension of multimedia just as they affect comprehension of written or spoken text.

Most research on comprehension has focused on comprehension of written text—that is, reading comprehension. However, given that reading and listening comprehension are often viewed as parallel processes, much of what can be said about comprehension during and after reading can be applied to the act of listening as well. We know much less about the process of comprehending visual stimuli, and until there is more definitive information to guide our efforts, it makes sense to assess student learning in that modality using the same basic principles that guide assessment of listening and reading comprehension.

The perspective of viewing comprehension as similar across reading, listening, and viewing is supported by Kintsch (1998). Kintsch regards comprehension as representative of cognition itself. Whether an individual reads, listens, or views, the products of comprehension are mental representations and the actions that result from them. Kintsch believes that all mental operations can be described as basic linguistic units or propositions that represent "meaning at multiple levels including the perceptual, action, linguistic and abstract-symbolic levels" (p. 47).

At Last! A Definition

Reading comprehension is "the process of simultaneously extracting and constructing meaning through interaction and involvement with written language" (RAND Reading Study Group, 2002, p.11). The same definition could apply to listening comprehension and comprehension of visual stimuli if we change "involvement with written language" to "involvement with oral language" or "involvement with visual stimuli." Comprehension encompasses three components: an active process of comprehending; the skill, knowledge base, and motivation of the comprehender; and the difficulty and characteristics of the text that is read, listened to, or watched. Let us begin our examination of comprehension by examining what we do when we read, keeping in mind that this probably applies to listening as well and may also describe comprehension of visual stimuli.

The Process of Comprehending

"Comprehension is not a single unitary process" (Kintsch & Kintsch, 2005, p. 7). The reader actively engages in a variety of simultaneous processes. First the reader moves from the words on the page to meaning in the mind. Kintsch and Kintsch (2005) refer to this activity as "decoding processes" involving both perceptual and conceptual components. The reader recognizes individual words, using memory and knowledge of letter and sound patterns, and matches the resulting pronunciations to meaning. The reader then connects these words into "chunks of meaning" or idea units, which are often referred to as propositions. Consider the following example:

> *Peter stroked the shivering cat and it began to purr loudly. He noticed how thin it was and wished he was drinking cold milk instead of hot coffee. The little thing seemed friendly as it rubbed against his leg. Peter had never owned a pet but he found the idea rather appealing. So, after a bit of thought, he picked it up and headed home.*

The reader who comprehends the first sentence will understand four idea units or propositions: Peter stroked the cat; the cat was shivering; the cat began to purr; and the purring was loud. The second sentence contains seven propositions: Peter noticed the cat; the cat was thin; Peter wished for something; the wish was to be drinking milk; the milk was cold; Peter was drinking coffee; and the coffee was hot. The reader connects these separate idea units within and across sentences. For example, the reader connects *Peter* in the first sentence to the pronoun *he* in the second sentence. The reader connects the pronoun *it* in the first and second sentences to *cat* and recognizes that it was the cat that was shivering, purring, and thin, not Peter. The reader identifies the "little thing" as the cat and recognizes that Peter was drinking, not the cat. This network of interrelated idea units is called a microstructure. As the reader continues to read, he or she eventually arrives at the gist of the passage, often referred to as the macrostructure. For example, the reader's gist of this short paragraph might be that Peter found a stray cat that he took home.

Together, the microstructure and macrostructure form the text base, "the mental representation that the reader constructs of the text" (Kintsch & Kintsch, 2005, p. 73). One may conceptualize the microstructure as the details and the macrostructure as the main ideas. A reader's retelling will probably include elements of both, although a good summary would primarily reflect the macro-structure. Kintsch and Kintsch (2005) caution that good comprehension does not involve the number of idea units recalled but the quality of those that are remembered. Good comprehension involves the recognition and recall of important idea units, not insignificant ones.

The text base remains close to the text or the author's meaning. However, much more goes into comprehension. The reader integrates the text with his or her prior knowledge, which can involve visual images, emotions, and personal experiences. In short, the reader constructs inferences based on information present in the text and his or her own prior knowledge. Inferences have often been termed "reading between the lines." Whenever a reader figures out something that the author does not explicitly state, he or she is making an inference. What does Peter look like? The author does not say. The fact that he was drinking coffee suggests an adult. The fact that the cat was shivering and the coffee was hot suggests that the day was cold and Peter may have been dressed accordingly. Where did Peter meet the cat? Again, the author does not say, but one reader may place Peter in his yard and another may place him in a city park. The reader is free to embellish the text in this way but only until the author specifically states, for example, that Peter was a middle-aged man strolling in the park. If the author describes Peter in this way, the reader must then adjust his or her text base to match the author's.

Emotions and personal experiences can play an important role in comprehension. A reader who owns cats may feel more sympathy for the cat than one who dislikes animals. The cat lover may also feel very positive toward the kindly Peter. Yet a reader who has had a bad experience with a stray animal may react very negatively to Peter's idea. These additions to the text base are idiosyncratic to each reader and form what Kintsch and Kintsch (2005) call a "situation model."

Suppose, instead of reading about Peter, you engaged in conversation with a friend who related the following:

> *The cat was shivering. When I petted it, it started to purr really loud. It was so thin, and I wished I had some cold milk instead of hot coffee. It was a friendly little thing, and it started to rub against my leg. I've never had a pet, but it seemed like a good idea. So I took it home.*

How would the comprehension process differ once you recognized the words? I suspect not very much. You would understand the propositions, relate ideas to form a microstructure, and arrive at the gist of what your friend was saying, the macrostructure. You would construct a text base and integrate this with your knowledge, your emotions, and your own personal experiences. If your friend does not tell you where and when this happened, you may infer that it was outside in somewhat cold weather. You may also infer that your friend probably does not understand the difficulties of adopting a stray cat, and you may ask some questions or offer some suggestions when your turn in the conversation arrives.

Suppose you watched a television show in which a character encountered a stray cat, picked it up, and headed home. How would your comprehension differ? You would have to make fewer inferences about the character's age, the weather, and the setting. However, you would still construct a text base and make inferences based on your knowledge base as to what might happen next or the wisdom of the character's action.

The Comprehension Process

Perceptual and conceptual decoding:
- Recognizing the meaning of individual words.
- Connecting words into idea units or propositions.

Connecting idea units, recognizing details, and forming the microstructure.

Arriving at the passage gist or main idea (the macrostructure).

Using the microstructure and macrostructure to identify important ideas (the text base).

Integrating the text base with prior knowledge, making inferences and building a situation model (idiosyncratic to each individual).

Learning: remembering the situation model and using it in some way at a later time.

Comprehension and Learning: Same or Different?

Comprehension and *learning* are terms that educators often regard as synonyms and use interchangeably. Gambrell and Mazzoni (1999) define learning as "making meaning" (p. 14) and describe it as an active process of continuously constructing, reconstructing, and connecting new and more complex meanings. This seems very much like the previous definition of comprehension. Is comprehension different from learning? In other words, can we comprehend something but not learn it?

Learning versus Comprehension

Kintsch and Kintsch (2005) define learning as constructing "a situation model that will be remembered and can be used effectively when the information provided by that text is needed in some way at a later time" (p. 76). Learning thus involves remembering, applying, and connecting, components that may not be part of the comprehension process. You may comprehend something but quickly forget and never use or apply it. Learning cannot occur without comprehension, but comprehension can occur without learning, that is, without retrieval and application. Although comprehension can occur in a relatively automatic and unconscious fashion, learning, particularly that fostered in schools, requires a high level of consciousness and intention (Kintsch, 1998).

Every moment of every day is filled with the act of comprehending what we read, see, and hear. We could not function if we did not comprehend the world around us. We comprehend the mood of a coworker, instructions for assembling a toy, or directions to a friend's house, but we do not remember everything we comprehend. Therefore, we cannot make future applications. In short, we do not learn everything we comprehend. As a result, we may misinterpret a coworker's mood in the future. When the toy breaks, we have to find the original directions to repair it. I am often embarrassed about how many times I must request the same directions to a friend's house. At one point I wrote them down, but then forgot where I put the written directions.

Comprehension and learning occur together so often and so naturally that we are not always aware of the process. Suppose you watch a garden show on television and comprehend that the use of a certain pesticide, although effective in getting rid of insects, also has a tendency to harm the root system of a plant. You remember this, and the next time you are in your garage, you apply your knowledge. You check to ascertain whether you have purchased this product, and the next time you buy pesticide, you read the list of contents on the label very carefully to make certain that the offending ingredient is not present. In this case, you learned something; you remembered a piece of content, and you applied your new knowledge to your purchasing practices.

Learning is not always so effortless. In school, the primary goal is to comprehend and learn new content and new skills, and students are often confronted with textbooks, lectures, and media presentations on unfamiliar subjects. Although learning can be an almost automatic process with familiar subject matter, it becomes a deliberate, controlled, and effortful process with unfamiliar content. Comprehending and learning about a pesticide may be an easy and natural process to a gardener. Comprehending and learning about the lytic and lysogenic cycles of viral reproduction is quite another matter.

What about memorization? If people memorize something, haven't they learned it? Unfortunately, people often confuse memory with learning. It is important to remember that learning involves three components: comprehension, memory, and application. If one is missing, there is no learning. I remember my elementary school days when the penalty for rule breaking was to memorize an assigned page of poetry. In this case, I remembered something but I seldom comprehended it. Because I did not understand what I so laboriously memorized, I was not able to make any connections to the works of other authors or to real-life situations. In short, I did not learn.

> ### Categories of Knowledge
>
> Linguistic knowledge
> Unschooled or informal knowledge
> Schooled or formal knowledge
> Subject matter knowledge
> Performance procedures or strategies

Categories of Knowledge

What exactly do we learn? Or, to put it another way, after we have learned, what do we know? Alexander and Jetton (2000) describe several categories of knowledge: linguistic knowledge, schooled and unschooled knowledge, and subject matter knowledge. We acquire linguistic components such as vocabulary knowledge and awareness of different text genres and structures. Unschooled or informal knowledge refers to what we learn, often unconsciously, through everyday experiences, communications with peers, and interactions with different forms of media. For example, we learn to avoid bees when we get stung. We learn the importance of sunscreen when we get sunburnt and the benefits of exercise from our increasing strength and agility. We learn about diabetes from a friend who has the disease, about the necessity of keeping accurate records from our tax preparer, and about the benefits of a cruise vacation from an acquaintance who recently returned from one. We watch television and movies and we read magazines and newspapers. In so doing, we learn about historical events, different cultures, different forms of government, and sports that are not generally known in our area. We are not able to actually identify the sources of most of our unschooled knowledge, which is quite vast and, unfortunately, occasionally inaccurate and colored by individual perceptions and biases (which we have also learned). Formal or schooled knowledge is that body of knowledge acquired through formal schooling. Subject matter knowledge is a form of schooled knowledge that "consists of bodies of conceptual knowledge organized around concepts and principles judged by experts as core to that field" (Alexander & Jetton, 2000, p. 293).

We also learn procedures for performing or for doing something (Bovair & Kieras, 1991; Paris & Paris, 2001). Such procedures are often referred to as strategies. Alexander and Jetton (2000) describe strategies as "how to" knowledge, which can take the form of step-by-step algorithms or broad performance guidelines. Procedural knowledge can be schooled or unschooled. In schools, students learn a variety of strategies for comprehending, for writing, for performing experiments, and for preparing reports. In our everyday life, we also learn a variety of procedures such as pumping gas, taping a television program, running a snow blower, and accessing the Web to purchase an airline ticket.

So, simply put, our knowledge is made up of facts and concepts about many topics as well as procedures for doing many things. An individual's knowledge base is generally quite extensive in some areas and very limited in others. Unfortunately, it can also be accurate or inaccurate and shaped by emotion and previously learned perceptions and prejudices.

Distinguishing between Comprehension and Learning

Why is it important to distinguish between comprehension and learning? This is a book about comprehension assessment, and in the next chapter assessment validity is discussed. A valid assessment instrument measures what it says it measures. To judge validity, it is important to know what an instrument actually assesses. Perhaps some examples can help. A teacher asks students to memorize a certain number of items on the periodic table. The students orally recite these or write them down. Does this assessment measure comprehension or address knowledge application? Probably not. A student can memorize without comprehending the content, and reciting a series of items is not application as Kintsch and Kintsch (2005) define it. Yet the teacher may erroneously describe it as learning. A teacher asks students to read a short selection and retell what they read. In this example, the teacher is assessing comprehension but not application. The teacher may feel confident that the students understood what they read, but the assessment does not indicate that they learned something that can be applied at a later date. But what if the teacher asks students to compare the theme of a short story to selections read earlier in the year? Because the teacher is asking students to retrieve previously learned information and apply it to a new situation, he or she is assessing learning.

What allows individuals to apply knowledge to new situations? They need a body of knowledge about a topic that goes beyond a list of multiple and disjointed facts. Their factual knowledge must be connected and organized around important ideas and concepts (Alexander & Jetton, 2000). Unfortunately, learning is often confused with the accumulation of information and seldom tied to central concepts or principles. "Many curricula fail to support learning with understanding because they present too many disconnected facts in too short a time—the 'mile wide inch deep' problem. Tests often reinforce memorizing rather than understanding" (Bransford, Brown, & Cocking, 2000, p. 24). As a result, students may construct a knowledge base that is "disjointed and piecemeal" (Alexander & Jetton, 2000, p. 287).

There are situations that demand assessment of comprehension and others that require the assessment of learning or application. For example, if I ask a salesclerk to recommend a coffeemaker to meet my specific needs, I am, in a sense, assessing his or her comprehension of my explanation. I do not expect the clerk to remember this at a later date or even to apply it to another customer. However, the role of schools is to promote learning. So it is important that educators understand the difference between comprehension and learning. There will be situations in which they assess comprehension. There are many facts and concepts that students must understand before they can apply their understanding to a new context or situation. A teacher needs to know that these are understood. For example, students must understand the purpose and structure of the League of Nations and the United Nations before they apply that knowledge and compare the two entities. The key is to understand the difference between comprehension and learning and to label the purpose of an assessment accurately.

The Role of the Comprehender

The skills of the comprehender are important components in the comprehension process. Because readers, listeners, and viewers approach the experience with different skills and skill levels, two individuals reading, listening, or viewing the same text may not comprehend it in the same way.

Word-Level Skills

At the most basic level, the listener must recognize that sounds and sound groupings stand for meaning. The reader must recognize that letter and letter chunks such as consonant blends, vowel patterns, prefixes, suffixes, and roots stand for specific sounds. When combined, these sounds represent meaning. In other words, C-O-F-F-E-E can be pronounced as "coffee." The ability to recognize the pronunciation of both familiar and unfamiliar words is one aspect of skilled reading and listening. However, it is only the beginning. Decoding, although necessary, is not sufficient for comprehension to occur.

What else do listeners, readers, and viewers need to do? Hearing "coffee" or pronouncing "coffee" will be meaningless unless the meaning of "coffee" is part of their background knowledge. Possessing an extensive vocabulary base is a critical aspect of comprehension.

Recognizing and comprehending words occurs in short-term memory, which has a limited capacity. Thus, word recognition and word comprehension compete for space. If a reader or listener is fluent, that is, if he or she can automatically and rapidly recognize letter and sound patterns and words, more short-term memory space becomes available for meaning activities. In general, word recognition fluency leads to better understanding of a word's meaning. In the same way, fluency in recognizing spoken words leads to greater understanding. Think about a time when you were learning a new language and your painful efforts to understand what your teacher said.

Text-Level Processes

The importance of prior knowledge in comprehension has been well established (Recht & Leslie, 1988; Alvermann, Smith, & Readance, 1985; Taft & Leslie, 1985; Lipson, 1983; Pearson, Hansen, & Gordon, 1979). Knowledge of the topic or a similar topic permits the reader, listener, or viewer to make inferences, that is, connect clues in the text with what he or she already knows. Inferences embellish the text base; that is, they turn it into a situation model.

> *Helen mowed the undergrowth at the back of her yard. She raked and packed the clippings into large plastic bags. Later that night, her arms and hands broke out in an angry red rash.*

If the reader or listener has some basic knowledge of poison ivy, he or she can infer what probably happened to Helen. One with more extensive knowledge, who knows how long poison ivy rash lasts and how painful it is, will probably have feelings of sympathy for the ordeal that she is facing. The more knowledgeable reader or listener may also conclude that Helen did not wear gloves and feel some exasperation for her stupidity. And of course, a more knowledgeable reader or listener will also have a vivid mental picture of Helen's itching and oozing hands.

Strategies Used to Comprehend and Remember

Overviewing	Constructing diagrams
Paraphrasing	Questioning
Summarizing	Hypothesizing
Rereading	Drawing analogies
Using imagery	Monitoring comprehension
Taking notes	

Comprehension Strategies

There are conscious and controllable processes or strategies that we employ to comprehend and remember text especially when faced with the demands of difficult and unfamiliar selections (Kintsch & Kintsch, 2005; Pressley &

Afflerbach, 1995). These strategies include a variety of possible activities: overviewing, using headings, pictures, and diagrams; paraphrasing; summarizing; selectively rereading; elaborating the content through imagery; making relationships between ideas in the text visible by taking notes and constructing diagrams; formulating questions; drawing, evaluating, and revising hypotheses; forming analogies; revising prior knowledge; and monitoring comprehension. Readers have different levels of skill in each of these areas. Some readers have no knowledge of the effectiveness of such strategies and have little understanding of how to employ them. Other readers use them effectively. Some of the strategies, such as overviewing and rereading, are not options for listeners; other strategies may not be relevant for viewers. However, taking notes, formulating and revising hypotheses, generating questions, producing visual images, and monitoring comprehension are all activities of effective listeners and viewers.

Motivation

Motivation also plays a role, as does the reader's, listener's, or viewer's purpose and interest in the topic. If one is motivated or interested, one is more persistent and tenacious in the face of difficulty. Consider our intent perusal of an insurance form to determine if we qualify for certain benefits, or the care with which we listen to the insurance agent. The difficulty level of a task also influences motivation. Tasks that are too easy become boring; tasks that are too difficult lead to frustration. In addition, learners are more motivated if they can see usefulness in what they are learning or understand how they can use it to positively impact others (Bransford et al., 2000).

Comprehender's Goal

The reader's, listener's, or viewer's goal is another factor. Are we content with a superficial understanding of the text? This may be all we want as we skim a sports story to determine why our favorite team lost or listen to a radio talk show on the way to work. However, if the reader, listener, or viewer is preparing for a test, he or she may engage in a number of the previously mentioned strategies.

Anxiety

Anxiety is another issue. If the reader, listener, or viewer feels threatened, comprehension can suffer. One cannot help but wonder about the effects of high-stakes testing. When well-meaning parents and teachers pressure students to do well, this can cause test anxiety, which may have a negative effect on performance. An additional factor is age. The comprehension of younger readers, listeners, and viewers differs from that of older and more expert comprehenders (Paris et al., 2005).

Word-Level Skills

Pronunciation
Pronunciation fluency
Word comprehension

Text-Level Processes

Existence of prior knowledge
Use of comprehension strategies
Motivation
Interest
Purpose or goal
Anxiety
Age

The Role of the Text

When we think of text, we generally think of written material. In fact, common thesaurus and dictionary synonyms for *text* are *book, manuscript, copy, textbook,* and *wording,* and research on text factors that affect comprehension have primarily focused on written text. However, if we are expanding the definition of comprehension to include listening and viewing, we need to similarly expand our definition of text to include auditory and visual stimuli. Although research has not established the role of various text factors in listening and viewing, it makes sense to consider possible and similar effects of structure, difficulty, and coherence on listening and viewing comprehension.

Text Structure

A variety of intertwining factors make a text easy or difficult. Chief among these is the structure of the text. Is it narrative or expository text? Narratives tend to follow a predictable structure of setting-character-goal/problem-events-resolution and are easier to comprehend and remember than expository texts (Leslie & Caldwell, 1989; Grasser, Golding, & Long, 1991). Consider the ease with which we follow a narrative performance on television or in the movies. This may be because we engage in goal-directed events in our everyday lives and narrative is the primary structure of television and movies. Much of what we listen to is narrative in format as well. We listen to our children describe their day at school, we listen to a friend's summarization of a movie, and we listen to our relatives' account of their vacation. In addition, when reading to children, either at home or at school, we generally read narratives. Thus, the structure of a narrative tends to be familiar to most of us.

The structure of expository text is much less obvious and uniform. Expository text is usually organized around any of five patterns (Taylor, 1982; Jennings, Caldwell, & Lerner, 2006): sequence or time order, listing or description, compare and contrast, cause and effect, and problem and solution. Skilled readers recognize these patterns and use them to facilitate comprehension and memory (Goldman & Rakestraw, 2000). However, these patterns are not always clearly signaled by the author, who may combine two or more patterns in one segment of text. Consider the following text (Cooney et al., 2000).

Clouds are mostly water. To understand how clouds form, remember how changes in temperature affect humidity. Think of a clear spring day where the sun warms the ground, which in turn warms the air. Warm air holds a certain amount of water, and warm air rises. Eventually the warm air cools when it joins the cooler air away from the ground. At the cooler temperature the air cannot hold as much water vapor. As the water vapor separates from the air it connects with dust and microscopic particles of salt to form tiny drops of water. They are so small and light that they float in the air. Collections of millions of these droplets form clouds.

What expository patterns are apparent in this passage? A pattern may be time order, as the text lists the steps in cloud formation. It may also be cause and effect, as the text describes the causes of cloud formation. Another reader may describe the pattern as simple description of a process. It is perhaps less important that a reader, listener, or viewer recognize a specific or "right" pattern; the issue is to recognize some pattern and use it to facilitate comprehension and recall. Skilled comprehenders tend to structure recall according to the dominant structure of the text, as opposed to simply listing facts (Meyer, 2003).

Expository Text Patterns

Sequence or time order
Listing or description
Compare and contrast
Cause and effect
Problem and solution

Listeners regularly encounter expository text throughout the day. They listen to explanations of why the car needs new brakes (cause–effect) and how best to avoid the construction on the freeway (problem–solution). They listen to descriptions of various processes such as how to program the remote or assemble a new kitchen utensil (time order). They listen to news reports and watch television shows about historical events and scientific phenomena (description), and they listen to the family debate various vacation options (compare–contrast). And, of course, much listening and viewing that occurs in the classroom involves exposition. Describing the circulatory system or the structure of matter does not involve a narrative format.

Some text is mixed; that is, it has properties of both narrative and expository structure. This occurs when textbooks insert biographical information regarding individuals in expository chapters.

Text Difficulty

Many factors make a text easy or difficult. I have already discussed the contribution of text structure and noted that narrative text is generally easier than expository. Obviously, text on unfamiliar topics is more difficult than text on familiar concepts. Contrast a descriptive selection on the replication process of viruses with an account of how the ancient Egyptians mummified their dead. Although both employ the descriptive pattern, clearly the selection on viruses would be more difficult for readers who know about mummies, have seen them in a museum, and have probably watched horror films involving mummies returning from their tombs, but who are unfamiliar with viruses.

Familiarity with the topic of the text is closely allied to the vocabulary load of the selection. Vocabulary difficulty is a powerful predictor of text comprehension (RAND Reading Study Group, 2002). A reader who encounters an unfamiliar word has several options: skip the word, attempt to determine its meaning from context, or stop reading and look it up, all of which impede the comprehension process. A listener in the same situation can repeatedly stop the speaker and ask for clarification, but this can be threatening to both speaker and listener. If the reader or listener encounters too many unfamiliar words, difficulty in comprehension may cause the individual to give up and stop reading or cease paying attention to the speaker. Multimedia presentations can also be easy or difficult and can contain a reasonable vocabulary load or one involving multiple new or unrecognized words.

Vocabulary overload often occurs with expository material. Consider a six-paragraph high school science passage that contains at least 30 new words, such as *mitochondria, nanometers, capsid,* and *organelles.* The same passage also includes a number of relatively familiar words used in new ways: *envelope, agent, core, recognize,* and *complimentary.* An accompanying visual includes an equal number of unfamiliar terms. Active and skilled comprehension processing may not make up for this challenge, and comprehension may well be impaired. Listeners also encounter difficult text.

Another factor that can increase text difficulty is the syntax of the text or how phrases are organized into sentences. "Sentences with complex syntax may present comprehension problems or a high load on working memory" (RAND Reading Study Group, 2002, p. 95). For example, sentences with clauses and phrases that occur before the main verb tend to be more difficult. Contrast the following two sentences: *On a cold and windy day in mid-March, Suzie looked out her window* and *Suzie looked out her window on a cold and windy day in mid-March.* In order to comprehend the first sentence, an individual must hold partially interpreted information in memory before arriving at the main proposition explaining Suzie's action. Sentences that contain many clauses and numerous adjectives and adverbs modifying the main noun and verb can also pose difficulty. These are only a few examples of how syntax can impede comprehension.

Usually, spoken syntax is somewhat easier because considerate speakers tailor their messages to the level of the listener. For example, we speak differently to an adult than to a child. We speak differently to a peer than to someone who is not well versed in our discipline. However, that does not mean that listeners do not encounter difficulties. Consider an adult listening to the slang language of adolescents!

Text Coherence

Coherence involves the overall structure of the text and is often referred to as the top-level structure (Meyer, 2003). Coherent texts are cohesive; that is, they are well organized. At the sentence level, authors or speakers clarify how each new piece of information relates to what has already been presented. For example, they signal the relationship between two clauses by using syntactic markers such as *because* and *although,* rather than requiring readers or listeners to infer the connection. At the gist level, authors and speakers clarify the relationships between ideas represented in paragraphs by signaling the introduction of a new topic and by organizing their ideas according to their importance. Coherent texts are easier to read and listen to and are recalled more successfully (Loxterman, Beck, & McKeown, 1994). Consider the following two paragraphs (Davidson, Castillo, & Stoff, 2002):

> *Many immigrants who came to the United States between 1866 and 1915 were farmers of small farms or farm workers who did not own land. The farms were too small to adequately support the families who worked them. Increasing the*

size of the farm was seldom an option. Land was both scarce and expensive. In addition, new farm machinery reduced the need for farm workers.

Persecution pushed many people to immigrate to the United States. During the late 1800s, the Russian government actively supported organized attacks against the Jews. In a similar fashion the Ottoman government killed over a million Armenians between 1890 and 1920. These persecuted groups fled their home land to find sanctuary elsewhere.

Which passage is more user friendly or coherent? Both offer explanations for immigration, but the second one is more explicit. A topic sentence states the main idea of the paragraph and a final summary sentence repeats it.

Another aspect of coherence is the clarity of top-level structure used by the author or speaker (Meyer & Rice, 1984), which was previously discussed under "Text Structure." In addition to the use of pictures, the inclusion of graphs and diagrams can help comprehension if they serve to illustrate important ideas in the text, but they can also confuse the reader if they are irrelevant, distracting, or contain too many unfamiliar concepts (Kintsch & Kintsch, 2005).

Listeners, as well as readers, are influenced by coherence or its absence. How many times have you listened to a poorly organized presentation full of unnecessary repetitions, rambling and confusing explanations, detours into subject matter unconnected to the topic, and an excess of irrelevant examples? When we are talking with peers, we can stop and ask for clarification, but many listening experiences do not allow for this. I remember an advanced statistics class in which I did not have the nerve to raise my hand and tell the professor that I did not understand a word he was saying.

Research has examined the coherence and effectiveness of multimedia presentations on student comprehension. Mayer and Moreno (1998) suggest that multimedia should use two modes of representation instead of one. That is, a presentation that combines listening with viewing is more effective than one that asks students to simply listen or view. If the presentation combines reading with viewing, it is more effective to present the two modalities at the same time, rather than separately. Words presented in an auditory format are easier to comprehend than visual on-screen text. Short, focused presentations that highlight relevant words and pictures are more coherent and thus more effective than longer and denser ones.

Readability Level

The use of readability formulas to determine the difficulty level of text is widespread. Such formulas are used for informal reading inventories, to structure their passages from easy to more difficult. Publishers use these formulas to indicate the difficulty levels of their textbooks. The idea of a single number indicating the difficulty level of a selection is appealing but somewhat unrealistic.

Readability formulas are based on items that can be counted, such as the number of words in a sentence and the number of syllables in a word. It is assumed that shorter sentences and shorter words are easier than longer ones. Some formulas also count the number of unfamiliar words in a selection on the basis of word frequency. Very frequent words are considered familiar, and infrequent ones are not. Thus, *mother* would be regarded as familiar and *matriarch* would be unfamiliar.

The typical practice is to describe text difficulty as a grade level. A text with a readability level of 5.3 is considered more difficult than one at a 2.5 grade level. It is generally assumed that text labeled at a fourth-grade reading level could and should be read by fourth graders or, if one is assessing listening comprehension, should be understood by fourth graders when it is read to them. Assessment of struggling readers is often based on the discrepancy between the readability level of the text they read and their chronological grade levels (Leslie & Caldwell, 2006). Thus, a fourth grader who can only read second-grade text would be considered in need of intervention. Similarly, a fourth grader who can only understand second-grade text in a listening mode would also need intervention.

Other formulas use descriptors other than grade-level designations. Lexiles (MetaMetrics, 2001) are based on sentence length and semantic difficulty and are reported on a scale ranging from 200 to 2,000. Typical Lexile scores are used to describe reader proficiency and test difficulty at different grade levels. Whereas typical readability formulas are primarily based on samples, Lexile scores are determined for entire novels and textbooks.

Readability methods based on sentence and word length and word frequency do predict 49–85% of the variance in comprehension (Meyer, 2003). However, readability in terms of a single number that indicates difficulty is still a limited index if one considers the complexity of the comprehension process (Zakaluk & Samuels, 1988). As indicated earlier in this chapter, many components affect comprehension beyond word and sentence length and word frequency. A reader may be able to comprehend a fourth-grade narrative but fail miserably with a fourth-grade expository selection. A reader may do well with selections on familiar topics and struggle with those on unfamiliar topics. "It makes no sense to talk about the readability of a text as if it were a single characteristic of the text or about the reading ability of a student as if it were a single characteristic of the student" (Kintsch & Kintsch, 2005, p. 85). The difficulty level of a text depends on a variety of components: structure, coherence, reader's prior knowledge, and reader's strategies, to name a few. Acknowledging this complexity, other methods of determining text difficulty have moved beyond sentence length and word difficulty to take account of such factors as text length, layout, illustrations, structure, content, and themes (Chall, Bissex, Conrad, & Harris-Sharples, 1996; Fountas & Pinnell, 1996).

Text Factors

Text structure: narrative and expository
Text difficulty: familiar versus unfamiliar; vocabulary load
Text syntax
Text coherence
Readability

Summary

• A set of language processes is probably common to both reading and listening. Although verbal material and visual material may be processed differently, until there is more definitive information, it makes sense to use the same basic principles to guide assessment of both listening and reading comprehension. The perspective of seeing comprehension as similar across reading, listening, and viewing is supported by Kintsch (1998).

• Comprehension is the process of constructing meaning through interaction and involvement with written language, oral language, and/or visual stimuli. Comprehension involves three components: the active process of comprehending; the skill, knowledge base, and motivation of the comprehender; and the difficulty and characteristics of the text that is read, listened to, or watched.

• The comprehension process involves a variety of simultaneous processes: decoding or moving from letters and sounds to meaning; forming idea units or propositions; connecting idea units to form a text base composed of a microstructure and macrostructure; and building a situation model through interaction with prior knowledge.

• Comprehension and learning are two separate entities. Learning involves comprehending, remembering, and applying. Learning cannot occur without comprehension, but comprehension can occur without learning.

• There are various forms of knowledge that individuals learn: linguistic knowledge, schooled and unschooled knowledge, subject matter knowledge, and procedural knowledge.

• The skills of the comprehender are important components in comprehension. These include word-level skills and text-level processes such as prior knowledge, use of comprehension strategies, motivation, and anxiety.

• Text components affect comprehension. These include text structure, text difficulty, text coherence, and readability level.

Professional Development Activities for Developing Understanding of Comprehension

- Think of something you comprehended very well. Perhaps it was something you read or listened to. Perhaps it was something you viewed, such as a television show. What factors enabled you to comprehend so well? Consider text factors such as structure, difficulty, and coherence. Consider such factors as word-level skills, prior knowledge, strategy usage, motivation, interest, purpose, and anxiety. Which of these factors were primarily involved in your successful comprehension?

- Now consider something that you found extremely difficult to comprehend. (I hope it was not this chapter!) Again, describe those factors that primarily impeded your comprehension.

CHAPTER 2

Defining Assessment
A Four-Step Process

Overview

This is a book about comprehension assessment. I attempted to define comprehension in the first chapter, so it makes good sense to do the same with the concept of assessment. Most people consider assessment primarily in relation to school activities. They think of spelling and math quizzes, yearly standardized test scores, tests following textbook chapters or curriculum units, and tests that qualify students for entrance into certain programs or schools. However, assessment is a much broader concept. It is something that all of us do every day, and we do it so often and so efficiently that we seldom think about it. We take it for granted, and we just do it.

When we assess, we collect evidence and we analyze this evidence. As a result of our analysis, we make a judgment that leads to a decision or to some form of action. For example, every morning most of us assess the weather. Our evidence may be what we see as we look out the window, the local weather report, or a combination of the two. On the basis of our analysis of this evidence, we may choose certain clothes, decide to take an umbrella to work, or make certain that no windows have been left open. After we dress, we usually assess our appearance and, as a result of the evidence, we may change a tie or add a scarf. As we drive to work, we assess the amount and flow of traffic on the freeway and perhaps turn off at the next exit and seek an alternate route. When we arrive at work, we assess the mood of our coworkers by listening to what they say, considering their tone of voice as they say it, and noting their body language. As a result, we may decide to avoid them for the rest of the day.

Assessment: A Four-Step Process

Assessment involves four steps. First, we identify what we want to assess. We usually do this in the form of a question. For example, before we leave for work, we may ask, "Do I need to stop at the grocery store before coming home?" Second, we determine how to collect information or evidence and then we collect it. We probably do a quick check of the contents of our kitchen cupboards and refrigerator. Third, we analyze the evidence. There are enough leftovers for dinner but milk is low, we are into the last loaf of bread, and there is no dessert. Fourth, as a consequence of our analysis, we make a decision. We decide to stop at the grocery store before coming home and, at this point, we may decide to have something else for dinner besides leftovers. After all, if we are going to the store, we might as well get something else.

Four Steps of Assessment Process

Identify what to assess.
Collect information or evidence.
Analyze the evidence.
Make a decision.

Most of the time the assessment process runs so smoothly that we tend to take it for granted. However, when the process fails us, we become very much aware that something has gone wrong. We can run into problems with any of the four steps. Sometimes we are not specific enough as to what we are assessing. Asking, "Do I have to go to the store after work?" may be less effective than asking the more specific question, "Do I have what I need to prepare chicken casserole?" Of course, the effectiveness of any assessment depends on the quality of the evidence we select. A quick glance in the cupboards or refrigerator may provide less sensitive evidence than a more careful perusal based upon a proposed menu or recipe. Sometimes our analysis of the evidence is faulty. We may assume that the box of rice on the shelf contains enough rice for the casserole and discover, too late, that it doesn't. I remember once believing that I had what I needed for a particular dish only to find, when I began to prepare dinner, that the can contained stewed tomatoes, not the chopped tomatoes called for in the recipe. Finally, we can make a wrong decision. Anyone who has ever begun cooking, only to find that key ingredients were missing, knows how that feels.

This four-step assessment process is an integral part of our lives and allows us to function quite efficiently most of the time. It is the same process we use in schools when we assess our students. We identify what we are assessing: word identification, punctuation, math computation, knowledge of specific science content, or another target. We collect evidence, using a variety of formats: observation, questions, essays, projects, formal tests, and the like. We analyze the evidence by correcting and scoring papers and projects. Finally, we make decisions regarding the learning of students and the effectiveness of our instruction. And, of course, we assign grades.

Educational Assessment: A Serious Endeavor

Have you ever taken a test that you thought was unfair or poorly constructed? Or a test that you thought seriously underestimated your knowledge, or one that contained unfamiliar items or items that were not covered in class? I'm sure you have. If you are an educator, you have taken a lot of tests throughout many years of schooling. I suspect we all remember certain examples that represent positive or negative assessment experiences.

I have never forgotten an experience during a freshman biology class in college. The instructor lectured extensively, and we performed a variety of experiments. Although we had a text, the instructor seldom referred to it or even seemed to care whether we read it. When it was time for the first test, I felt confident. I had taken careful notes on the lectures and the experiments, rewritten and reorganized them several times, and studied them extensively. When the test was handed out, the format and printing indicated that it was a published instrument accompanying the textbook. The contents of that test did not match the contents of the lectures and experiments. It contained items I had never heard of and addressed topics that were never addressed in class. Of course, I did poorly. Although the experience taught me a valuable lesson (read and study the text even if the instructor does not seem to stress this), I felt then and I do now that it was a very unfair assessment of my knowledge. That biology test violated an important tenet of good educational assessment: Assess what you have taught or, in other words, align class content with test content.

Educational assessment has serious consequences for students and educators alike. Assessment has a variety of functions. It is used to evaluate individuals and programs. It is also "used to hold particular groups accountable for some specified set of outcomes . . . to inform instruction, either for individuals or whole classes, and finally to determine who gains access to particular programs or privileges" (Sarroub & Pearson, 1998, p. 97). If students do not do well, a variety of things may occur, depending on the type of assessment. Students can be denied entrance to specific programs or courses, as well as to certain schools. Report card grades can reflect poor performance and may block promotion to the next level. As anyone who has ever received a low grade knows, it can have serious consequences for student motivation and self-esteem (Assessment Reform Group, 2002). Poor performance can result in lowered expectations on the part of the teacher as well as the student, and it can cause friction and unpleasantness at home.

We live in an era increasingly characterized by high-stakes assessment, in which poor test performance can also result in negative consequences, not only for students but also for schools or districts. Standardized test scores can label a school or district as successful or failing, and this can positively or negatively impact community support. For example, it is a common practice in my state for realtors to include published district test scores as part of the information given to prospective home buyers. Although there is much controversy about the viability of high-stakes testing, the public generally supports the practice (Afflerbach, 2004), believing such instruments to be both fair and scientific. I return to the issue of high-stakes testing later in the book.

Types of Assessment

Assessment is generally divided into two broad categories: formal and informal. Formal assessment includes an extensive array of commercially produced and published instruments that have specific procedures for administration and scoring. Standardized tests are examples of formal assessment measures, so called because they are administered and scored in a uniform or standardized manner. Informal assessment measures, however, are flexible, and educators can modify procedures and adapt them to the needs of specific students or classroom situations. The popular informal reading inventory is an example of an informal test. Although general guidelines for administration and scoring are included in the test manual, the examiner is free to adapt the instrument with regard to choice of passage, scoring guidelines, and administration of different diagnostic options. Typical classroom assessment is a form of informal assessment.

Many people consider informal assessment to be more authentic than formal assessment because the format of the assessment more closely parallels the actual activities that students perform in schools. For example, in informal assessments students read longer passages than those included in most formal tests and demonstrate comprehension by composing summaries or constructing projects.

Instead of answering multiple-choice questions and filling out scoring sheets, they construct diagrams, report the results of experiments, and engage in discussion with their peers.

Assessment can also be divided into formative and summative assessment. Suppose you have been teaching a unit on weather and you are unsure as to how well the students understand the concept of relative humidity. You need to know if you should reteach this component or move on to the next part of the unit. You ask students to complete a short activity to ascertain what they have learned and what they still find confusing. You do not assign a grade to this exercise, but use it to evaluate your own teaching and to provide feedback to your students. This is an example of formative assessment, which is associated with greater interest, effort, and learning on the part of students (Black & Wiliam, 1998; Assessment Reform Group, 2002).

After you have completed the entire unit on weather, your purpose shifts. Now you are interested in what individual students have comprehended and learned. Have they met your instructional objectives? You administer a unit test, carefully grade it, and record the results in your grade book. This is summative assessment. Trice (2000) makes an important distinction between the two forms of assessment. In formative assessment "the teacher accepts responsibility for student learning. . . . In summative assessment the teacher shares responsibility with the students" (p. 70). The focus of formative assessment is instruction; the focus of summative assessment is student comprehension and learning.

Good Assessment Practices

People often equate assessment with testing; however, assessment is a much broader concept. *Testing* refers to an instrument used specifically to arrive at a grade or some numerical description of performance. Basically, a test audits learning. *Assessment* refers to any process involved in evaluating performance. McMillan (2000) describes assessment as a process of professional judgment that can involve a variety of related activities such as writing questions, designing classroom assessments, creating rubrics, scoring student work, arriving at grades, and interpreting standardized test scores. Assessment can have a positive or negative influence on the motivation and learning of students (Black & Wiliam, 1998; Assessment Reform Group, 2002), and given the seriousness and sometimes unpleasant consequences of assessment, it is important that educators carefully adhere to good assessment practices.

The Joint Committee on Testing Practices (2004) developed a code that delineates major obligations in test usage. The code lists practices for test developers and test users and is primarily directed at commercially developed instruments and those used in formal testing programs. The code focuses on four broad areas: development and selection, administration and scoring, reporting and interpreting results, and informing test takers. Although the code does not specifically address classroom assessment, the practices have much relevance for teachers and provide a useful framework for improving classroom practice.

Test Development and Selection

First, assessments should be developed and/or selected that meet the intended purposes for assessment and are appropriate for the students who are taking them. In the classroom, this means that the content of an assessment should be aligned with instruction and with the developmental levels of the students. This is the first step in the assessment process: Identify what you want to assess. If you are clear in regard to your assessment purposes, it will be easier to construct and/or evaluate an activity to evaluate student performance. This is also related to the concept of validity. A valid assessment accurately measures what it was designed to measure.

Administration and Scoring

Tests should be administered correctly and scored fairly. This is aligned with the second step of the assessment process: Collect evidence. Those who administer and score tests should be adequately trained to do so. In the classroom, some assessment measures are quite easy to score: The word is or is not spelled correctly, or the answer to the math problem is right or wrong. However, what about scoring an essay question? Are there guidelines for the kind and number of important concepts that should be included in the answer?

Test takers should have opportunities to become familiar with test formats, and accommodations should be made for students with disabilities and those with diverse linguistic backgrounds. With regard to the classroom, McMillan (2000) suggests that it is important for students to have knowledge "of learning targets and the nature of the assessment prior to instruction (e.g., knowing what will be tested, how it will be graded, scoring criteria, anchors, exemplars and examples of performance" (p. 5). When teachers explain the purpose and expectations of their assessment practices, student self-efficacy increases (Assessment Reform Group, 2002). In the classroom, we readily provide oral test administration for students who are visually challenged, but we do not always do this for struggling readers. If, for example, a test is intended to measure content knowledge of atoms, ions, and atomic numbers, wouldn't oral administration be more appropriate for students who cannot read well or for those who are just learning the English language? Otherwise, how would we know if a low score was due to lack of knowledge, unfamiliarity with the language, or low reading ability?

Reporting and Interpreting Results

Test results should be interpreted accurately and clearly. This practice aligns with the third and fourth steps of the assessment process: Analyze the evidence and make a decision. In the classroom, score interpretation rests on how the score was derived. Does each question count for one point? A unit test may contain items that focus on important concepts and some that address relatively unimportant details. Are all items weighted identically, or are some given more weight because they are more important? How are essays or projects scored? Does the teacher use a rubric as a guide for evaluation, or is evaluation a relatively subjective process? To what extent will teacher bias affect scoring interpretation? Will the performance of students whose behavior is often disruptive and unpleasant be judged by the same criteria as that of well-behaved students?

Educators should also avoid using a single score for making decisions, but should interpret student performance in combination with other information. All assessments contain some margin of error, but error can be reduced through use of multiple assessments (McMillan, 2000). Given the complexity of the comprehension process and the many factors that shape it, multiple samples just make good sense.

Informing Test Takers

Educators should inform test takers about the nature of a test and how scores will be derived and used. What is the purpose of the test? What test formats will be employed? Will the test be timed? How will it be scored? In the case of classroom measures, how important is this assessment to the students' report card grades? Students and parents have a right to answers to these and many other questions regarding formal standardized assessment as well as classroom assessment. In my university classes, I explain the exact format of a proposed test, the nature of the content that will be tested, and the weighting attached to certain items. This tends to astonish my students, who seem to regard test format, content, and scoring as great unknowns to be deciphered by them (they hope) during the testing session.

Nobody wants to fail, and tests can indicate failure, at least in the mind of the test taker. In my graduate classes, I am always amazed at how educators fear tests. Even when I tell them what to study and assure them that they can take another version of the test if they are dissatisfied with their grades, their nervous behavior indicates apprehension and negative expectations of success. Over the years I have resorted to a variety of practices to allay their fears. I administer short quizzes that do not count toward their grades but offer examples of items similar to those on the midterm and final. I hand out worksheets that contain problems and activities parallel to the test items. I answer questions about interpretation of the questions during test administration. But nothing seems to help. Where did this fear of testing come from? It cannot have come from repeated failure, as educators are notoriously successful in school. Could it be that past violations of good assessment practices have created this negativism?

Validity and Reliability

When educators talk about validity and reliability, it is usually in the context of formal standardized testing, not classroom assessment. After all, aren't validity and reliability concepts that properly belong in a statistics or measurement text or in the pages of the thick manual that accompanies formal instruments? Nothing could be farther from the truth! Of what earthly use is any assessment that is not valid or reliable? It is important that educators understand these concepts in the context of informal classroom assessment. In Chapter 10 I return to them as related to formal standardized measures.

Test Validity

A valid test measures and accurately reflects what it was designed to measure. What would be the purpose of administering a test that did not yield meaningful results? We inherently know this and apply it in our everyday assessments. For example, we recognize that taste is not a valid measure of nutritional value. How many times have we said something like, "This is probably bad for me, but it sure tastes good"? We acknowledge that the ability to run 3 miles is not a valid assessment of cholesterol level, and we accept the validity of a blood test in this regard. Similarly, we accept the validity of our car's gas gauge and stop for gas when it reaches the danger point.

Validity is related to knowing the exact purpose of an assessment and designing an instrument that meets that purpose. This is easier said than done. Educators are often not specific enough in their delineation of assessment purpose. Sometimes they mislabel an assessment, calling it a test of learning when it is actually a test of factual recall. (Remember, in Chapter 1, learning is defined as involving application of some kind.) Sometimes educators choose published instruments that do not accurately reflect what has been emphasized in the classroom. One criticism of government-mandated standardized assessment is that the contents of a test do not accurately mirror classroom learning. In fact, the increasing emphasis on such instruments may actually "confine and constrict" the curriculum (Afflerbach, 2004, p. 8).

Does the assessment adequately reflect the skills, behaviors, or content to be measured? In other words, is there a match between the assessment and classroom instruction? This is called *content validity*. For example, suppose giving a weekly spelling test of 10 words is a common practice in a school or district. If the test includes the words that were studied during the week, then the measure has content validity. Similarly, if a unit test reflects what was demonstrated and studied during a science unit, it has content validity. However, if the teacher emphasizes understanding reasons and processes in a unit on westward expansion but asks students to recall dates, names, and events, the assessment does not have content validity. The biology test I described earlier in the chapter did not have content validity. Teachers who design their own classroom tests "should make sure that items on the test correspond to what was covered in class in terms of content, behaviors and skills" (Ravid, 2000, p. 264).

A factor that weakens the content validity of classroom assessments is that teachers often use a single score to represent performance on very different skills and abilities. Marzano (2000) offers the example of a math quiz with completion items that address knowledge of multiplication and a word problem that assesses organization of quantities, deductive reasoning, and mathematical communication. A single score on the test is ambiguous; two students could receive the same number of correct answers but demonstrate very different patterns of strengths or weaknesses.

Test Reliability

A reliable test is consistent, that is, it yields similar results over time with similar students in similar situations. We expect a degree of reliability or consistency in medical assessments. We accept that a blood test will yield reliable indications of our cholesterol level, blood sugar level, and so on. If we did not accept this, we would expect, and doctors would order, multiple blood tests over a series of days, a process that would be expensive, time-consuming, and, to one who dislikes needles, quite threatening. Similarly, a reliable test would be scored similarly by different teachers, and two students of similar ability should receive the same score. This may be the case with objective measures such as multiple-choice tests, but what about essay tests and class projects? Do they possess reliability? Would two or more teachers assign identical scores to the same student? What about classroom grades? How reliable are they? Does a B in one class mean the same in the classroom across the hall?

Educators use a variety of assessments to describe student performance, and these are based on the assumption of their consistency or reliability. For example, asking questions is probably the most frequently used assessment format. Instead of asking students to "talk about the experiment" or "tell what you think about the story," educators use specific questions to direct students' attention to key content. Why do they do this? Because they know that answers to such questions are easier to score and yield more reliable and consistent results. Unfortunately, such questions often focus on literal content (Black & Wiliam, 1998) and ignore the inferential and application levels of comprehension.

Reliability does not just refer to scoring an assessment; it also extends to grading. Marzano (2000) questions the reliability of classroom grading, because teachers may raise or lower a grade on the basis of their individual perceptions of student effort and/or behavior. Of course, this also represents an issue with content validity. If an assessment is supposed to measure mathematical computation or knowledge of the structure of matter, the insertion of effort or behavior lowers both its reliability and its validity.

Throughout the rest of this book, I continually return to the issues of validity and reliability in classroom assessment. Although there can be no perfect assessment of comprehension, educators can improve their classroom assessment practices, and it is the purpose of this book to offer suggestions for doing so.

General Guidelines for Classroom Assessment

• *Guideline 1. Define the purpose of assessment as clearly and specifically as possible.* Accept that no assessment is perfect. All assessments contain error of some kind. However, error can be reduced if you define what you want to assess in terms that are as clear and specific as possible. In working with student teachers, I see them expending much effort in designing class projects and unit tests; however, they are often unclear as to what they want students to learn and do. Last year our museum hosted a traveling exhibit of ancient Egyptian artifacts, and many schools capitalized on this by including attention to ancient Egypt in the social studies curriculum. I remember watching fifth graders present their reports on such topics as Egyptian agriculture, art, religion, government, and burial practices. When I asked the student teacher how she was assessing student comprehension of important content, she was genuinely confused. She had not clarified in her own mind what constituted important content, nor had she clarified it for her students. As a result, she accepted a report on Egyptian art that included lists of various media but completely ignored the significant relationship of the art to Egyptian religious beliefs.

• *Guideline 2. Tie assessment activities and instruments to classroom objectives and instruction.* This will increase the validity of your assessment process. If, for example, a published test that accompanies your textbook contains content that you did not emphasize in class, strike these items from the test or, better still, have the students do it. There is something inherently motivating in drawing a black line through a number of questions on a test. Don't expect students to comprehend and learn what was not covered in class.

• *Guideline 3. Describe the assessment to the students.* What is its purpose?

What should they know? Describe the assessment format and how you will grade it. Assessment should not be a huge mystery known only to the teacher. If students understand what they should know and do, there is a greater chance that they will actually know and do it. Have you ever prepared for a test, only to discover that you studied the wrong thing or missed a key component? I'm sure you have, and wasn't it a frustrating experience? I remember hearing a student at my university ask an instructor what would be on a test, and he answered, "Me to know, you to find out." How misguided! Assessment should represent collaboration between the teacher and student, with the teacher sharing the purpose, format, and grading guidelines of the assessment.

• *Guideline 4. Use multiple methods and assessment experiences to evaluate a student's performance.* Short, well-designed assessments that are repeated multiple times are better than a major assessment that is used once or twice a year. Teachers often assess as they were assessed. The all-important unit test is still a fixture in many classrooms, and a student's report card grade is often determined by a few major assessments. Although such assessments can be weighted more heavily in the final grade, multiple smaller samples of a student's performance over time are perhaps more meaningful. Use both formative and summative assessment. Testing as a summative experience is often overemphasized in classrooms. However, student learning is heavily dependent on the quality of formative assessment.

• *Guideline 5. Keep assessment simple.* There is only so much time in a day and only so many days in a week. Assessment that is very time-consuming is assessment that will be soon discarded.

Summary

• Assessment is a four-step process: identifying what to assess, collecting evidence, analyzing evidence, and making a decision.

• Educational assessment is a serious endeavor, and poor test performance can have a variety of unpleasant consequences for students.

• Tests fall into different categories: formal and informal, formative and summative.

• Good assessment practices include matching test content to its purpose, administering and scoring the test correctly and fairly, interpreting results accurately and clearly, and informing test takers about the format of the test and how scores will be derived and used.

• Assessments should be valid; that is, they should measure what they were designed to measure.

• Classroom assessments should have content validity; that is, test items should correspond to what was taught.

- Tests should also be reliable or consistent, that is, yield similar results over time with similar students in similar situations.
- Classroom assessments do not always have reliability, and two teachers may score the same test and arrive at different grades.

Professional Development Activities for Increasing Understanding of the Assessment Process

- Consider the four-step assessment process described in this chapter. Choose something outside the field of education and describe the assessment steps. For example, how would you assess the condition of your garage or basement? How would you go about assessing the state of your winter wardrobe?
- Think about the many times you have taken tests or been assessed during your academic career. Describe an example of valid assessment, that is, an assessment that measured what it was supposed to measure. Describe an example of invalid assessment.
- Examine your own testing practices. How do they conform to the code of good assessment practices? What areas do you need to work on?
- Consider the general guidelines for classroom assessment. Do you agree with them? Which ones do you follow now? Which ones do you need to work on?

CHAPTER 3

Assessing Comprehension

What, How, and for What Purpose

Overview

Schools are expected to teach children to read, listen, and watch a variety of visual presentations, and students are expected to do these in order to learn new things. At the heart of reading, listening, and viewing (indeed their very soul) is that incredibly complex process called comprehension. Reading, listening, and viewing basically involve two skills: decoding written, spoken, or visual stimuli, and comprehension. Decoding can be assessed in relatively uncomplicated ways, but "there is no uniform comprehension process to be measured" (Kintsch & Kintsch, 2005, p. 86). As indicated in Chapter 1, comprehension varies, depending on the student, the text, and the context of the situation.

Comprehension is something that can be examined only indirectly. We cannot actually see what is occurring in a student's head as he or she comprehends. We can only observe "indirect symptoms and artifacts of its occurrence" (Pearson & Hamm, 2005, p. 19). If a student correctly answers a question, we infer that comprehension has occurred. Similarly, if a student composes a coherent summary, accurately fills in a diagram, or correctly completes a problem, we make the assumption that the student has comprehended. Because we can only observe the products of comprehension, "any attempt to assess reading comprehension is inherently imperfect" (Francis, Fletcher, Catts, & Tomblin, 2005, p. 376).

As described in Chapter 1, comprehension is an extremely complex entity. "There are many different processes entailed in the broad thing called 'comprehension,' and 'comprehension' proceeds very differently for different kinds of text, different topics and different reading purposes" (Duke, 2005, p. 93). However, we often talk of comprehension as if it were relatively straightforward, simple, and unitary. Educators discuss students' comprehension scores on standardized tests. Some districts list comprehension as an item on the report card. Students are referred to as good or poor comprehenders. Many formal measures, as well as classroom activities, use general titles such as "reading," "language arts," "social studies," and "math" to describe their intended purpose. This masks the specific purpose of the activity and often leads to confusion in interpretation of results with regard to comprehension. Referring to comprehension in these ways suggests that it is a single entity that can be assessed as such. Nothing could be farther from the truth.

Assessing What?

What should educators assess in regard to comprehension? This is intimately connected with how we have defined comprehension. Educators need to know exactly what they assess as comprehension; however, this has always been a complex and inexact science.

In regard to schools and classrooms, comprehension is generally defined as a series of subskills. Pearson and Hamm (2005) describe the genesis of this definition as emanating from the work of Davis (1944), who conceptualized comprehension as involving two major factors: word knowledge and reasoning. Davis sorted these factors into the following general categories: remembering word meaning; recognizing word meaning in context; understanding explicitly stated content; connecting ideas; drawing inferences; following passage organization; recognizing literary devices; and understanding the author's purpose, mood, and tone. Although Davis focused on reading comprehension, the same skills can also be applied to listening and, with some modifications, to viewing.

Over time, the lists of comprehension skills grew longer and longer and evolved into what was referred to as *scope and sequence charts.* Such charts were very lengthy and could include as many as 30 different comprehension skills (Pearson & Hamm, 2005). However, these skills were seldom discrete entities.

For example, finding the main idea is very similar to determining importance, although both might be on the same chart. Making predictions and drawing inferences were often listed as different skills, but a prediction is a form of inference. And are drawing conclusions and making judgments really different, or are they both facets of the same component, inferential comprehension? The scope and sequence charts became the basis for comprehension testing. Each skill was repeatedly assessed and reassessed at different levels until a student attained some semblance of mastery. Test items required a single "right" answer, even after educators acknowledged that experience and prior knowledge could influence a student's response. Such testing required complex management systems to facilitate classroom and district implementation.

Lengthy scope and sequence charts have not gone away. Many districts have simply recycled them, using different terminology. Skills are now called performance expectations, benchmarks, learning objectives, or grade-level targets. However, they are still confusing and impossible to keep track of in regard to individual students. What do I mean by this? Consider a classroom of 30 students. Suppose the teacher is expected to address and assess 30 grade-level targets carried over from the old scope and sequence chart. This means that the teacher has to keep track of 900 different points of assessment, an impossible task. For this reason and despite district efforts to tie these performance expectations to state standards, I suspect that many have gathered dust on classroom shelves. Comprehension of subject matter text has been similarly confusing. Some state standards for comprehension of science and social studies, for example, are extremely broad; others are quite narrow and delineate a large number of specific facts that should be learned at a particular grade level. Textbooks compound the problem. The number of facts included within a single chapter is overwhelming. Are all of these equally important? I suspect not. And although facts are important, there is much more to comprehension than understanding and remembering facts. If educators are to assess comprehension in a more valid and meaningful way, then perhaps we need a different system.

Components of Comprehension

As mentioned repeatedly, comprehension is extremely complex and we have sought ways to simplify it in order to make both instruction and assessment more manageable. Wiggens and McTighe (1998) describe six facets of understanding or comprehension. The first is explanation or understanding of why and how. For example, a student can explain why the ancient Egyptians mummified their dead or how a cactus stores water in order to survive. The second facet is interpretation. A student recognizes the importance or significance of an event or idea. For example, the student is aware of the far-reaching effects of the

Homestead Act on settlement in the Great Plains, or distinguishes family and cultural influences that led Patricia McKissack to become a writer. The third facet is application or the ability to use knowledge in new situations and contexts. A student applies his or her interpretation of the influences on Patricia McKissack's life to a different author, or applies understanding of the Homestead Act to the effects of other government initiatives. The fourth facet is perspective. A student understands different perspectives on an issue and evaluates the validity of each. For example, the student examines the Treaty of Versailles from both the German and the Allies' point of view, understands the position of both sides, and evaluates the justice of the treaty in this regard. The fifth facet is empathy for the feelings and views of others. Basically, a student is able to walk in another's shoes and imagine the thoughts and feelings of others. For example, the student understands slavery and discrimination from the point of view of Biddy Mason (a former slave) or Malcolm X. The final facet is self-knowledge, knowledge about what we think and why we think it. A student recognizes his or her ideas or biases about a specific culture and is able to identify the source and evaluate the validity of these perceptions.

Bloom's taxonomy of educational objectives (Bloom & Krathwohl, 1956) is a familiar device for breaking comprehension into manageable parts: knowledge, comprehension, application, analysis, synthesis, and evaluation. Knowledge is defined as recall of information, usually factual or literal in nature. Comprehension is the ability to interpret information in one's own words, and application entails applying learned content to new situations. Analysis is the identification of patterns and relationships. Synthesis involves organizing knowledge from different areas, and evaluation includes making judgments and assessing the value of ideas and theories. This taxonomy has been used for many years to describe different facets of the comprehension process.

Both Wiggens and McTighe (1998) and Bloom and Krathwohl (1956) focus on six separate components of comprehension, and there is some similarity between their categories. For example, both address application and move well beyond the factual or literal level. To put it another way, both systems recognize the importance of doing something with the facts that were understood. However, the systems are more different than alike. Yet because comprehension is such a complex entity, both probably tap into the comprehension process in some way.

Can educators use these two systems effectively to describe the comprehension of their students? Of course. However, the issue is the ease with which this might occur. Six components may be too many to handle efficiently in the world of the busy classroom. In addition, distinguishing between the separate components is not always easy. The line between interpretation and perspective, or application and evaluation, for example, often tends to blur, and many activities actually represent more than one component. No matter how well intentioned and dedicated an educator is, describing a specific comprehension assessment in terms of six separate elements may be too unwieldy for effective long-term use.

The RAND Reading Study Group (2002) offers a more efficient taxonomy and differentiates between three components of comprehension: knowledge, application, and engagement. What does the student know? Can the student use this knowledge to do something new? Is the student engaged or actively involved? It is interesting that Wiggens and McTighe (1998), Bloom and Krathwohl (1956), and the RAND Group (2002) all identify application as an important component of comprehension, which seems to support Kintsch's (2005) definition of learning as application.

An examination of question taxonomies (explained in Chapter 4) suggests that the categories of literal, inferential, and application may represent a viable system for describing comprehension in the classroom. Dividing comprehension into literal, inferential, and application presents more specificity than simply calling an assessment activity "comprehension." Three components are more manageable than the six proposed by Wiggens and McTighe (1998) and Bloom and Krathwohl (1956) and offer educators something that is more controllable than recycled scope and sequence charts. Elements of state standards can easily be tied to these three components. If a teacher or school uniformly describes student performance in terms of a manageable number of chosen components, comprehension assessment becomes more meaningful and more manageable.

Verbs as Indicators of Comprehension Components

How does a teacher know if a comprehension activity is literal or inferential in nature, or if it involves application? It is relatively easy to identify literal comprehension; the student answers a question, offers a comment, or identifies a concept that has been explicitly stated in the text. Unfortunately, differentiating inferential and application components is not as clearcut, and teachers do not have time to engage in lengthy examinations of questions or activities to determine which component of comprehension is best represented. However, we do have a guideline that, although not perfect, makes a relatively workable distinction between inferential and application comprehension, at least as far as we are able to take it at this point in time. We have verbs that describe what students are supposed to do, words like *describe, analyze, evaluate, compare, justify,* and so forth. A teacher can use these performance or question words to determine whether a question, activity, or student comment represents inferential or application comprehension. There may still be times when a teacher is unsure, but applying the guideline allows one to be right more often than wrong in the long run. Remember, comprehension assessment is still an inexact science, but differentiating it according to three manageable components is better than some past and present practices.

Text and Topic

In addition to choosing a workable model of comprehension components, we also have to consider the underlying text and the topic of that text. Is the student reading or listening to a narrative? Is the student grappling with expository material? Is the student viewing a video of familiar or unfamiliar content? Many students comprehend well in reading narratives but falter when dealing with unfamiliar expository material. Caldwell and Leslie (2004/2005) described proficient middle school readers who performed very differently with narrative versus expository text. They were able to effectively retell and answer questions about a narrative describing a family's capture during the Vietnam war, but failed miserably to comprehend an expository selection on viral replication. The difference between comprehending a family's struggle in a war and comprehending viral replication points out that, in addition to the text genre, topic is another issue in assessing comprehension.

Comprehension can also depend on familiarity and knowledge. It is often assumed that there is a single grade level for a written text and that fifth graders, for example, should be able to read, listen, and/or understand all text written at that level. This is an erroneous belief. I have asked many students to read passages on familiar and unfamiliar topics at the same grade level. Students who comprehended a narrative selection on the familiar topic of Abraham Lincoln evinced serious difficulties in comprehending an expository passage on temperature and humidity. Similarly, fourth graders who read and comprehended a passage on Johnny Appleseed struggled with a fourth-grade selection on plant structure. Is it fair to describe a student as having difficulties in comprehension on the basis of performance with a text structure and/or topic that is relatively unfamiliar? In reality, we can expect that students may comprehend very differently in literature, social studies, math, and science.

We do not presently have, nor can we ever construct, a single assessment that adequately measures something as complex and multifaceted as comprehension. There is no such thing as a single measure of comprehension that we can administer, score, record in a grade book, and relate to parents. Our assessment of comprehension must necessarily involve multiple samples of different kinds of behavior. When we choose or construct a test or assessment activity, we must determine what components of comprehension we are assessing and qualify the word *comprehension* with appropriate modifiers such as *literal, inferential,* and *application.* This applies to published instruments as well as assessments constructed by the teacher. Knowing exactly what an assessment instrument measures is the first step toward establishing validity. Perhaps the most difficult task facing educators regarding comprehension assessment is to stop thinking and talking about it as a single entity and instead attach appropriate modifiers to the word *comprehension.*

Assessing How?

We all know how fast some plants grow. The seed germinates and the first leaves poke through the soil. The plant grows taller and bushier, blossoms appear, and finally there is a tomato or squash ready to be picked and enjoyed. As we weed and water our garden, we note changes in the plant but we do not actually see the process unfold. However, time-lapse photography can record the entire progression and reduce the time so that over a matter of minutes, we can watch a growth process that spans several months. Unfortunately, we cannot do the same with comprehension; we cannot see it as it happens. There is no way we can get into a person's head and watch what occurs when comprehension "clicks." We have to be content with "residual traces of the comprehension process—indirect indexes of its occurrence" (Pearson & Hamm, 2005, p. 62).

In Chapter 1, I discussed how comprehension varies, depending on the knowledge and skill of the comprehender and the structure and difficulty level of the text. Comprehension also varies according to how we measure it, according to those indirect indices of its occurrence that we choose to assess its presence or absence. Do we ask students to retell or answer questions? Do we expect students to answer questions from memory, or do we allow them to locate the answers in the text? What form do our questions take? Do we ask for factual or literal recall, or do we ask higher-level inferential questions? Do we use formats such as multiple choice, fill in the blanks, and true/false, or do we assign essay questions? Do we assess comprehension by evaluating research papers, group projects, lab experiments, or oral presentations?

How we assess comprehension also relates to our methods of scoring the assessment instruments that we choose. If we choose questions as our index of comprehension, do we weight all questions the same? Or do we assign more weight to questions that tap higher-level comprehension skills such as inferring and applying? If we assign essay or open-ended questions, do we construct a rubric to guide our scoring, thus establishing a measure of reliability for the process and ensuring that all students are evaluated in a relatively consistent way?

How we assess and score comprehension can have a powerful effect on the process itself and may underestimate or overestimate a student's comprehension. I used to regularly employ true/false items in a graduate class until I overheard one student say, "If she had asked me to write the definition, I could have done this, but I got all mixed up with true and false. I hate true and false questions!" I took the student aside and asked her to define the concept in question and she did so quite adequately. That was some years ago, and it taught me a valuable lesson. Not all comprehension assessments are equal.

Questions

There are many ways to assess comprehension. Perhaps the most common testing format is asking students to answer questions. However, questions take many forms and not all are similarly sensitive to the existence of comprehension. A student may correctly answer a multiple-choice question by clever guesswork without ever really understanding what was read. With true/false questions, students have a 50% chance of being correct. There are questions that students can answer just from their own knowledge without ever reading or understanding the text. Educators will always ask questions to evaluate comprehension. The trick is to know what a student's answer tells us about his or her comprehension. Has the student comprehended or learned? Does the question tap literal understanding of facts or understanding at a higher inferential level? Chapter 4 includes guidelines for using questioning as an effective measure of comprehension assessment.

Open-Ended Assessment

Another index of comprehension is gained by evaluating students through open-ended tasks such as answering essay questions; doing science experiments, projects, and presentations, and developing portfolios. By open-ended I mean that a student must construct something, as opposed to choosing a correct answer from two or more choices. We can learn a lot more from open-ended assessments than from multiple-choice and true/false questions, but only if we know exactly what we are looking for. An open-ended assessment probably encompasses all three components of comprehension—literal, inferential, and application—and it may be impossible to separate these during the assessment process. However, an educator can decide which of the three is most clearly represented by the assignment and use this for a more fine-tuned description of a student's comprehension. Scoring open-ended assessments presents challenges. A true/false question is either right or wrong, but 25 students turning in the same essay question can represent 25 very different interpretations of the assignment. Moreover, student performance variables can obscure comprehension. A student may understand the material quite well, but difficulties with writing, organization, or oral presentation can suggest the opposite. Chapter 5 addresses guidelines for describing and assessing comprehension through open-ended activities.

Student Dialogue

Teachers listen to students every day and, by so doing, can learn quite a bit about their comprehension or lack of it. Unfortunately, much dialogue in the classroom is teacher centered and offers students few opportunities for discussing what they have read, heard, or viewed. Fostering student-centered dialogue through practices such as thoughtful talk and thinking aloud provides another window on the comprehension process, and students' dialogue can be evaluated according to the nature of their comments: literal, inferential, and application. For many teachers, this represents a dramatic shift in how they structure classroom dialogue. Chapter 6 addresses guidelines for fostering student-centered dialogue and using it to assess comprehension.

Word Comprehension

There is a strong relationship between word knowledge and comprehension. To put it simply, people who know more word meanings tend to comprehend more effectively. Although there is almost uniform agreement that word knowledge should be taught in all classrooms, little attention has been paid to the assessment of vocabulary knowledge. Good assessment is always tied to instruction, and the same activities recommended for teaching vocabulary can be used to assess it. As demonstrated in Chapter 7, these same activities can be designated as literal, inferential, or application in nature, thus tying word knowledge to the comprehension process.

Comprehension Proxies

There are also a variety of assessments that we can label *comprehension proxies*. A proxy is an individual appointed to act for another; basically, a proxy is a substitute. Popular comprehension proxies are measures of word recognition and oral reading fluency. These are used as proxies because they are strongly correlated with comprehension. Correlation is a statistic that shows a relationship between two sets of scores. Two correlated variables share something in common. Obviously, the ability to accurately and quickly recognize words is necessary for comprehension but, as indicated in Chapter 1, it is not the whole of comprehension.

Because assessments of word recognition and fluency are relatively easy to administer and score, it is tempting to use these as comprehension proxies. There are other measures, such as the cloze technique and the sentence verification technique, that can also be called proxies. In using the cloze technique, students fill in missing words in a piece of text. With the sentence verification technique, they indicate whether or not a specific sentence was present in the text they read or listened to.

There are problems with the use of comprehension proxies no matter how attractive the process may seem. First, they are, at best, only an indirect measure of the comprehension process. The ability to fill in a missing word sheds little light on a student's ability to understand facts, draw inferences, and/or apply knowledge. Second, educators often interpret correlation as establishing a causal relationship, and they regard word recognition and fluency as causes of comprehension. Correlation establishes the existence of a relationship but not a causal one. There are students who read accurately and fluently and still demonstrate comprehension problems. Comprehension proxies may have a place in the assessment cycle, but they are not substitutes for more direct assessments of comprehension. Comprehension proxies are addressed in more detail in Chapter 8.

Assessing for What Purpose?

The basic purpose of any assessment is to gather information in order to make a decision of some sort. In regard to comprehension assessment, the primary purpose is to gather information in order to decide if students are comprehending and learning. Farr (1992) states that "the bottom line in selecting and using any assessment should be whether it helps the students" (p. 46). Comprehension assessment should assist educators in evaluating the effectiveness of schools, in fostering student growth, and in designing and planning instruction.

School Effectiveness

One purpose of comprehension assessment (and the one receiving most emphasis at present) is to judge the effectiveness of schools. The No Child Left Behind (NCLB) Act, signed into law in 2002, requires that schools document the adequate yearly progress of their students. The instruments chosen to do this are formal standardized tests. These are the measures most often reported in the media and responded to by the general public. These are the measures that possess face validity in that they are generally (and perhaps unfortunately) accepted as valid measures of student comprehension and learning. But are they? To what extent do standardized measures actually assess comprehension? Chapter 10 focuses on what standardized measures tell us and what they don't.

Assessments using formal standardized measures are becoming more and more high-stakes evaluations in that state and federal approval and funding depend on acceptable levels of performance by students. Unfortunately, at the present time few schools or districts have any alternatives to the standardized tests. That is, if student performance is suspect on the standardized measure, there are no schoolwide alternatives based on state standards, district goals, grade-level curricula, or classroom expectations. Even if schools or districts have implemented schoolwide assessment programs, rarely are the data summarized and disseminated to the public in such a way as to counter the standardized results. Or, to put it another way, rarely are the data used to build a case for the face validity of less formal assessment instruments.

Student Learning and Progress

Another purpose of comprehension assessment is to measure the learning of students and to monitor their progress across a school year. Such assessment is at present very idiosyncratic across teachers and schools. Although schools and districts may construct a uniform plan of what to assess based on state standards, how this is translated into classroom practice generally varies from teacher to teacher and from grade to grade. Measuring learning and monitoring progress are tied to grading practices, and there is no agreed-upon system for designing assessments or assigning a specific grade (Marzano, 2000).

Some schools and districts mandate certain assessments at specific grade levels, such as the use of running records at the primary level. Content teachers often use identical unit tests to assess student learning. However, for the most part, teachers in different classrooms design different assessments to measure comprehension. This lack of uniformity is both a strength and a weakness. It is a strength in that it dignifies the knowledge, professionalism, and creativity of individual educators. It is a weakness in that the reliability of assessments across a school or grade level is suspect. Chapter 9 focuses on classroom assessment and grading practices.

Designing, Planning, and Improving Instruction

Using assessment of student performance to plan instruction is formative in nature and measures teacher effectiveness more than student learning. The teacher assigns a short activity to ascertain whether certain material needs to be retaught or presented in a different way. Allied to this practice is the provision of feedback to students, which is closely allied to the promotion of student self-reflection on performance. "What did I know?" "What am I still confused about?" "How can I improve?" These are questions that are seldom tied to the evaluation process in our schools. Typical classroom practice provides feedback in the form of a single grade. Students know the grade they received but not often why they received it. Assessment should be a collaborative activity involving both teacher and students. Unless the assessment actively includes the student, the following scenario is all too common: A teacher carefully evaluates a paper or project and provides extensive comments to help each student to understand his or her strengths and weaknesses. When such papers are returned to the students, many totally ignore the comments, look at the grade and toss the paper into the trash.

Pulling It All Together: Sampling and Categorizing

How can we pull together what we know about comprehension assessment in a workable fashion? That is, how can we address the what, how, and purpose of comprehension assessment in such a way as to offer specific guidelines to students, parents, and the general public, as well as to the educator? Whatever method we choose will be imperfect and inexact, but it can only improve upon the present methods of assessing and scoring that elusive and complex entity called comprehension. We can design and implement a workable system for assessing comprehension by using two components that are integral parts of our everyday life: taking samples and categorizing objects, events, and experiences.

Using Samples

Comprehension assessment relies on the use of samples of performance, but samples that are clearly labeled as to what is being assessed. Perhaps an analogy will help. Suppose you visited a new restaurant and did not enjoy the taste or presentation of the food. If a friend asks you about your experience, you probably reply, "The food wasn't too good." As a result, your friend may decide to avoid that particular establishment. Now, was your assessment a complete or fair evaluation of the restaurant's food? After all, you tasted only your selected salad, a single entree, and the dessert you chose. Could it be that other salads, entrees, and desserts might have been very different? In order to evaluate the total menu, you would have to taste all the foods on the menu. This would be a massive task, and even then it may not represent a fair appraisal. Different cooks cook on different nights, and ingredients can vary in their quality and freshness. A dish ordered on Saturday during a peak time may be very different from the same dish ordered on a relatively calm night. It is probably not realistic or possible to completely assess all the dishes offered by the restaurant. Instead, when we evaluate restaurants, we use samples to determine if the restaurant meets our expectations. We also naturally group our samples into general categories such as appetizers, salads, entrees, and so on. We might report on a dining experience by praising an appetizer, criticizing an entree, and going into raptures over a dessert. And because we inherently understand this idea of sample usage, even if we have a bad experience on one night or in one category, we generally return to give the cook another try.

Our lives are basically made up of samples and we inherently understand this. A sample is a small part of a whole; it may or may not reflect the quality of the whole. We use samples to make decisions about the wholes they represent. In other words, samples of the world around us provide data, information, or evidence for the decisions we make. The traffic on the freeway at 6:30 in the morning, the attitude of a salesperson late in the day, the reaction of a coworker to a national issue, and the music we hear on a specific radio station are all samples, and we react to them in a variety of ways. Usually we evaluate several samples before making a judgment and taking action. For example, we may have a first impression of a new coworker, but we generally interact with that individual over several instances before deciding that the person is someone we might like as a friend. We may take the same route to school several times before deciding that the traffic is too heavy and choosing an alternate path. We probably allow for one or two instances of rude salespeople before we decide to avoid a store. Generally, we take samples, look for patterns, and make decisions based on these patterns, not on single instances. Of course, sometimes a single sample is so pleasant or unpleasant that our decision is formed immediately. I well remember my first taste of anchovies and I have never attempted them since.

We need to carry our everyday practice of sample analysis into comprehension assessment. Instead of looking at a test or activity as representing a student's comprehension, we should regard it as only one sample of comprehension. It may be an accurate sample, but it may not be. For example, think about high-stakes testing and the pressure put on students by both parents and teachers. This can lead to a high level of anxiety, which may have a very negative effect on comprehension. Consider a group project in which negative group dynamics hinders comprehension. I remember when mandated certification tests in my state moved to a required computer format. At that point in time, many students found this awkward and unfamiliar and their scores indicated their unease. Because so much can go wrong with a single assessment, collecting multiple samples makes good sense.

Our role is to look for patterns in multiple samples of comprehension behaviors. But don't educators already do this? Not if they label an activity or assessment "comprehension" without categorizing it in some more specific way. Not if they describe it in a grade book as "Chapter 4 Test." Not if they use one form of assessment such as mandated standardized assessments as the primary basis for deciding about a student's ability. An educator who takes the grades of all tests, projects, worksheets, and homework assignments and averages them for the report card is basically saying that all are of equal importance and all reflect the comprehension process in a similar way. Given the contents of Chapter 1 and the first part of this chapter, we should actively question the validity of that assumption.

Categorization

Using samples for decision making works only if it is combined with categorization. Categorizing objects, events, and emotions is a natural cognitive process, so natural that we are not even aware of doing it. We categorize samples as good or bad, needed or unneeded, acceptable or unacceptable, tasty or nasty, convenient or inconvenient, and so forth. This natural categorization process is an integral part of our decision-making procedure. And so, if we are to make a decision about the quality of a student's comprehension, we need a system for categorizing comprehension samples. We need a simple coding system that can allow educators to detect patterns of comprehension behavior. When an assessment sample is entered into a grade book, it should be accompanied by a code that specifically categorizes it. Many grade books use one- or two-word descriptions of an assessment activity, such as page number, unit/chapter title, or a brief description. Although these suggest the subject matter topic, they are inadequate to categorize that complex entity called comprehension.

What are the basic elements of comprehension categorization? Consider some possible elements and whether they are workable for school and classroom assessment. The first is mode of input. Was comprehension assessed during or after reading, listening, or viewing? In most cases, it is impossible to separate these components. During an instructional unit or classroom activity, a teacher may ask students to read segments of the textbook and the print on a media presentation, view illustrations and computer simulations, and listen to the teacher's explanations and the comments of their peers. How can this complexity be easily categorized as representing primarily reading, listening, or viewing? It can't. In such cases, categorizing the mode of input is clearly unworkable.

However, there are instances when categorization of input may be important. Differentiating the mode of input is important when assessing students who are struggling academically. This usually occurs when a student is not reading at the level of his or her peers. Because listening comprehension is strongly related to reading comprehension (Daneman, 1991; Sticht & James, 1984), it makes sense to determine if the listening comprehension process is similarly impaired. Many students who are learning English as a second language can understand through listening much more than they can through reading, and it makes good sense to separate the two. In fact, students who are English language learners are often given the option of taking tests in an auditory as opposed to visual format. In summary, whereas an assessment specialist will probably differentiate mode of input, a classroom teacher will generally not do so.

Another comprehension category is type of text, narrative versus expository. For content teachers who teach social studies, science, math, or other specific subjects, this is not an issue. Almost all text used in a content classroom is expository in nature. However, English teachers and reading teachers should pay attention to possible comprehension differences in narrative versus expository material. A variety of genres are presented in English and reading classes, and it is important to differentiate narrative from expository. Many students demonstrate much higher comprehension after reading a narrative selection than after reading expository text. Assessment should inform instructional planning, and this can suggest a need for greater attention to comprehension of expository text structure.

Another category is familiarity or unfamiliarity of the topic. Again, for math, social studies, science, and other subject matter disciplines, this is probably not an issue. Most, if not all, text is unfamiliar in nature. However, in the reading or language arts classroom, familiarity can be an issue. I recall watching a teacher read a story to a second-grade class of urban children and assess their understanding through discussion. Unfortunately, the story was about a farm, and none of the children had any idea of the nature and purpose of a farm. Although some had gone to the zoo and watched monkeys and lions, none had seen a pig, chicken, or cow. None understood what such animals eat or how they must be cared for. Their comprehension reflected this lack of familiarity. Another time, in the same classroom, a totally different picture emerged as the children eagerly discussed their reactions to a story about washing the family car. If the teacher intended to keep some record of both experiences, one should certainly have been categorized as unfamiliar and the other as familiar.

Yet another category is the format of the assessment activity. Although there are many ways to categorize assessment formats, I suggest that, for the purpose of describing comprehension, teachers focus on the following two kinds: selected response assessments and constructed response assessments. Selected response items are often referred to as objective assessments. The student is presented with several possible choices for an answer and chooses one. Most standardized instruments use the selected response format. Constructed response assessment requires that the student construct something. It can be a written answer, an oral summary, or a project of some sort. We often call such assessments open-ended or subjective assessments. All assessments can fall into these two broad categories, which allows for a simple form of categorization. Did the students select an answer or construct the answer? Very often, teachers find very real comprehension differences across the two kinds of assessment formats.

But what about an assessment that utilizes both formats, for example, a unit test that employs a series of selected response questions with several constructed response questions? It is important to separate the two when analyzing student performance. They represent different forms of comprehension, and we cannot assume that a student will do well in both. This subject is discussed in more detail in later chapters.

In addition to the aforementioned elements of comprehension categorization (mode of input, type of text, familiarity, and format), educators should choose a limited number of components to describe the nature of the comprehension process itself. Perhaps the simplest way is to categorize comprehension as literal, inferential, and application.

The following table suggests categories of comprehension with simple coding symbols that can be easily entered into a grade book. Note that the categories Assessment Format and Comprehension Component are listed first and are italicized. This is to stress that these are the basic and required codings for all assessments. Mode of Input, Type of Text, and Familiarity may have relevance for some teachers in some specific situations, but differentiating comprehension in terms of assessment format and comprehension component is basic to detecting patterns of comprehension in all students. This allows an educator to move away from thinking of comprehension as a unitary entity and provides modifiers for educators to use in describing comprehension performance.

Categories of Comprehension

Assessment format	Comprehension component	Mode of input	Type of text	Familiarity
SRF—Selected response format	L—Literal	R—Reading	N—Narrative	F—Familiar
CRF—Constructed response format	I—Inferential	Ls—Listening	E—Expository	U—Unfamiliar
	A—Application	V—Viewing		
		C—Combination		

The following table summarizes categories that may be applicable for different educators.

Assessment of Comprehension Components

Assessment specialist	Mode of input	Type of text	Familiarity	Assessment format: SRF, CRF	Comprehension component: Literal Inferential Application
Reading teacher		Type of text	Familiarity	Assessment format: SRF, CRF	Comprehension component: Literal Inferential Application
English teacher		Type of text	Familiarity	Assessment format: SRF, CRF	Comprehension component: Literal Inferential Application
Content specialist				Assessment format: SRF, CRF	Comprehension component: Literal Inferential Application

Suppose an educator assessed comprehension following a science unit using a traditional question-based unit test. Using this coding system, the educator might describe the assessment as usual in the grade book (e.g., Test Chapter 6 or Test Structure of Matter) but append the following: SRF (the assessment employed selected response items such as multiple-choice and true/false) and L (the assessment primarily involved literal or factual comprehension).

Consider another example. The English or reading teacher assesses students' comprehension following discussion of a short story and records this by coding N (it was a narrative), U (it was on an unfamiliar topic or theme), CRF (the assessment employed an open-ended constructed response activity), and L/I (the assessment involved both literal and inferential comprehension). Of course, in the grade book, there would be two columns: one for a literal score and one for an inferential score.

When it is time to enter report card grades, talk with students, or confer with parents, the educator identifies any salient patterns. An assessment specialist would probably note any clear differences in reading and listening comprehension. Students who are English language learners often demonstrate better listening and viewing comprehension than reading comprehension. Young children who are just beginning to make sense of letters and sounds also show better listening comprehension. In fact, it is important to note this, because poor listening comprehension can be an indication of problems with language development in general.

The assessment specialist, the reading teacher, and the English teacher would note any comprehension differences between narrative and expository text. A student who displays acceptable comprehension with narrative text but falters with expository material is not a poor comprehender. This student is a poor comprehender of a certain kind of text, but comprehension in general seems intact. I would certainly look like a poor comprehender if you assessed my ability to interpret income tax directions. For content teachers of math, social studies, and science, almost all of the written or oral text used in the classroom is expository in nature, so this level of analysis can be skipped.

The assessment specialist and the reading teacher would also note any differences between familiar and unfamiliar material. Inability to comprehend familiar text is more serious than inability to comprehend unfamiliar topics. For many content areas, all subject matter is basically unfamiliar, so this level of analysis can be skipped.

All educators should determine whether a student experiences difficulty with an assessment format. Some students do well with selected response questions but experience difficulty with constructed response assessments' essay questions. Some students can answer multiple-choice questions but are not able to conduct a science experiment or coordinate an open-ended project. At this level of analysis, you are identifying information that not only describes your students but also suggests areas for instructional emphasis.

Finally, which comprehension components showed a student's strengths? Which ones need more instruction? Again, you are not only determining a student's strengths and weaknesses, you are also discovering how to focus subsequent instruction.

At first glance this process seems unwieldy and, like any new endeavor, it takes a bit of getting used to. In the beginning it may seem quite time-consuming, but as you become familiar with the process, it takes much less time. However, this process offers a workable system for categorizing multiple samples of a student's comprehension behavior. It allows the educator to use general but meaningful descriptors to specify comprehension. I return to the notion of sample categorization again and again in succeeding chapters.

Comprehension Assessment and Response to Intervention

Response to intervention (RTI; Fuchs & Fuchs, 2006) will no doubt have a profound influence on an assessment of student comprehension, learning, and progress. The passage of the Individuals with Disabilities Education Act (IDEA, 2004) allowed schools and districts to classify students as learning disabled on the basis of their response to instruction. In the past, classification of learning disability rested on an identified discrepancy between level of intelligence, as measured by a standardized IQ test, and level of functioning in listening, thinking, speaking, reading, writing, spelling, and/or mathematical calculation. That is, a child with normal intelligence who was functioning below the level of his or her peers in reading, writing, or math, for example, could be considered learning disabled, and the school or district would receive federal funding to provide instructional intervention. Today, the identification of learning disability can rest on lack of student response to instruction. "Response to intervention is, simply put, a process of implementing high-quality, scientifically validated instructional practices based on learner needs, monitoring student progress, and adjusting instruction based on the student's response. When a student's response is dramatically inferior to that of his peers, the student may be determined to have a learning disability" (Bender & Shores, 2007, p. 7).

RTI is often conceptualized as embodying three tiers. The first is classroom instruction. Assuming the presence of effective classroom instruction and valid and sensitive classroom assessment, lack of student progress can signal a need to move to the next tier. Tier 2 provides focused intervention in addition to regular classroom instruction. It can be delivered by the classroom teacher or by personnel external to the classroom such as reading specialists or subject matter experts. Such instruction usually involves small-group instruction offered two to three times a week (McCook, 2006). Lack of progress in this tier leads to Tier 3, individualized intervention and the probable identification of a learning disability.

RTI emphasizes "the role of data for decision-making" (Brown-Chidsey & Steege, 2005, p. 18). Student progress is monitored using "short, quick and easy-to-administer probes" (McCook, 2006, p. 14). In Tier 1, universal classroom screening occurs three times a year and identifies those students who are not progressing as well as their peers. In Tiers 2 and 3, the same measures are used more frequently to identify progress as a result of intervention. Classroom screening establishes a baseline for scores, and the performances of individual students are compared to that baseline to determine progress or lack of it.

What forms do the short and quick assessments take? They primarily focus on what I describe in Chapter 8 as proxies, that is, measures that predict comprehension but do not directly assess it. The most popular RTI assessment is oral reading fluency, a measure of the number of words read correctly in 1 or 2 minutes. Other RTI probes assess number of sounds and letters recognized and number of words correctly spelled, all within a 1- to 3-minute time frame (Wright, 2007). If assessed, comprehension generally takes two forms, neither of which parallel what readers, listeners, and viewers do when they comprehend. The student orally reads a passage for 1 minute and then retells it. Retelling is scored as the number of words in the retelling offered within a 1-minute time frame; the accuracy of the retelling is not judged. A second form of assessment is a 3-minute maze task in which the student reads a passage with words deleted and selects a missing word from three or four choices.

At the present time, the RTI assessment and intervention model primarily centers on reading performance (Bender & Shores, 2007; Wright, 2007; McCook, 2006; Brown-Chidsey & Steege, 2005) involving sound-based or phonological measures. Admittedly, these are highly predictive of future reading comprehension performance. However, Gersten and Dimino (2006) state that although such assessment is not inaccurate, "it is incomplete; it is only one part of the picture" (p. 104). There are other nonphonological measures that predict reading comprehension, such as oral language proficiency, expressive vocabulary, and passage recall. However, these do not necessarily lend themselves to short, quick, and easy-to-administer RTI probes.

RTI, as presently conceptualized, seems focused in the elementary school, but there is certainly a chance that the initiative will extend into the middle and secondary levels. When and if this occurs, assessment of comprehension will have to move beyond comprehension proxies and measures of letter and sound identification. Because federal funding is closely tied to RTI, the validity and reliability of comprehension instruction and assessment will be of increased importance in the next years and subject to a closer form of scrutiny than in the past.

RTI is basically quite new, and it remains to be seen how various schools and districts will interpret and implement the fairly general federal guidelines. As always, the devil is in the details. It is not a purpose of this book to suggest specific guidelines for RTI implementation. However, it is important to examine RTI in relation to classroom comprehension assessment. All teachers basically represent Tier 1, and their instruction and assessment should be sensitive enough to identify children in need of additional and more focused instruction whether or not a classification of learning disability ever applies. In succeeding chapters, I briefly examine the RTI paradigm in regard to comprehension assessment.

Summary

The following table provides a summary of the contents of this chapter.

What am I assessing?	How am I assessing?	Why am I assessing?	Pulling it together
Components of comprehension: literal, inferential, application	Formal standardized assessments	To evaluate school effectiveness.	Taking multiple samples
Mode: reading, listening, viewing	Informal classroom assessments	To evaluate student learning. RTI.	Categorizing comprehension
Text: narrative, expository, familiar, unfamiliar	Selected response assessments	To determine why students struggle academically. RTI.	Coding comprehension categories
Topic: literature, mathematics, social studies, science	Constructed response assessments	To evaluate instructional effectiveness.	
	Questions	To provide student feedback.	
	Student dialogue		
	Comprehension proxies, RTI		

Professional Development Activities for Increasing Understanding of Comprehension Assessment

- Examine a published test that you have used in the past or are planning to use. Identify sections that assess literal comprehension. Which ones assess inferential comprehension? Are there any that assess application or learning?

- Examine how you code entries in your grade book. Does your system allow you to note patterns across assessment formats and the three components of comprehension?

- Choose the most recent entries in your grade book. How would you code them with regard to assessment format and comprehension component?

CHAPTER 4

Questions

Promises and Pitfalls

Overview

Asking questions is the most common form of assessment. This is not surprising if one considers that asking and answering questions are integral parts of our everyday life. It is not just educators who ask questions to assess their students' comprehension. Questions are a natural way for us to assess and clarify, first our own comprehension, and second the comprehension of our families, friends, and acquaintances.

We can examine the role of questions in our own comprehension process. We listen to many people discuss and explain countless things. We listen to friends, family members, auto mechanics, doctors, salespersons, waiters, computer technicians, and so forth, and we ask them questions to make sense of what they say. We read a wide variety of texts: magazines, newspapers, novels, recipes, catalogues, directions, bills, insurance forms, and the like. In these situations, we cannot directly ask questions of the text authors, who are seldom present, but in our attempt to comprehend, we ask ourselves questions to focus our understanding. Then we continue reading and/or rereading, in hope of finding answers. We watch movies, television shows, videos, and DVDs, and we listen to the radio, tapes, and material downloaded to our iPods. As we do, we again use the self-questioning process to guide our comprehension even if we cannot interact with a real-live person. Self-generated questions play a very large role in our comprehension of what we hear, read, and see as we use them to clarify our own comprehension. In addition, as speakers or conversationalists, we use questions to assess other people's comprehension of what we say. Writers of informational text often attempt to anticipate questions that people may ask in order to address them. For example, many directions for new appliances include a section termed "commonly asked questions."

Educators obviously use questions to assess student learning. However, they also employ questions to scaffold student comprehension (Kintsch, 2005). Prereading questions direct students' attention to what they will read about. Postreading questions ask them to self-assess their understanding of key points. The insertion of questions throughout textbook chapters is a common practice for focusing the readers' attention. Teaching students to self-question is an effective instructional tool, and training students to employ the strategy of question generation improves comprehension (Rosenshine, Meister, & Chapman, 1996).

Questions come in many forms, and not all forms are equal. Given the wide use of questions in listening, reading, and viewing, it is no wonder that we tend to take questions a bit for granted. Because we formulate questions frequently, effectively, and somewhat unconsciously, we seldom examine the process. As a result, we are not always aware of the complexity of questions. Before we can begin to consider the use of questions as a tool for assessing comprehension in the school and classroom, we need to understand their structure. This involves understanding three areas: question format, question category, and question purpose.

Question Format

In Chapter 3, I suggested that all assessments can be categorized into two basic groups: selected response assessments and constructed response assessments. Similarly, there are two basic question formats: selected response questions and open-ended or constructed response questions.

Selected Response Questions

In selected response questions, students select the correct answers from several possible choices. Typical selected response formats are multiple-choice questions, true/false questions, fill-in-the-blank questions with an answer bank provided, and matching questions for which the student matches two columns of terms that are related in some way. Selected response questions can also take the form of a series of events or steps that the student must rearrange in sequential order. Selected response questions are often referred to as objective questions. This is because scoring such items requires no subjective judgment on the part of the teacher. The answer is either right or wrong and, given the answer key, all teachers will score an objective test in exactly the same way. Thus, objective questions possess a high degree of scoring reliability which is why high-stakes standardized tests usually employ such items. Selected response items are basically recognition measures; that is, a student does not have to recall an answer from memory but only to recognize or identify it from a group of possible alternatives.

Some people feel that selected response questions are easier than open-ended items because they are measures of recognition as opposed to recall. This may be true as a general rule; however, as discussed in Chapter 1, comprehension is heavily dependent on a student's prior knowledge. Thus, a selected response item on a very unfamiliar topic will probably pose difficulties for students that are unrelated to the format of the question.

Constructed Response Questions

Open-ended or constructed response questions require a student to supply or construct the answer; thus, such instruments are generally regarded as measures of recall. An open-ended question can require a one- or two-word answer and can be of the fill-in-the-blank form, in which possible choices are not available. Open-ended questions can also entail short answers of one or two sentences, as well as longer and more complex responses such as writing a paragraph or essay. Open-ended questions are considered subjective because scoring them requires judgment on the part of the teacher. Even scoring open-ended fill-in-the-blank questions can call for subjective decision making. For example, if the question is, "Pyramids were built as tombs for _____," will all scorers regard "pharaohs" and "mummies" as equally correct responses?

Comparison of Question Formats

There are promises and pitfalls connected with different question formats. Selected response questions certainly take less time, both for responding and for scoring. It takes much less time to choose the right answer out of four possible choices than to write a persuasive essay. It also takes less time to score such questions. However, selected response questions may be more time-consuming to write. Good selected response items that are closely tied to instructional objectives are quite difficult to construct.

Constructed response questions can involve more on the part of the student than knowing the answer. They may also demand skill in organization and writing. A short-answer open-ended assessment has been described as "a supply item that does not require organization" (Trice, 2000, p. 121) because such items are generally no longer than a few sentences and focus on content alone. Essay questions, however, demand knowledge of content and knowledge of the process of writing a well-structured essay. Unless students are taught to write essays prior to using this question format, the teacher cannot know whether poor performance reflects lack of content knowledge or lack of writing ability. Kintsch (2005) states that open-ended questions provide a more accurate measure of deep comprehension but acknowledges their problematic nature "because considerable human resources are needed to score essays and even short answer questions and reliability is not guaranteed" (p. 55). Because selected response and constructed response formats are so different, it is important that teachers evaluate a student's comprehension in terms of the type of questions used. For this reason, in Chapter 3, I suggested describing and coding all comprehension assessments as selected response formats (SRF) or constructed response formats (CRF).

Some students experience difficulty with certain selected response formats. I personally cringed when faced with a true/false question that contained multiple items. If one was erroneous, the entire question was false. However, when unsure about an answer, some students learn "tricks" for choosing a probable correct one, and test preparation materials teach such helpful strategies. It is clearly impossible for a teacher to know and keep track of each student's comfort level with a specific selected response format or to know which questions were answered correctly because the student actually knew the material as opposed to making a good guess. In Chapter 3, I discussed assessment as involving multiple samples of behavior. A teacher should vary question formats and not depend exclusively on selected response or open-ended items. Because comprehension assessment involves noting patterns across multiple samples, this can tend to negate the effect of student difficulty with a specific question format. Another consideration in choosing the question format is the distinction between recognition and recall. That a student recognizes an answer in a selected response format does not mean that he or she will be able to call it up from memory and use it at a later date.

Question Category

Different categories of questions tap different stages of the comprehension process. In Chapter 1, I described this process as follows: Once words are recognized, the reader, listener, or viewer connects idea units or propositions and builds a microstructure of interrelated idea units. This leads to the construction of the macrostructure or passage gist. The microstructure (details) and the macrostructure or gist (main ideas) form the text base, which remains very close to the author's meaning. Questions that tap into the text base focus primarily on what the author said or, to put it differently, what was explicitly stated in the text. However, comprehension moves beyond the text base. The reader integrates text base information with his or her prior knowledge and constructs inferences, creating what W. Kintsch (1998) and E. Kintsch (2005) call a situation model. Questions that focus on the situation model move beyond what was explicitly stated in the text and ask the student to connect the text to his or her knowledge base and make inferences. I also differentiated between understanding and learning. Learning involves taking what was understood and transferring or applying this knowledge to new situations or contexts.

Questions have been categorized in a variety of ways. The simplest and most common form of question categorization involves two question groups: literal or explicit questions and inferential or implicit questions. This division is critical in assessing comprehension; however, it is somewhat limited in that it does not address application (Kintsch, 2005; RAND Reading Study Group, 2002; Pellegrino, Chudowsky, & Glaser, 2001).

Bloom's Taxonomy

Bloom's taxonomy of educational objectives (Bloom & Krathwohl, 1956) is a familiar form of question categorization, described in Chapter 3. It involves six levels: knowledge, comprehension, application, analysis, synthesis, and evaluation. This taxonomy has been used for many years to categorize types of questions, with question words indicated for each component. Unfortunately, the question categories, although helpful, are not discrete. For example, *summarize* and *classify* are question words often tied to the comprehension component, but they could just as easily refer to analysis. Similarly, *interpret* and *predict* are also tied to the comprehension component, but could also be used to construct synthesis questions. I suspect that Bloom's taxonomy is seldom used by classroom teachers, partly because of the fuzziness of the categories but also because there are six of them. In the busy world of the classroom, six categories may be just too much to handle with any degree of efficiency. There is another consideration. Teaching students to generate questions on their own is an important instructional strategy that improves comprehension (Mayer & Wittrock, 2006; Nokes & Dole, 2004; Beck, McKeown, Hamilton, & Kucan, 1997). Bloom's taxonomy may be too complex and imprecise to serve as an instructional model for student question generation.

Applegate et al. Question Categorization

Applegate, Quinn, and Applegate (2002) categorize questions as literal, low-level inference, high-level inference, and response items. Their classification was devised to evaluate questions in published and current informal reading inventories. Literal questions demand answers that are stated explicitly in the text. Low-level inferential questions take several forms. A question can ask the student to infer on the basis of information that was explicitly stated but in words that are different from those in the question. For example, the text says, *After the wool is removed, it must be washed very carefully,* and the question asks, *After people shear the wool, what is the next step?* (Leslie & Caldwell, 2006). Low-level inferential questions can ask students to identify relationships between ideas that were not clearly signaled in the text. For example, the question is, *Why did Mary go to the store?* and the text says, *Mary went to the store. She bought bread and milk.* The text did not include *because,* thus forcing the student to make a low-level inference of causality. Other low-level inferential questions focus on relatively irrelevant material or ask the reader to answer questions on the basis of prior knowledge as opposed to text content. For example, after reading a story about washing a car, such a question might be, *What do you think is the most efficient way to wash a car?* Low-level inferential questions perhaps tap the comprehension text base to a greater degree than the situation model.

High-level inferential questions require students to integrate prior knowledge with text content and draw logical conclusions. Such questions involve providing explanations, alternatives, predictions, and descriptions of processes. Response items ask students to focus on broader ideas, underlying themes, and passage significance. They require longer answers than high-level inferential items because they ask the student to "react to the underlying meaning of the passage as a whole" (Applegate et al., 2002). Clearly, high-level inferential questions and response items draw upon the situation model constructed during the comprehension process.

Kintsch Question Categorization

Kintsch (2005) regards questioning as a method for developing comprehension as well as for assessing it. There are two general groups of questions: text-based items and inference items. Text-based items have three levels. Level 1 questions are prompts to summarize. Level 2 questions are open-ended, require short-answer responses, and refer to explicitly stated important information. Level 3 questions focus on who, what, when, or where and serve as a check of basic factual understanding. Inference questions go beyond explicitly stated text-based information and ask students to integrate, explain, predict, and speculate.

Ciardiello Question Categorization

Ciardiello (1998) describes four categories of questions: memory questions, convergent thinking questions, divergent thinking questions, and evaluative thinking questions. These categories can not only guide the teacher in choosing or constructing questions but can also be used to teach students how to generate and answer such questions on their own.

Memory questions begin with *who, what, where* or *when.* Students answer a memory question by naming (*What is a synonym for humidity?*), defining (*What is a nebula?*), identifying (*Who was Stephen Douglas?*), designating (*Where was the armistice signed?*) or offering a yes or no response (*Are viruses the same as cells?*). Memory questions are tied to comprehension of the text base. They assess recall of content but they may not indicate understanding of that content. In fact, a student may have memorized the information without understanding it or may be simply parroting the words of the text.

Convergent thinking questions begin with *why, how,* and *in what way.* Students answer such questions by explaining (*Why did Wilson offer compromises at the Paris Peace Conference?*), stating relationships (*How did the Nile River influence the development of civilization?*), and comparing and contrasting (*How are the red giant stage and the black dwarf stage of a star's life different?*). Answering such questions requires an understanding of the content and the construction of a situation model.

Divergent thinking questions begin with the signal words *imagine, suppose, predict, if . . . then . . . , how might . . . , can you create,* and *what are some possible consequences).* Students use their situation models to move beyond the text and apply what they have understood. In answering divergent thinking questions, students predict (*Predict how the terms of the Versailles Treaty paved the way for Hitler's rise*), hypothesize (*Suppose the United States had not entered World War I? What might have happened?*), infer (*What might have been the possible consequences of excluding Germany and Russia from the Paris Peace Conference?*), and reconstruct (*Create a new Treaty of Versailles that might have prevented World War II*).

Evaluative thinking questions begin with *defend, judge, justify, what do you think,* and *what is your opinion.* In answering evaluative thinking questions, students value (*How do you feel about giving benefits to illegal immigrants?*), judge (*Were the actions of American factory owners justified in offering low wages to immigrants?*), defend (*Should immigration quotas have been imposed during the late 19th and early 20th centuries? Why do you think so?*), and justify choices (*Why would you prefer to attend a school that has a large percentage of immigrant students?*). Again, as with divergent thinking questions, students use their situation models to move beyond the text and apply or transfer what they have understood to new situations.

Question–Answer Relationships

Another form of question categorization is that offered by Raphael (1982, 1986) and Raphael, Highfield, and Au (2006), who differentiated questions as to where the answers can be found. Raphael calls her system Question–Answer Relationships, or QARs, and it represents a simple and effective scheme for teaching question types to students. Answers to questions can be found in two places: In the Book and In My Head. There are two forms of In the Book questions: Right There questions and Think and Search questions. The answer to a Right There question can be found explicitly stated in the text, usually in a single sentence. Often the words in the question parallel the words in the text. Right There questions correspond to knowledge questions (Bloom & Krathwohl, 1956), memory questions (Ciardiello, 1998), and literal items (Applegate et al., 2002). The answers to Think and Search questions are also in the text, but the reader may have to find them in different parts of the text, and the words in the question and the words in the text may not be the same. Think and Search questions are still literal in nature and, like Right There questions, tap into the text base of the comprehension process.

There are two In My Head questions: Author and Me and On My Own. The answers to In My Head questions are drawn from the situation model of the comprehension process. Author and Me questions are inferential in nature and correspond to Ciardiello's (1998) convergent thinking questions or the higher-level inferences of Applegate et al. (2002). The answers to Author and Me questions are not in the text; instead, readers must identify text clues and match these to what they already know. On My Own questions ask the student to move beyond the text to engage in what Ciardiello (1998) calls divergent and evaluative thinking and what Applegate et al. (2002) term response questions. QARs are perhaps best fitted for elementary students, whereas Ciardiello's question classification seems more appropriate for middle and high school students.

Comparison of Question Categories

All of the question categorizations are quite similar. All identify literal questions as one form of question, although they call them by different names. All pay attention to different levels of inferential questioning and distinguish between inferences that are tied to text content or, in other words, the situation model, and inferences that ask students to move beyond the text and apply what they have understood.

Different question categorizations can easily be divided into the three components of comprehension: literal, inferential, and application (Table 4.1). Similarly, question words or question stems can also be grouped into the three comprehension categories (Table 4.2).

It is important for teachers to consider question categories if they are to assess comprehension. In fact, question categories are more important than question format because they are directly tied to content and it is comprehension of content that is the focus of assessment. Teachers either choose questions that have been written by others, such as those included in a textbook or teacher's manual, or they

TABLE 4.1. Comparison: Question Categories

	Literal questions	Inferential questions	
		Text inferences	Application inferences
Ciardiello (1998)	Memory	Convergent questions	Divergent questions Evaluative questions
Raphael (1982, 1986)	In the Book: Right There questions In the Book: Think and Search questions	In My Head: Author and Me questions	In My Head: On My Own questions
Kintsch (2005)	Text-based questions: Levels 1, 2, 3	Inference questions: integrating, explaining	Inference questions: predicting, speculating
Applegate et al. (2002)	Literal questions	Low-level inferences High-level inferences	Response questions
Bloom and Krathwohl (1956)	Knowledge questions Comprehension questions	Application questions Analysis questions	Synthesis questions Evaluation questions

construct questions on their own. In either case, it is critical that teachers recognize the different levels of comprehension tapped by a question. This can allow them to perform a more fine-tuned assessment of student comprehension.

To practice recognizing the different question categories, read the following selection taken from a middle school social studies text and identify the ques-

TABLE 4.2. Question Words

Literal question words	Inferential question words	
	Text inferences	Application inferences
who, what, where. when, define, label, list, name	why, how, in what way, interpret, discuss, explain, describe, summarize, classify, demonstrate, show, relate, order, connect, compare, categorize, analyze	imagine, suppose, predict, how might . . . , create, what might happen if . . . , if . . . then . . . , what are some possible consequences of . . . , modify, invent, design, plan, defend, judge, justify, what do you think . . . , evaluate, what is your opinion of . . . , appraise, conclude, recommend

tions that follow as literal questions, text inference questions, and application inference questions.

The Khmer Kingdom*

The Khmer kingdom was one of the wealthiest kingdoms in Southeast Asia. Khmer is also the name of the people who lived in the kingdom. In the sixth century, the Khmer ruled the lands we know today as Cambodia and Laos on the Indochina Peninsula. The Khmer civilization was influenced by Indian culture. Buddhism also flourished, along with the worship of Shiva and other Hindu gods.

Internal conflicts divided the kingdom during the eighth century. But Jayavarman II reunited the kingdom in 802. He was crowned king according to Hindu rites, which declared he was a deva-raja or god-king. Being a deva-raja allowed Khmer rulers to act with absolute power, or the power to control every part of society. They used this power to form large armies that could defend the kingdom, as well as to invade its neighbors. In addition, the kings could force both the Khmer and slaves to work on the extensive irrigation system.

The irrigation system was key to the successful economy. During the monsoon season, the large reservoirs, levees, moats, and ponds helped prevent the farmland from being flooded. They also stored water to be used during the dry season. The irrigation system allowed farmers to grow crops as many as two to three times a year.

Agricultural surpluses helped strengthen the kingdom's economy. For more than 500 years, the Khmer kingdom was an important influence in Southeast Asia.

The first royal city was built at Angkor in the tenth century. This marked the beginning of the empire's golden age. Under Suryavarman II the empire reached its peak in the early twelfth century. During his rule from 1113 to 1150, he oversaw the construction of the magnificent towers of the temple Angkor Wat.

In 1431, the Thai people invaded and destroyed the capital city of Angkor. The Khmer kingdom never recovered. In addition, Angkor was ruled by one or another of its neighbors for hundreds of years. In the late 1800s, the French began to colonize the area. But by 1953, Cambodia won its independence. The Khmer, as a people, remained in Cambodia and today make up some 90 percent of the people who live there.

Label the following questions as literal questions, text inference questions, and application inference questions. There are three of each but they are in mixed up order. Don't be tempted to peek ahead to the answer key. The purpose of this activity is to determine if you truly understand different question categories, an understanding that is critical to comprehension assessment.

*Excerpt from *Scott Foresman Social Studies: The World*, Grade 6 (2003, pp. 357–358). Copyright 2008 by Pearson Education, Inc. Reprinted by permission.

1. Predict what might have happened to the Khmer kingdom if the irrigation system had failed.
2. Why did Jayavarman II allow himself to be crowned according to Hindu rites?
3. What is a deva-raja?
4. Do you believe that absolute power is a good thing? Why or why not?
5. Why did the Khmer kingdom become an important influence in Asia?
6. For how many years was the Khmer kingdom an important influence?
7. How did the position of deva-raja influence the expansion of Khmer rule?
8. What percentage of the Khmer people remain in Cambodia today?
9. Why would the French be interested in colonizing the Khmer region?

Answers

1. Predict what might have happened to the Khmer kingdom if the irrigation system had failed. <u>Application inference.</u> *In order to answer the question, the student must move beyond what is stated in the text and infer that floods and drought would damage crops which, in turn, would weaken the economy. A weak economy would make the kingdom less powerful and open to invasion.*
2. Why did Jayavarman II allow himself to be crowned according to Hindu rites? <u>Text inference.</u> *The student must infer that he sought the absolute power that this would give him.*
3. What is a deva-raja? <u>Literal question.</u> *The answer is stated in the text.*
4. Do you believe that absolute power is a good thing? Why or why not? <u>Application inference.</u> *This question asks the student to move beyond text content, use what was understood about the Khmer kingdom with regard to forced labor and military invasion, and make a judgment as to the value of absolute power in any situation.*
5. Why did the Khmer kingdom become an important influence in Asia? <u>Text inference.</u> *The student must infer that the successful agricultural economy brought great wealth to the kingdom. Such wealth allowed the kingdom to expand and control others.*
6. For how many years was the Khmer kingdom an important influence? <u>Literal question.</u> *The text states the answer.*
7. How did the position of deva-raja influence the expansion of Khmer rule? <u>Text inference.</u> *The student must infer that absolute power allowed the kings to force people to join armies and work on projects that would expand Khmer rule.*
8. What percentage of the Khmer people remain in Cambodia today? <u>Literal question.</u> *The answer is stated in the text.*
9. Why would the French be interested in colonizing the Khmer region?

<u>Application inference.</u> *The student must move beyond the text and explain that France or any nation might need or want to extend its power to Khmer because of its resources and wealth.*

Literal questions are easy to construct and recognize. Inferential questions are more difficult. Yet inferences are at the heart of the comprehension process. There is a temptation to get somewhat hung up on whether a question represents a text inference or an application inference. Don't fall into that trap. Use question words to help you construct or evaluate your questions. Make a decision as to the type of question and move on. Perhaps there will be times when you mistakenly identify a text inference as an application inference and vice versa. But remember, we are dealing with multiple samples of assessment items, and a few questions that are mislabeled will not really matter.

Question Purpose

At a global level, we can agree that our purpose for asking questions is to ascertain whether students have comprehended what they read, listened to, or viewed. But question purpose goes beyond this to address additional concerns. The first and primary concern is the validity of the question itself, why a specific question was asked in the first place. What exactly does the teacher want to know about the students' comprehension? Were the instructional objectives of the lesson met? Did the students understand important facts? Were they able to make inferences on the basis of these facts and their own prior knowledge?

A second purpose addresses what the teacher intends to do with the questions after they are asked and the answers are evaluated. In other words, was the purpose of a question formative or summative in nature? Formative questions help the teacher to improve instruction; summative questions require the teacher to make a decision about a student's learning.

In Chapter 2, formative assessment was defined as assessment for learning. Such learning takes two forms: teacher learning and student learning. The teacher asks questions to determine what the students understand for the purpose of changing instruction. If the questioning process suggests that students are still confused about certain concepts or processes, the teacher uses this knowledge to repeat, adapt, or vary instruction for the express purpose of fostering learning.

The teacher also uses feedback to foster student learning. Feedback is crucially important in any learning task (Bransford et al., 2000). Formative assessment involves giving specific feedback to students in the form of comments and additional questions for the purpose of improving student performance. Such feedback can be written on first drafts of papers and projects or can take the form of an oral discussion of what students understood and what still needs clarification. Formative questions allow a teacher to determine not only if a student knows the answer but also why the student answered as he or she did. Formative feedback revises student thinking and fosters the skill of self-assessment. No grades are assigned to formative assessment experiences.

Summative assessment requires the teacher to assign a grade and/or make a judgment about a student's comprehension. Typical summative assessments are grades on tests, papers, worksheets, and report cards. Many summative assessments include valuable teacher feedback on the quality of the product but, unfortunately, such comments come too late to affect or improve student learning. We have all seen what generally happens when such papers are handed back. The students look at the grades and ignore the comments.

Guidelines for Assessing Comprehension through Questions

If questions are to be used effectively to assess comprehension, there are certain guidelines that should be followed. Because asking questions is the most common form of assessment, it is also the most commonly misused; improving comprehension assessment involves paying more attention to question design and usage.

• *Guideline 1. Differentiate between literal, inferential, and application questions.* Use the coding system described in Chapter 3 to do this. Consider the typical content test composed of perhaps 25 selected response questions such as multiple-choice, true/false, and a few short-answer items. The objective items generally receive 1 point each; the short constructed response items may be assigned 2 or 3 points each. Each test receives a single numerical score based on the number of correct answers. Often this score is translated into a letter grade and entered in the grade book. The assessment is described according to the content it represents—that is, structure of matter, nineteenth-century immigration, the Elizabethan age, and the like. There is no differentiation between a student's ability to remember literal items and his or her ability to deal with the inferential ones. It is entirely possible that two students may receive the same grade and present very different profiles in ability to comprehend literal versus inferential content. Marzano (2000) offers several examples of single scores that mask very different student profiles on test items.

If an educator does only one thing to change his or her grading practices, it should be to differentiate between literal and inferential comprehension questions. This contributes to the validity of the questioning process as reflecting the complexity of the comprehension process. In Chapter 3, it was suggested that assessments be coded according to literal, inferential, and application comprehension components. This is important because it allows the teacher to note which students are adept at literal comprehension but may need instruction in dealing with inferences. I recall quite vividly a middle school student I tested not long ago. Dominic's grades had been acceptable throughout elementary school, but in middle school he soon began to evince difficulty in all subject areas. I asked Dominic to read several middle school passages covering literature, social studies, and science content. After he finished each one, I asked both literal and inferential questions. In analyzing Dominic's comprehension, I carefully differentiated between the two. A pattern soon emerged. Dominic was very successful in answering literal items. If he missed a literal question, he was generally able to look back in the text to find the answer. Yet Dominic found it very difficult to answer inferential questions. Nor was he able to look back in the text to identify clues that might help him. In summary, Dominic comprehended explicitly stated items quite well but he was not able to draw inferences. Nor did he seem to understand the process of matching text clues to his knowledge base. If I had not differentiated between these two kinds of questions, I would have had little insight as to how to help Dominic.

At the most basic level, a teacher should differentiate between literal and inferential questions; however, a teacher can also draw distinctions between literal questions, inferential questions, and application questions, as delineated in Table 4.1. What does it mean to differentiate such questions? First, the teacher should identify the category of each question that he or she writes or chooses, using the question and performance words in Table 4.2 as a guide. Then the teacher can code a question as L (literal), I (inferential), or A (application). Ideally, if a grade is to be assigned, the student should receive separate grades for the three kinds of assessment questions: literal, inferential, and application. This may mean that separate grades are entered in the grade book. If separate grades are not an option, the three forms of questions should be analyzed separately and weighted differently to arrive at a final grade. Such weighting is based on the notion that the ability to answer inferential or application questions represents a higher-level comprehension skill than the ability to respond to literal items.

• *Guideline 2. Differentiate between selected response and constructed response questions.* Selected response questions measure recognition, but constructed response questions tap recall. As such, they represent a higher level of difficulty. Just as students exhibit differences between literal and inferential comprehension, they can also demonstrate different patterns in their ability to answer selected response versus constructed response items. A teacher will not know this unless he or she differentiates and codes questions as SRF (selected response format) or CRF (constructed response format). Knowing the possible differences between students allows you to better match your instruction to their needs. But what about an assessment that involves a combination of selected response and

constructed response items, each of which includes literal, inferential, and application items? In such a case, the analysis of a student's performance can become
rather complex, and, as mentioned in a previous chapter, complex assessments
tend to be quickly discarded.

The solution to the dilemma is to treat the selected response and the constructed response items as two separate assessments and code each one for literal,
inferential, and application components. If you are constructing your own assessment (as opposed to using a published one), you have two options. You can use a
single assessment format, consisting of selected response questions only or constructed response questions only. In this case, you just code for components of
comprehension. Or you can physically separate selected response and constructed response questions and grade them separately. Another solution is to
always limit application questions to a constructed response format, which
makes sense. Given the complexity of an answer to an application question, it is
extremely difficult to adequately tap this level of comprehension through a
selected response question.

• *Guideline 3. Tie questions to the objectives of the instruction.* This strategy
seems relatively basic; that is, assess comprehension in terms of what you, the
teacher, deem important for the students to understand. However, in reality and
in the busy world of the classroom, several things occur that work against a
merger of assessment and instruction. First, teachers are often much too general
in terms of their objectives. As a result, all questions are regarded as equally
important. Second, content specialists who are deeply in love with their subject
matter tend to have unrealistic expectations of what a student can comprehend
and remember after reading a chapter, listening to a lecture, or viewing a video. A
few years ago, I sent some high school teachers excerpts from textbooks in their
specific disciplines: literature, history, and science. I asked them to highlight
those parts of the text that they thought students should understand and remember. The pages were returned to me transformed from white to the color of the
highlighter they used. In other words, they highlighted almost everything! From
their point of view as content experts, it was clear that they thought almost
everything was important to comprehend, but was that realistic? In unfamiliar
and concept-dense text, is it reasonable to expect students to remember everything? For example, in reading about the characteristics of viruses, is it realistic to
think that students who are approaching this concept for the first time should
understand all the characteristics that differentiate viruses and cells, all the components of a virus, the steps in the replication process of a virus, including the
lytic and lysogenic cycles, ways of classifying viruses, how and why viruses are
very specific, the functions of different viruses, and the distinction between
viruses and nonviral particles?

Wiggens and McTighe (1998) describe curricular content in terms of three
components. The first is enduing understandings, those really big ideas that you

want students to remember 5 years later. "Enduring understandings go beyond discrete facts or skills to focus on larger concepts, principles or processes" (p. 10). They are fundamental to the discipline and applicable to new situations. Perhaps an enduring understanding regarding viruses would be an understanding of how all living things are affected by cell alteration. The second component represents a more detailed level and reflects the basics, or key concepts and processes, of the discipline. These are things that it is important for students to be able to know and do, such as describing how a virus replicates using a host cell. The third component represents those things that students should be familiar with but may not remember in detail. Given these three components, instructional objectives and assessment should focus primarily on the first two. Application questions assess enduring understandings. Literal questions and text inferential questions assess important concepts and processes.

In determining instructional objectives, the teacher needs to determine those big ideas or enduring understandings and the key concepts or processes that students should know and do. At this point we are talking about *key* concepts, not *all* concepts. Once you have determined specific objectives based on big ideas and key concepts, construct questions or select questions that specifically reflect these and reject the temptation to include questions that are less important.

To what degree should questions tap factual knowledge? Knowledge of facts is important and crucial to knowledge application. "The ability to plan a task, to notice patterns, to generate reasonable arguments and explanations, and to draw analogies to other problems are all more closely intertwined with factual knowledge than was once believed" (Bransford et al., 2000, p. 16). Go back to the text on the Khmer kingdom. If a student does not understand certain facts, it is impossible for that student to use this knowledge to apply it. Teachers should not apologize for asking factual questions; however, they should ask factual questions that tap key content and are critical for application to new contexts. Returning to our first guideline, comprehension assessment should not just focus on factual content but should include inferential questions, tapping both the text base and the situation model of the comprehension process.

• *Guideline 4. Differentiate between formative and summative assessment questions.* Under "Question Purpose," I described the difference between formative assessment for the purpose of improving learning versus summative assessment for the purpose of assigning a grade. Unfortunately, many teachers do not make this distinction and grade everything, be it homework, practice exercises, quizzes, projects, and unit tests. I remember once, during a district inservice session, suggesting the practice of assigning grades only to important or summative assessments. Many of the teachers became very upset at the thought of not assigning a grade to every piece of written work. In fact, one teacher angrily stated that she would not be doing her job if she returned papers without a grade. Although I can appreciate the dedication of these teachers, they failed to understand the critical difference between formative assessment, or assessment that forms learning, and summative assessment, or assessment that summarizes learning.

Think about a skill that you recently learned. Perhaps it was playing a new sport such as tennis or engaging in a new craft such as scrapbooking. Think about how faulty and tentative your first efforts were. Think about how important feedback was as you struggled with new learning. Think about how you avoided demonstrating your skill to others until you had achieved some measure of competence. I well remember learning to knit, and I completed three sweaters before I was willing to wear one or to admit that I had knitted it and, in a sense, receive a grade in the form of another's judgment. So it should be in the classroom. Students need feedback on what they did not understand and what they did not recognize as important. Such formative feedback fosters comprehension. Only after adequate feedback should a summative grade be assigned.

This does not mean that teachers should not keep records of formative assessments. Such records are invaluable in helping students and in differentiating between learner needs. Formative assessments can take the form of a letter grade; that is, a student can receive a grade of C on a formative assessment. However, a formative grade should always be accompanied by feedback describing why the grade is a C, as opposed to B or A. Selected response tests can also be formative in nature. I know of one teacher who has students correct missed items on such formative instruments by locating the answers in the text or discussing their answers with peers.

In summary, teachers should ask both formative and summative questions, but only summative assessments should contribute to the report card grade. Students need to know the difference, that is, when a grade will "count" and when it represents an opportunity for feedback and improvement. I have talked with teachers who express concern that students will not attach importance to formative questions because they do not affect report card grades. Perhaps this way of thinking occurs in the beginning, but it seldom lasts. As students begin to see the value of formative questions and how they lead to higher performance on summative measures, they eagerly embrace the concept of formative assessment.

• *Guideline 5. Do not assume that a wrong answer always means that the student did not comprehend the content.* In truth, the student may not have comprehended the question. This may be more problematic for younger students and for students who are learning English as a second language, but it can apply to older students as well. Gunning (2006) discovered that students who were not able to answer a question could often do so if the question was rephrased. Younger students and those who are English language learners often do not have a fine-tuned understanding of question words and fail to differentiate between *when, where, how,* and *why.*

The structure of selected response questions can also mask a student's real understanding of the content. For example, some true/false items focus on a single fact, whereas others include multiple facts of which one is false. Consider the following example of two true/false selected response items.

Boysenberries are an example of an aggregate type fruit.

Boysenberries, raspberries, and blueberries are examples of aggregate type fruit.

Only one decision is required to answer the first question. The second question requires three decisions before a true or false judgment can be made.

Trice (2000) suggests that a true/false item should never include more than three facts. In fact, he recommends testing one fact at a time until grade 6 and then including two facts but never moving beyond three. Questions with more than a single fact make it difficult to assess a student's learning. If the student missed the question, which fact was the cause? If the question contains only one fact, it is easier to recognize where gaps in student learning occur.

Multiple-choice questions are made up of a question stem, the true answer, and the wrong answers, which are called distracters. Test format can act as a pitfall, with students failing an item because of the difficulty with such possible choices as both a and b, all of the above, or none of the above. Teachers and publishers often include such items in order to have a uniform number of choices across all test items. Actually, there is no rule that says there should be a uniform number. Negative question stems also pose difficulty, such as when students are asked which of the following choices are not true.

The difficulty of understanding questions became very apparent to me when I took an 8-week master gardening course through the state university extension office. The final activity was a 50-item multiple-choice open-book test. Some teachers think that open-book tests are too easy. Not so! However, I was challenged not by the content of the questions but by the structure of the question stems and the answer choices. Often, choice rested on one seemingly innocuous word. Double negatives were prevalent; that is, there were items in which the stem and one or more choices contained a negative. Consider the following example.

> Which is not true of about the dynamics of wildlife?
>   a. Mortality occurs annually.
>   b. Population is not impacted by changes in habitat.
>   c. The process of nasality does not occur annually.
>   d. Reproduction corresponds to periods that are favorable to survival
>   of the young.

Both the question stem and choices *b* and *c* contain negatives, which places additional processing demands on the student. The term *nasality* is not defined.

It refers to annual production of young. The student may not remember the technical term even though he or she understands the concept, and as a result the student may well miss the question.

I had read the material, attended the classes, and was generally able to locate where an answer could be found but was often confused by what the question was really asking. I wondered as I worked on the test, and I still wonder, why the test maker felt he or she had to include such confusing questions. Was it to trick the students? Was it to make an open-book test so difficult as to force some form of deeper processing? Unfortunately, it only raised my anger and damaged my motivation to persevere. I don't think the test measured my understanding or comprehension; instead, it tested my ability to ferret out details and tricks of question generation.

Somehow it never occurs to us to teach students how to answer the selected response questions we compose or select. We are placing more emphasis on test-taking skills as schools struggle with the impact of high-stakes standardized tests. One very effective strategy is to have students construct their own selected response items and try them out on their peers. This helps them to deal with the pitfalls of poorly constructed questions. The purpose of a question is to assess understanding of content, not to trick or confuse the student.

• *Guideline 6. When asking subjective open-ended questions, know exactly what you are looking for.* In other words, construct guidelines to minimize the subjectivity of scoring. Determine which information should be included in the answer. For essay tests, prior to testing, determine how much of the student's score will depend on content knowledge, structure or organization of the essay, and composition mechanics such as spelling and punctuation.

I am basically talking about rubrics, which I examine in more depth in Chapter 5. People tend to think of a rubric as something that is written, used to evaluate performance, and often shared with students. A written rubric can be handed out with an assignment, which lets students know exactly what the teacher is looking for. Rubrics are often used as explanatory feedback in formative or summative assessment. I have found that students perform at a higher level when they have the benefit of a rubric that details what should be included in an open-ended question. Rubrics do not have to be written; that is, a teacher can mentally determine the guidelines he or she will use to evaluate the students' answers. However, the very activity of writing a rubric tends to clarify thought and thus makes the resulting evaluation criteria more precise.

• *Guideline 7. Consider using look-backs to assess comprehension.* By look-backs, I mean open-book assessments. Instead of expecting students to answer from memory, allow them to find the answers in the text. Look-back or open-book tests discriminate between understanding and memory. A student may have understood a concept while reading, listening, or viewing but forgot it and therefore answered incorrectly, made a bad guess, or skipped the question. If allowed to look back, the student may be able to correctly answer the question. Standardized tests allow for students to engage in look-backs but, unfortunately, many students do not utilize this opportunity. If a student can look back to locate an answer, that is a good indication that the student understood it in the first place.

Look-backs work for both literal and inferential items. For literal items, the student locates an explicitly stated answer, what Raphael (1982, 1986) referred to as Right There answers. For an inferential question, the student locates the text clue that directs the inference process, what Raphael referred to as an Author and Me question. Look-backs are particularly relevant for application questions when understanding and memory for facts must be applied to novel contexts. Some teachers feel that look-back questions are too easy. I would counter that they are a sensitive measure of a student's understanding that is not confounded by memory. Leslie and Caldwell (2001, 2006) determined that students with reading levels at or above third grade were able to answer more comprehension questions by looking back after reading, and, at a high school level, comprehension after look-backs correlated significantly with standardized test scores.

Guideline 8. Organize your questions in a user-friendly way. I am referring particularly to summative test items. Group the questions according to key concepts. Learning occurs in chunks; that is, as students encounter new learning, they tend to place it with similar concepts (Bransford et al., 2000). Memory is not a haphazard process. For example, if a student learns what a ratel is, the student may include that new knowledge in the concept of animal and immediately see how a ratel is like or unlike other animals. In constructing or choosing selected response test items, group questions according to similar concepts. To return to the example of the test in my master gardening course, there was no grouping of the items. Questions on growing fruits might be items 5, 17, 29, 35, and 42, and questions on soil analysis might be 1, 6, 24, and 44. I know of one social studies teacher who not only groups test questions but also provides labels for each grouping.

Questions and Response to Intervention

As mentioned in Chapter 3, most RTI assessments do not involve asking questions after reading, listening, or viewing, probably because asking questions requires more time than administering a 1-minute oral fluency measure or asking a student to identify letters or sounds. This is unfortunate, because well-designed questions that differentiate between literal, inferential, and application levels can offer much information about the quality of a student's comprehension. At the upper elementary, middle, and high school levels, it is imperative that student response to instruction include more direct measures of comprehension. Very often, poor performance at these levels occurs for reasons other than word identification or fluency issues. As mentioned in Chapter 1, there are many factors that impact comprehension—reader background, the presence or absence of comprehension strategies, and text structure, to name a few.

Questions can be incorporated into RTI assessment, but such probes take more time than 1–3 minutes. Bender and Shores (2007) describe a tenth grader who was having difficulty in history class. His teacher worked with him outside class and taught him a strategy for summarizing text. Each week, the teacher monitored the student's progress by administering a test made up of questions similar to those used in the classroom.

If a teacher intends to work with an individual or small group and monitor weekly progress through questions, this is not difficult to do. The teacher selects passages that are representative of materials used in the classroom and writes questions to accompany each passage. Passages should be of similar length and structure (narrative or expository) and, if possible, should have a similar level of familiarity or unfamiliarity. The assessment can be administered in either of two ways: individually or silently. For individual administration, the student reads a passage orally or silently, and the teacher asks questions. The teacher can also read the passage to the student in order to assess listening comprehension. For group administration, all students in the class or group listen to or read the passage at the same time and answer the questions in writing.

There are pros and cons to both formats. Individual assessment takes more time; the teacher will have to find a way to occupy the other students while he or she is involved with an individual. The advantage to group administration is that the entire class or group can be assessed at one time. However, writing answers to questions may compromise the quality of comprehension for students whose writing skills are poor or who do not like to write.

For both formats, the quality of the questions is critical. They can involve a mixture of literal- and inference-level questions, but these should be differentiated and reported separately. Some students can answer literal questions but evince much difficulty with drawing inferences. The questions should all follow the same format: selected response, constructed response, or a mixture of both. Selected response questions are faster to score but take more time to construct. The selected response format also minimizes the negative effect of poor writing skills. However, constructed response questions are easier to write but more difficult to score. Because of these differences the two formats should be reported separately in the screening or progress report. Whatever choice the teacher makes, that format for assessment and administration should be followed throughout the school year for Tier 1 classroom screening or for the duration of the intervention for Tiers 2 and 3 progress monitoring.

Summary

- Asking questions is the most common form of assessment. Educators use questions to assess student learning and to scaffold student comprehension.

- There are two basic question formats: selected response and open-ended questions. In selected response questions, a student selects the correct answer from possible choices. Open-ended or constructed response questions require the student to supply or construct the answer. Selected response questions are considered measures of recognition, whereas constructed response questions are measures of recall. Selected response questions are faster for responding and for scoring. Constructed response questions can involve skill in organization and writing.

- Different categories of questions tap different stages of the comprehension process. Questions have been categorized in a variety of ways, the simplest being literal and inferential. Question categorizations include knowledge, comprehension, application, analysis, synthesis, and evaluation (Bloom & Krathwohl, 1956); literal, low-level literal, inference, high-level inference, and response (Applegate et al., 2002); memory, convergent thinking, divergent thinking, and evaluative (Ciardiello, 1998); In the Book and In My Head (Raphael, 1982, 1986). All categories are quite similar and can be grouped into three major categories: literal questions, text inference questions, and application inference questions.

- There are different purposes for asking questions. Is the purpose formative or summative in nature? Formative assessment is assessment for learning. The teacher learns whether the instruction should be repeated or modified. The student receives specific feedback for improving his or her performance. Summative assessment requires the teacher to assign a grade or make a judgment about a student's comprehension.

- Certain guidelines should be followed when using questions to assess comprehension.

- Differentiate between literal and inferential comprehension questions.

- Differentiate between selected response and constructed response questions.

- Tie questions to the objectives of the instruction. Application questions tap enduring understandings; literal questions and text inferences assess important concepts and processes.

- Differentiate between formative and summative assessment.

- Do not assume that a wrong answer indicates lack of comprehension of content; it may reflect lack of comprehension of the question format or language.

- Construct guidelines for evaluating open-ended questions.

- Consider using look-backs to assess comprehension.

- Organize questions in a user-friendly way by grouping questions according to key concepts.
- Questions can be incorporated into the RTI model, but only if question formats and comprehension levels are carefully differentiated.

Professional Development Activities for Improving Question Use

The following activities can be done individually or with other teachers. Actually, working with your peers is much better than working alone. It allows for different perspectives, for discussion, for clarification, and for collaboration. The old adage about two heads being better than one is especially true for activities designed to change existing practice. Although change is always difficult, having the support of your peers makes it easier.

- Choose a summative assignment involving questions that you have administered or intend to administer. Identify the level of questions by choosing a question taxonomy as your base. You may decide to use Ciardiello's (1998) four question types: memory questions, convergent questions, divergent questions, and evaluative questions. You might use Raphael's (1982, 1986) grouping of In the Book and In My Head questions. Or you might choose the three question groupings shown in Table 4.1: literal questions, inferential questions, and application questions. Now, go through the questions in your summative measure and label each one. Which question category was most prevalent? Was there an imbalance between the question types? If so, add, delete, or rewrite questions to achieve a balance.
- Go through your textbook or teachers manual. Choose a chapter or similar segment of text and examine the questions. These can be prereading questions, during-reading questions, or postreading items. Label the questions according to the taxonomy you have chosen. Is there a balance between the different question types? Does the manual emphasize one type over another? How would you change the questions? Which ones would you keep, delete, or rewrite?
- Consider question format. Again examine past summative assignments and published materials. Are the questions primarily selected response or open-ended? Is there a balance?
- Choose a unit of instruction that you have taught recently or one that you are planning to teach. What are your instructional objectives? Do the questions match the objectives? If not, change the questions by keeping some, deleting others, and writing new ones.
- Inspect your assessment practices. Do you differentiate between formative and summative assessments? If not, go through the information in your grade

book. Which recorded activities might be formative in nature? Which could be summative?

• Do you presently differentiate between literal and inferential comprehension when assigning a grade or offering formative feedback? If not, choose an assessment that you intend to administer in the near future. Label the questions according to the question taxonomy you have chosen. If this is your first effort in question differentiation, you might begin with just differentiating literal from inferential. Administer the measure and score it. Each student should receive two grades, one for literal questions and one for inferential items. You might simply count the number correct in each category, or you could figure out the percentage of items correct relative to the total number of literal or inferential items. For example, if there were 10 literal items and the student had 5 correct, the literal score would be 50%. If there were 6 inferential items and the student had 4 correct, the inferential score would be 66%. Construct a simple table (see below) to record the grades. Now examine your students' performance. Do you see differences between the two question categories? I am sure you will!

Student name	Literal score	Inferential score

CHAPTER 5

Open-Ended Assessments

Powerful but Problematic

Overview

In Chapter 3, I suggested that all assessment falls into two broad categories: selected response and constructed response. In selected response assessment, students choose an answer from several possible choices. In constructed response assessment, often referred to as open-ended, students supply the information from memory. This chapter focuses on constructed response open-ended assessment of comprehension, a powerful measure of comprehension but problematic in many ways.

Open-ended assessment of comprehension in the classroom can take multiple forms. Much of it is driven by teacher inquiry in the form of short-answer items and essay questions. However, there are other forms of open-ended assessment, often referred to as project and performance assessment. *Performance assessment* is a relatively generic term that can apply to a variety of open-ended evaluation options. The National Research Council Committee on the Foundations of Assessment (2001) defined it as the "use of more open-ended tasks that call upon students to apply their knowledge and skills to create a product or solve a problem" (p. 30). Wiggens (1989) described such assessments as "authentic" because they seem to possess intrinsic task value and more closely parallel real-life activities. Instead of answering multiple-choice or true/false questions, students construct diagrams, design projects, write reports, build models, and conduct experiments. They keep journals, compose and deliver oral reports, and maintain portfolios. Most forms of performance assessment strongly tap the inference and application levels of comprehension. Such activities can be extremely revealing to a teacher and can indicate not only if a student has comprehended a body of content, but also the extent to which he or she can apply it.

Open-ended assessment is generally viewed as drawing on a higher level of comprehension than selected response assessment. First, constructed response assessment is regarded as a measure of recall, that is, a measure of what a student has understood and committed to memory, as opposed to what a student may recognize from a list of possible choices. The difference between recall and recognition can be illustrated by the following two questions:

Name one of the first five presidents of the United States.
Which of the following was one of the first five presidents of the United States: Jackson, Cleveland, Monroe, Lincoln?

It is clearly easier to play the elimination game and come up with the correct answer *Monroe* than to recall a possible name from memory. Second, selected response assessments call for inert knowledge; the student is not required to create or reconstruct the solution to a problem (Calfee & Hiebert, 1991). Because open-ended assessment generally moves beyond short one- or two-word answers, it requires more than just an answer. It demands some organization on the part of the student. The student must not only construct the content of the answer from memory, but must also organize it in some coherent fashion. If the assessment measure is written, as so many are, it requires some proficiency in the mechanics of writing if it is to be understood. If it is an oral report, it demands skill in delivery and the possible construction of visual aids. If the measure is a cooperative group project, student participation and the ability to interact positively with peers becomes an issue.

Constructed response open-ended assessments, like selected response items, can address all three levels of the comprehension process: literal, inferential, and application. Such assessments can assess the comprehension of facts and concepts, as well as processes and cognitive strategies such as composition, problem solving, and summarizing. An open-ended assessment can focus on what is explicitly stated in the text and ask students to recall the text base. It can tap into the situation model and ask students to draw inferences. Or it can ask students to apply their knowledge in some way and thus demonstrate learning. In most cases, open-ended assessments, particularly complex performance assessments, address all three levels, which makes them quite complicated and problematic to evaluate.

Open-ended assessments can possess validity. Remember that *validity* means that the assessment measures what it was supposed to measure. An open-ended essay question or a science project can be extremely valid in assessing a student's comprehension of content or process, but only if the teacher knows exactly what he or she is assessing. To put it another way, open-ended assessments are valid to the extent that they match the teacher's specific instructional objectives. The major problem for open-ended assessment is reliability. That is, there is a strong subjective element involved in evaluating such assessments. Two teachers reading the same essay or evaluating the same project may assign very different scores. Teachers clearly recognize the subjectivity of scoring open-ended assessments. In fact, they often refer to them as "subjective tests," with selected response items designated as "objective tests."

The purpose of this chapter is not to offer suggestions for constructing open-ended assessments in areas such as reading, science, or social studies. Teachers are infinitely creative, and most have already designed and implemented a variety of projects, exercises, and activities included under the open-ended umbrella. Textbooks also offer many suggestions in this area. The design and choice of appropriate open-ended assessments demand the knowledge and expertise of the content specialist. The purpose of this chapter is to offer suggestions for increasing the validity and reliability of any open-ended assessment, those that already exist as well as those that have yet to be created.

Validity of Open-Ended Comprehension Assessment

> **To establish the validity of open-ended comprehension assessments:**
>   Match the open-ended assessment to specific instructional objectives.
>   Focus on important or significant content and processes.
>   Differentiate the levels of comprehension expected: literal, inferential, application.
>   Acknowledge the possible interference of performance variables.

Match the Open-Ended Assessment to Specific Instructional Objectives

The first step in any assessment process is to identify what to assess. The Joint Committee on Testing Practices (2004) states that assessment instruments should meet their intended purpose; that is, the teacher should know exactly what he or she is assessing and why. In other words, the assessment is clearly tied to classroom instructional objectives and its purpose is to demonstrate that students have comprehended and learned what the teacher intended to teach.

Unfortunately, many classroom assessments lack validity. This occurs when educators do not specifically define what they are teaching. Sometimes they describe their purpose in terms so general as to be meaningless, such as "teaching reading" or "teaching writing." Sometimes they define their objectives in terms of general content, such as "teaching the circulatory system" or "teaching the industrial revolution." Sometimes they refer to the text organization itself, such as "teaching Chapter 4." If instruction is to promote student comprehension and lead to effective and valid comprehension assessment, there must be more detail. You may have assigned text readings, shown visual diagrams, offered explanations, and matched students to interactive websites. What specifically do you want the students to understand about the circulatory system or the industrial revolution? What factual knowledge is important? What processes do you want them to acquire? What do you want the students to do with their knowledge?

I vividly recall watching a social studies lesson conducted by a student teacher. The teacher asked the students to take turns orally reading sections of the text. Some read fluently and expressively; many did not. Few paid attention during the reading and, when called upon to take their turns, had to be directed to the location of the proper text segment. After each reading, the teacher asked the student to retell the content. If the student was unsuccessful (and many were), she asked a few questions, primarily literal in nature. Some focused on key concepts, but many involved relatively unimportant details. If the student's response was inaccurate, the teacher supplied the answer and moved on to the next section. At no time during the entire lesson was there any mention of lesson purpose, of what the students should be learning about the topic, of what they should be able to do with their knowledge. When I asked the teacher about this, she seemed genuinely confused and reminded me that she was following the teachers manual. When I asked her what she wanted the students to do with their learning, she answered that she hoped they would pass the unit test. When I asked her about the content and format of the unit test, she admitted that she had not yet looked at it.

Trice (2000) suggests composing instructional objectives as if you were doing so for a substitute teacher. Instead of using such imprecise terms as *teach, go over,* or *cover,* compose your objectives in terms of the three levels of comprehension: factual, inferential, and application. Is your objective to focus on the comprehension and recall of factual content? Then ask the students to define, list, label, or name. Do you intend to concentrate on inferential comprehension? Then ask them to summarize, explain, categorize, compare, and contrast. Is your primary purpose to apply content to previously learned concepts? Ask the students to design, defend, or justify. Use the question words listed in Table 4.2 to help you clarify and specify your instructional objectives.

Brookhart (2006) refers to the teacher's instructional objectives as learning targets, which is an apt analogy. An effective target is visible; that is, it can be clearly seen. Targets that are hidden do not allow individuals to demonstrate their skill. For example, the archer must see the bull's-eye in order to hit it. The basketball player must discern the basket in order to direct his or her aim. These may seem like simplistic analogies, but they illustrate that learning targets (or instructional objectives) are effective only to the extent that they are recognized and understood by both teachers and students. Such targets can involve understanding of content such as facts and concepts. They may also include a focus on processes and procedures such summarizing, comparing and contrasting, conducting experiments, writing essays, or delivering speeches.

We all remember (probably not fondly) constructing behavioral objectives in education classes. Such objectives listed what the students should learn or do in minute detail, the degree to which they should learn or do it, and the circumstances under which learning or performance should occur. I suspect that most of us constructed such objectives only in our education classes and seldom, if ever, engaged in the process once we entered the classroom. It would be nice if teachers had the time to specify instructional objectives in such minute detail, but they do not. What, then, should you do about constructing objectives? Simply and specifically state what you want your students to learn and do by focusing on the descriptive verbs listed in Table 4.2. Keep your objectives clear and simple, and use them to focus both your instruction and your assessment.

Focus on Important or Significant Content and/or Processes

Just as instructional objectives must be specific, they must also be significant. In other words, what big or significant ideas or processes do you want students to comprehend or do? Wiggens and McTighe (1998) call these enduring understandings. At the next lower level, what important concepts or processes do you want to foster? Do you want students to learn literal content, draw inferences based on that content, or apply what they have comprehended and committed to memory? You can design valid assessments only by first identifying what is important for your students to comprehend, learn, and do.

I admit this is not easy when one considers typical classroom textbooks. They seem to grow bigger and heavier with each new publication cycle. The amount of information presented on a single page is overwhelming. How can a student comprehend and remember all of it? And is it all equally important? Here is where specificity comes in. The teacher, as the content specialist, needs to carefully decide what is most important and teach to that and only that. And, of course, assessment should focus on what the teacher identifies as important.

Consider the example of a middle school textbook on United States history. The chapter on the first colonies contained four parts, one of which focused on the English colonies. This segment of approximately 10 pages included the following information: the geography of the 13 English colonies; a description of the New England colonies, including brief biographical information about Puritan leaders; a description of the Middle Colonies with a focus on Pennsylvania; a description of the Southern Colonies with a focus on Georgia; a biography of William Penn; an account of the persecution of Roger Williams and Anne Hutchinson; and a page-length chart comparing and contrasting the 13 colonies. And this was only one segment of one chapter!

Recall the first step of the assessment process. Identify what to assess. In order to do that, the teacher must determine what is important for students to understand and, we hope, learn. Once that has been determined, the assessment can be designed.

A teacher may utilize a variety of open-ended activities to assess comprehension of text content. The history text I described offered several suggestions for this assessment, such as having students summarize how religious dissidents were persecuted in the colonies, design a newspaper to chronicle colony events, or write a letter to relatives in England describing colony life. How will a teacher assess such open-ended projects? If the teacher evaluates the projects on the basis of his or her instructional objectives, then the assessment possesses validity. Suppose the teacher chose the following enduring understanding or big idea (Wiggens & McTighe, 1998): *Students will comprehend the hardships suffered by the colonists in their pursuit of the religious freedom that we take for granted today.* Then, if the assessment possesses validity, the teacher evaluates the summary, newspaper, or letter in terms of that purpose. Did the students' work describe the hardships of living in the colonies? Did it express the importance of religious freedom?

Identify and Differentiate the Levels of Comprehension Expected: Literal, Inferential, Application

Assessing comprehension requires that teachers indicate the level of comprehension that is expected (Trice, 2000). This refers to the three levels of comprehension discussed in Chapters 3 and 4: literal, inferential, and application. To return to the lesson on the 13 colonies, the teacher's objective certainly suggests a focus that extends beyond the literal level. Students would need to comprehend and infer hardships in terms of their own lives, such as winter cold without furnaces, sickness without medical clinics, hunger without supermarkets, and communication without computers or cell phones. At an application level, it would involve judging whether the hardships were worth religious freedom or even if such freedom was a reality in the colonies. The summary, newspaper, or letter could be evaluated at three comprehension levels. At a literal level, did the student describe the hardships and motivations mentioned in the text? At an inferential level, did the student expand on items mentioned in the text and include inferences related to the difficulty of life and the importance of freedom? At an application level, did the student make a judgment or offer an opinion about the value of freedom and the price that is often paid to gain it?

Assessing comprehension through open-ended assessments also demands that the teacher prioritize the importance of facts, which are usually at a literal level. The chapter segment mentioned previously contained many explicitly stated facts: how the colonies were founded; names of mountains, rivers, oceans, and towns; lists of natural resources; crops grown in the colonies; descriptions of laws governing the colonies; biographical accounts of specific individuals; information about the Native Americans; and explanations of climate patterns. Are all these facts equally important? Not really. The facts that are important are those that relate to the teacher's instructional objectives. Facts regarding why the colonies were founded and the persecutions suffered by some individuals are germane to the teacher's objectives and thereby appropriate for inclusion in an open-ended assessment.

Acknowledge the Possible Interference of Performance Variables

There is more to validity than matching open-ended assessments to instructional objectives and comprehension levels. Open-ended assessments can be quite complex. The students must do something to demonstrate or indicate their understanding; that is, they must perform in some way. And it is the performance that often gets in the way of comprehension assessment. A student may comprehend but be unable to demonstrate his or her comprehension because of performance demands attached to the assessment. In such a case, comprehension is obscured by performance interference, as described in the table on the following page.

To return to our history example, evaluating the summary, newspaper, or letter as including hardship and appreciation of freedom is a valid measure of comprehension, because the teacher's instructional objective focused on that outcome. But what about the performance elements associated with writing, such as organization, sentence structure, and spelling? And if the newspaper project was a cooperative project, what about the interference of such elements as a student's contributing to the joint effort or taking a leadership role in group activities? Such performance variables can hinder or mask comprehension. For example, poor writing skills or an unwillingness to write can conceal the depth of a student's understanding; the student may have understood much more than his or her writing suggested. Lack of positive interactions between group members can also obscure comprehension or even obstruct it. For these reasons, in order to establish validity, it is important that teachers differentiate such performance variables from comprehension of factual, inferential, or application content in the assessment process.

There are times when a teacher's instructional objectives may include aspects

Type of assessment	Student response	Level of performance interference
Written selected response question	Student points to the answer, underlines the answer, or fills in a circle.	Little performance interference
Oral question	Student responds orally.	Some performance interference in terms of language ability
Written essay question	Student responds in writing.	Performance interference in terms of the writing process: organization, sentence structure, spelling, punctuation, and willingness to write
Oral report/presentation	Student composes and presents orally.	Performance interference in terms of organization, use of visual aids, and vocal delivery
Group project/ presentation	Students work together to compose and present.	Performance interference in terms of organization, use of visual aids, delivery, and group dynamics

of performance. That is, the teacher may intend to assess both comprehension of subject matter content and writing performance through an essay test. Or the teacher may propose to assess both comprehension of subject matter content and performance through construction of a research project. For example, the middle school history teacher might focus teaching on content such as the hardships endured in pursuit of religious freedom and, at the same time, teach students how to summarize or write a factual newspaper account. In such a case, the performance component becomes a clearly defined instructional objective.

If teachers identify both content and performance objectives as their instructional focus, they must assess both. In the example of colonial history, if the teacher evaluates on the basis of spelling and punctuation alone, the assessment lacks validity because it is not tied to the instructional objective of understanding hardship in pursuit of freedom. Suppose the teacher's objectives did include a performance objective, that of communicating understanding through writing. If the teacher measures only the process of writing, the assessment still is not valid. For it to have validity, the teacher must evaluate the summary, newspaper, or letter in terms of both content and performance objectives. And what if the teacher's instructional objective included a third component: for students to cooperate positively with peers? Then the teacher would also have to assess such cooperation. A valid assessment measures what it was supposed to measure; it measures what the teacher intended to teach and what the teacher wanted students to comprehend, learn, and do.

Content specialists, especially at the middle and high school levels, generally prefer to focus on their content and the students' understanding of literal, inferential, and application components. Despite multiple efforts to increase reading and writing instruction across the curriculum, many content teachers do not see it as their role to instruct students in reading, writing, and oral presentation skills. And yet they recognize the importance of a well-written essay question or an effective oral report and often include performance components in their grading criteria. In such cases, a teacher should acknowledge that comprehension of content and the performance aspects involved in assessment are two separate things. If teachers choose to include performance variables in the grade, that is their choice. What is important for validity is that they clearly differentiate between comprehension and application of content and how the student performs in order to demonstrate that comprehension. Such differentiation allows a teacher to recognize that students with poor writing skills or limited language proficiency may have truly understood the enduring understandings, or big ideas, represented by the open-ended assessment.

To review: In order for an open-ended assessment to be valid, the teacher must set specific and important instructional objectives and indicate the level of comprehension required: literal, inferential, or application. The teacher may include objectives that focus on content, as well as performance aspects needed to complete the open-ended assessment such as writing, group cooperation, and so forth. If the instructional objectives focus only on content, then the teacher assesses only content. If the teacher sets both content and performance objectives, then both should be addressed. If the teacher focuses only on content but expects that performance skills have been learned elsewhere, the two components should still be differentiated in the evaluation process and the teacher needs to decide if, and to what extent, performance components such as writing and speaking should factor into the grade.

Reliability of Open-Ended Comprehension Assessment

To establish the reliability of open-ended comprehension assessment:
Construct rubrics to match instructional objectives.
Keep rubrics simple and specific.
Share or construct rubrics with students.
Teach students the format of open-ended assessments.

What makes an assessment reliable? A reliable assessment is an accurate measure of what it was designed to measure. "Put another way, reliability is the extent to which error is eliminated from the assessment process" (Trice, 2000, p.

29). If no error was present, five teachers evaluating the same essay test, for example, would all arrive at the same score or grade. Five teachers evaluating the same oral report would arrive at the same score or grade. Unfortunately, this seldom happens. In research, open-ended assessments such as oral retellings or essay answers are scored by two or more individuals using a carefully crafted list of guidelines. The agreement between scorers is generally reported as percentage of agreement. I have read research studies in which the percentage of agreement was high, but it was never 100%, even under circumstances in which raters were extensively trained.

We acknowledge the issue of reliability even if we do not use the terminology. When you were in college, did you ever seek out teachers reputed to be "easy graders"? If you did, your motivation was likely based on an understanding that teacher evaluations are not always reliable. On tasks that are not selected response (or objective) measures, some instructors just give higher grades than others, possibly because they use less stringent or different guidelines for evaluation. Two instructors teaching the same class and using the same project or essay question as an assessment can assign very different grades.

Subjectivity in grading does not just occur across different teachers. It can also occur with a single educator. Think about what might happen when a teacher sits down to evaluate a stack of papers or projects. In the beginning, the teacher may pay careful attention to a variety of issues, but what happens when fatigue sets in? Evaluation can become less fine-tuned and may degenerate and become somewhat sloppy. Think about the differences that can occur if evaluation happens very soon after a project is assigned, as opposed to much later, when the teacher gets to the stack of projects that have sat on his or her desk for 1 or 2 weeks. Think about teacher mood, teacher fatigue, and the environment in which the evaluation takes place. Is the teacher grading or scoring with television blaring in the background or with noisy children continually interrupting the process, or is the evaluation occurring at a quiet, private time? Does the teacher feel well or is he or she suffering from a cold or headache? All of these circumstances can reduce the reliability of an assessment. The same paper, scored at different times and under different circumstances, by the same teacher might receive very dissimilar grades.

Construct Rubrics to Match Instructional Objectives

How can subjectivity in comprehension assessment be reduced, thus increasing the reliability of the assessment process? One tool for doing this is a rubric. Trice (2000) defines a rubric as "a system for assessing a complex response by a student" (p. 161). Rubrics provide criteria for describing student performance at different levels of proficiency. In other words, rubrics describe and scale levels of student achievement (Solomon, 1998). Rubrics can take a variety of forms, ranging from short-item checklists to lengthy descriptions of desired behaviors. They can describe levels of performance in terms of descriptors such as *excellent, good,* and *needs work,* or they can involve complex scoring systems.

Rubrics are not something added to make a teacher's job more difficult—they actually help. I well remember a paper I assigned in a graduate-level class back in the days when I knew very little about assessment or rubrics. Before I began the grading process, I mentally listed, in rather general terms, what should be included in the paper. I began grading, and for a short time the process went quite well. Then I encountered a paper that included components that seemed extremely significant to the purpose of the assignment. However, I had not seen such items mentioned in the papers I had previously graded, even papers to which I had assigned a grade of A. Quite frankly, in my hurried mental overview of what should be included in the paper, I had not even thought of those particular items. What should I do? Leave the grades as they stood or go back and grade each paper again? If I had thought out specifically what should be included in an A paper, if I had constructed a rubric, and if I had that rubric in front of me as I graded, I would not have encountered my dilemma. What did I do? I stopped grading and thought long and hard about what should be in the paper and the differences between the grades of A and B. Not trusting my memory, I wrote down what I had decided on. Basically, I designed my first rubric (I have certainly improved upon my rubrics since) and used it to grade all of the papers.

In the 1980s and 1990s, interest shifted to authentic or performance assessment. As a result, the construction and use of rubrics became quite commonplace. A variety of articles and textbooks suggested guidelines for constructing rubrics and offered a variety of rubric examples for teachers to use (Billmeyer, 2001; Burke, 2005, 2006; Glickman-Bond, 2006; Hill, Ruptic, & Norwick, 1998). In addition, the Web provides rubric examples, rubric templates, and interactive activities for building rubrics. Unfortunately, my experience with teachers suggests that ready-made rubrics do not work very well. Although it seems both convenient and time-saving to use them, much of the time they are not a close match to the teacher's specific instructional objectives. They are often quite general; in fact, they must be in order to reach a wide audience. However, an effective rubric must be relatively specific. For example, if you are assessing a student's comprehension of the characteristics of viruses through an essay question or a project of some sort, the rubric must focus on the important content that should be included, perhaps the size of viruses, their shapes, and how they replicate. Because of this specificity, a rubric for assessing comprehension of the circulatory system will be quite different from one that evaluates student comprehension and application of the basic principles of heredity.

It is not the purpose of this book to offer more examples of rubrics that teachers can copy and use. The content of an effective rubric can best be determined by the teacher because it is specifically tied to his or her instructional objectives, what that teacher deems important for the students to know or do. Some websites allow you to create your own rubrics using their predetermined templates, and you may find these very helpful.

Rubric Criteria

A rubric is basically made up of three elements: criteria, gradations of quality, and a system for translating gradations of quality into a grade (Caldwell, 2008; Goodrich, 1996–1997). Criteria can include both literal, inferential, or application content and process and performance components. On the basis of his or her specific instructional objectives, the teacher decides what aspects must be included in an assessment to evaluate a student's comprehension. Suppose you are teaching about cell structure and your primary objective is for students to compare and contrast plant and animal cells. You decide to assess their achievement through an essay question. Comparing and contrasting is an inferential level of comprehension; however, it requires understanding and inclusion of literal content. What literal content should be included in a complete and accurate answer? For example, do you want the students to say that both types of cells contain a nucleus or do you, in addition, expect a definition or description of the nucleus? An effective rubric lists specific criteria for what should be included in a student's answer.

Suppose a teacher lists the following factual items that students should address in comparing and contrasting plant and animal cells: cell membrane, cell wall, nucleus, cytoplasm, and organelles. However, the text describes seven organelles. Should all seven be included? Perhaps the teacher decides that students should be able to list one organelle shared by both kinds of cells and one that is specific to either a plant or an animal cell. In addition, the teacher thinks that the function of each cell part should be described. Having thus tied the assessment to specific instructional objectives for factual content, the teacher can construct the following checklist of factual content criteria.

> The student's answer should include the following:
> Cell membrane/function
> Cell wall/function
> Nucleus/function
> Cytoplasm/function
> One shared organelle/function
> One specific organelle/function

However, remember that the inferential purpose of the essay question is to compare and contrast plant and animal cells. A student must tell how they are alike and how they are different. So this component must also be included.

The student's answer should:
　　Tell how plant and animal cells are alike.
　　Tell how plant and animal cells differ.

Rubric Gradations of Quality

Now gradations of quality must be considered. One student may describe only a single function of the cell membrane, whereas another student may describe two or more. Are both responses of equal quality? One student may describe the membrane but inaccurately call it the cell wall. Another student may erroneously identify golgi bodies as found only in plant cells. In short, student responses may include the criteria for inclusion of content but still be very different because of inaccuracy, incompleteness, and amount of detail.

In order to address this situation, the teacher needs to specify gradations of quality. Rubrics can employ a variety of quality gradations or scales, as indicated in the following table. Most rubrics employ a 4-point scale, but you can extend a scale to five or six levels of quality if you choose. However, going beyond six becomes very unwieldy. There is no rule for choosing one scale over another. Choose the one that works best for you, one that can help you to best differentiate the quality of a student's response.

Specific criteria are combined with chosen quality indicators to produce a basic rubric.

Types of Quality Scales

0	1	2	3	4
0	1	2	3	
Poor	Satisfactory	Very good	Excellent	Superior
Poor	Satisfactory	Very good	Excellent	Superior
Novice	Adequate	Apprentice	Distinguished	
Inaccurate	Partially accurate		Accurate	
Incomplete	Partially complete		Complete	
No evidence	Minimal evidence	Partial evidence	Complete evidence	
In progress	Meets standards		Exceeds standards	
Not effective	Slightly effective	Somewhat effective	Effective	
Minimal	Somewhat		Extensive	
High pass	Pass	Low pass	No pass	

The following rubric includes criteria for content and gradations of quality. Notice that the inferential components are marked with an *I* and the literal ones with an *L*. This is important for differentiating these in the grading process. The rubric now provides a guideline for the teacher to use as he or she corrects the essay question.

		Very complete and accurate	Generally complete and accurate	Somewhat complete and accurate	Inaccurate and incomplete
I	Tells how plant and animal cells are alike				
I	Tells how plant and animal cells differ				
L	Includes cell membrane/function				
L	Includes cell wall/ function				
L	Includes nucleus/ function				
L	Includes cytoplasm/ function				
L	Includes one shared organelle/function				
L	Includes one specific organelle/function				

Certainly, an individual teacher may quarrel with the quality indicators I have chosen. You may prefer five as opposed to four. You may prefer descriptors other than *very, generally,* and *somewhat.* If so, there are certainly a variety of indicators to choose from. None may be completely perfect, but all can serve in some way to increase assessment reliability. At this point the teacher needs to consider whether to include a rubric that evaluates writing performance. If the teacher feels that it is important to include writing performance as part of the grade, then a rubric must be constructed to evaluate such components as organization, sentence structure, spelling, grammar, and punctuation. Fortunately, you seldom have to construct such a rubric as there are many examples of writing rubrics in the references mentioned previously and on the Web.

Translating Quality Indicators into a Grade

The teacher now has one more task to pursue, that of turning the quality indicators into a grade. The easiest way is to award a limited number of points for each quality indicator. Then the teacher must determine what total number of points count for the letter grades that are used so extensively in our schools. A simple rule of thumb for a 4-point quality scale is to assign 4 points to the highest level, 3 points to the next highest, and so on. In other words, a student whose answer on the likenesses of plant and animal cells is very accurate and complete would receive a score of 4. A generally complete and partially accurate answer would be awarded a score of 3, and so on.

The highest score a student can obtain on the sample rubric is 32 points; the lowest is 8. How is this turned into a letter grade? I suggest two possible and simple solutions. One is to divide the total number of points (in this case, 32 points) into equal increments based on the number of quality indicators, in this case 4. Thirty-two divided by 4 equals 8, so each scale represents 8 points. A score of 32–25 represents a grade of A; a score of 24–17 stands for a B; C is the grade designation for a score of 16–9; and a total score of 8–1 represents a D/F. The problem with this solution is that you may want to assign five grades and are not happy with the D/F designation. If that is the case, divide the total number of points by the number of grades you intend to assign. Thirty-two divided by 5 (for the grades of A through F) equals 6.4—but don't get into fractions. Assign your grades as follows: 32–27 = A; 26–21 = B; 20–15 = C; 17–13 = D; 8–1 = F. Of course, because of the fraction, you have two additional points in the F category. If you wish, you can assign those points to another grade category, perhaps the category of C.

How can you differentiate between literal and inferential levels? Separate them in your rubric and determine a score for each, using the same simple numerical system. There are a total of 8 possible points for the inferential level. Eight divided by 4 equals 2, resulting in the following grade designations for the inferential portion of the assessment: A = 7–8; B = 5–6; C = 3–4; D/F = 1–2. The highest possible score for the literal components is now 24. So 24 divided by 4 equals 6, which results in the following grades: A = 24–19; B = 18–13; C = 12–7; D/F = 6–1.

The rubric on the next page shows how a student's performance may be scored using the system of dividing the total number of points by the number of quality indicators and differentiating literal and inferential levels.

Some will no doubt be tempted to turn this simple system into a more complex affair. For example, instead of assigning 4 points to a very complete and accurate explanation of the cell wall and its function, a teacher may consider awarding 3 points or 2 points in an attempt to differentiate gradations of quality in a very complete and accurate answer. Resist this temptation. The more com-

Inference level	Accurate and complete 4 points	Complete and partially accurate 3 points	Partially complete and accurate 2 points	Inaccurate and incomplete 1 point
I Tells how plant and animal cells are alike			2	
I Tells how plant and animal cells differ		3		
Student score	0	3	2	0
Total 5				
Grade inferential comprehension B				
Literal level	Very complete and accurate	Generally complete and accurate	Somewhat complete and accurate	Inaccurate and incomplete
L Cell membrane/ function	4			
L Cell wall/function				1
L Nucleus/function	4			
L Cytoplasm/function			2	
L One shared organelle/function		3		
L One specific organelle/function			2	
Student score	8	3	4	1
Total 16				
Grade literal comprehension B				

plicated the scoring system, the more inaccuracy raises its ugly head and the instrument becomes less reliable or consistent.

If the teacher included writing performance as part of the rubric, he or she must determine how to weight that score as well. Do content and writing each count for 50%, or does content count for more? These are questions for which there are no definitive guidelines. It is the teacher who makes such decisions, but it makes sense for groups of teachers to work together to decide such issues across a single grade level or even across an entire school.

Does a rubric remove all error or subjectivity in scoring? Of course not. One teacher's judgment of "Excellent" may be another teacher's rating of "Very good." However, rubrics do reduce a substantial amount of error both among teachers and for a single teacher. Some schools and districts have uniform writing assignments or projects administered at set grade levels. For example, in my state many fourth graders are expected to complete an essay assignment on state history. Although the requirements for such assignments are usually identical for all teachers at that designated grade level, each classroom teacher generally grades or scores the assignments of his or her students according to his or her criteria. If there is no agreed-upon rubric for scoring, subjectivity can creep in and destroy the reliability of the assessment. Students in some classes will receive lower or higher grades than other students, not because their performance differs dramatically from their peers, but because they were assessed by different teachers.

Keep Rubrics Simple and Specific

Various authors use different terms to describe rubric formats. For example, Burke (2006) distinguishes between *analytic* and *holistic* rubrics, and Trice (2000) categorizes rubrics as *checklist* or *descriptive*. I do not think one form of rubric is innately better than another or that it is even important to know the difference. An effective rubric meets the specific needs of the teacher, his or her instructional objectives, and the demands of the content. There are a variety of books, articles, and websites that offer examples, descriptions, and suggestions for rubric construction, and I encourage teachers to examine these to get a sense of different rubric formats. However, don't expect to find the perfect rubric that will fit all occasions. There is no such thing. An effective rubric is always tied to specific instructional objectives and the comprehension of specific content and/ or processes.

Keep rubrics as simple as you can. As chair of a curriculum committee at my university, I have seen extremely complex rubrics and even more complex scoring systems. For example, a single quality scale of "Excellent" can involve the awarding of 1 to 30 points! That is, instead of assigning a single score of 4 to the quality scale of "Very complete and accurate," a teacher can award any score from 1 to 30 points. People often consider such rubrics to be more fine-tuned and sensitive to gradations of excellence. However, what is the real difference between accuracy and completeness scores of 14 and 16, or of 8 and 12? Such rubrics actually decrease assessment reliability. Keep it simple. In the long run, a specific and simple rubric will serve you best.

A rubric is a tool of comprehension assessment, nothing more and nothing less. Some people turn rubrics into the assessment itself. They spend so much time constructing a rubric that will, they hope, tease out fine gradations of student performance that they often lose the point of the assessment process. Determine what you want students to comprehend. Determine the level of that comprehension: literal, inferential, or application. Use these factors to select rubric criteria. Choose a simple grading scale, understanding that no scale will ever be sensitive enough to reflect that multifaceted entity we call comprehension.

Share and Construct Rubrics with Students

Did you ever study for a test and then find out, after taking the test, that you studied the wrong thing? That has probably happened to you, as it has to me. Think of all the wasted effort you spent in studying something that did not count toward the teacher's evaluation of your performance quality. Is there some reason why the content of an assessment has to be a deep, dark secret and known only to the teacher? Doesn't it make more sense for students to know what the teacher wants them to comprehend and do? Recently, I watched a television show about a couple who were trying to sell their house. A real estate expert went through the house and pointed out specific things that had to be changed in order to get the best possible price. In other words, they knew exactly what they had to do before putting their house on the market. And that is what they did, without spending time and money on things that did not count. Comprehension and learning are a bit like that. If students know what they are expected to understand and do, they can focus on those elements instead of spending their energy and time on things that are not germane to the teacher's instructional objectives. To put it succinctly, they will learn more through a focused process of study than an unfocused one. If you want students to learn the function of a cell and nucleus, for example, tell them so by distributing the rubric prior to the test. Rubrics are tools for both teachers and students. They let teachers know what to assess and students know what to focus on.

There is no reason why you cannot construct a rubric with your students. I have seen this done successfully at all levels. The construction of a rubric acts as a powerful teaching and learning tool. Constructing a rubric with students allows them to take ownership of the assessment process.

Teach Students the Format of Open-Ended Assessments

If you are going to use a specific open-ended assessment such as an essay test, you have to be certain that students know how to deal with the format of the assessment, that is, know how to write an essay. Unfortunately, teachers often make assumptions about students' knowledge, and assessment of comprehension is blurred by their inability to write, lack of understanding of what should go into a project, or lack of awareness of how an oral report should be delivered. You can combine content and process components as part of your instructional objectives, but, as indicated previously, performance should always be separated from comprehension. In other words, they should be evaluated separately.

Basically, this means that you should teach the format of the assessment prior to using it to assign a grade. This is where formative testing comes in. Prior to using an assessment as a measure of student performance, determine, for example, whether a student can write an essay or construct a report. If not, teach the process by giving practice in test-like situations and delivering specific feedback to the students. If you do not think that it is your role to teach open-ended assessment formats, there are two basic options. One is to distribute, prior to the assessment, a rubric that clarifies your expectations in regard to an essay, an oral report, a group project, or a similar assignment. Second, assess student skill in these elements separately from comprehension of content.

Guidelines for Open-Ended Comprehension Assessment

Are there any open-ended formats that cannot be used to assess comprehension? I do not think so. There are many varieties of essay tests, projects, oral reports, portfolios, journals, experiments, and the like, and all can function as viable comprehension assessments, but only if certain guidelines are followed.

• *Guideline 1. Identify and code the components of comprehension that are represented by the open-ended assessment.* Your instructional objectives should establish whether you are focusing on one, two, or three of the comprehension levels. In truth, because of their complexity, open-ended assessments generally involve all three components: literal, inferential, and application, and it is probably impossible to accurately determine the relative contribution of each one to the overall assessment. So, you have two options.

The first is to separately evaluate each component. In such a case, your rubric will include categories of facts to be included, inferential statements to be made, and the application activities to perform. It is up to you to weight each of these. You can weight them equally or assign more points to inferential or application components. A second option is to decide which component is primarily represented by the activity and code the assessment accordingly. In the case of the social studies assessment that focused on religious freedom in the colonies, writing a summary, letter, or newspaper article probably best represents inferential comprehension. Refer to the question words in Chapter 4; such activities seem to require description, analysis, and interpretation, all activities associated with the inferential component of comprehension. The same can be said of the comparison of plant and animal cells. However, if students were asked to use their knowledge of the first colonies to predict difficulties in colonizing Mars, we would probably categorize the assessment as application. Similarly, if students were given a cell specimen and asked to identify it as plant or animal, application would better describe the comprehension activity.

Is one option better than the other? I do not think so. Remember, it all goes back to what you, the teacher and content specialist, want the student to learn and do. If you are concerned about all three levels of comprehension, differentiate your rubric. If you are primarily focused on application, then design your rubric with a focus on that component.

• *Guideline 2. Base assessments on important instructional goals.* Winograd and Arrington (1999) suggest that best practices in assessment are based on important instructional goals. Design your open-ended assessments to focus on meaningful standards, significant goals, and key ideas. Involve students in the assessment process. Make certain that they understand your goals so they can use information from a rubric to improve their performance.

• *Guideline 3. Maintain a focus on simplicity.* Construct your objectives and design your rubrics in a format as simple as possible. We know that comprehension is an extremely complex entity, but in order to conceptualize it at a classroom assessment level, we must keep the process somewhat simple. Our assessment is probably only a shadow of the real comprehension process that occurs in the minds of our students. However, a simple and focused assessment, although imperfect, provides more validity and reliability in the long run.

We use simple and focused assessment every day as we evaluate items to purchase, activities to choose, people to approach, and goals to achieve. For example, I remember when my son was inundated with materials from college admissions offices describing the numerous advantages of their institutions. However, his choice of university was directed by several simple criteria: family tradition (a beloved uncle had attended the university), relative nearness to home, and opportunities for work-study. I have questioned many undergraduates and have always found that their college choices were similarly directed by a few simple criteria.

Too much complexity can destroy the effectiveness of the assessment process. I remember shopping for a new computer; the salesperson kept offering more and more complicated information on topics that I knew little about—I retreated in confusion. Similarly, I have seen well-meaning individuals administer so many different tests to struggling readers that they are hard put to draw any conclusions as to how instruction should be conducted.

• *Guideline 4. Remember that any assessment is only a sample of student performance.* Any open-ended assessment is only one sample of a student's comprehension at that time, in that text, and using that measure of performance. Winograd and Arrington (1999) suggest gathering "multiple measures over time and in a variety of meaningful contexts" (p. 217). This reflects the idea of comprehension assessment as a collection of multiple samples of behavior. A single assessment, no matter how complex, does not represent the whole of a student's comprehension. Treat it as a sample and evaluate it in comparison to other samples. This means that when you enter a grade for the social studies assessment on the colonies, or the science assessment in cell structure, your descriptors will include L, I, or A to indicate the level of comprehension that is best represented by this sample of student performance. If the performance assessment spans a relatively long period of time, consider assessing student performance several times and noting possible changes in performance. Open-ended assessments of products such as portfolios, ongoing science notebooks, or journals lend themselves to this approach.

• *Guideline 5. Collaborate with others.* Establishing the validity and reliability of open-ended assessments should not be a solitary endeavor. It works best as a collaborative and cooperative activity in which teachers at the same grade level or in the same content field work together to design the best possible assessment.

This is easier said than done. There is an unfortunate tendency in our schools for teachers to go into the classroom, close the door, and do their own thing. Rarely do school districts provide teachers with the time or opportunity to collaborate on designing assessment activities (Schmoker, 2006). Districts provide myriad professional development activities on assessment but rarely provide teachers with the time to apply what they have learned.

Many schools and districts have common assessments at specific grade levels. Some have common assessments in content classes. Whenever possible, teachers should take advantage of the commonality and work together to focus their instructional objectives and refine the validity and reliability of their assessments (Schmoker, 2006).

But what if you are the only one who teaches physics in your high school or you are the only French teacher? You may not have peers who are immediately present in the teacher's lounge, but you have professional peers in other schools. Send them your rubrics or a description of your objectives for a unit and ask for their input. I never realized how lonely teaching could be until I team taught a statistics course. My teaching and my rubrics improved immeasurably through interaction with a peer who valued my subject matter as much as I did. And the students certainly benefited from assessments that were more closely tied to objectives and were more reliable because of the cooperative design of rubrics.

Open-Ended Assessment and Response to Intervention

Does open-ended classroom assessment have a place in RTI monitoring? Wright (2007) suggests that it does. In a list of methods for monitoring progress toward academic goals, he includes "Permanent Work Products (Classroom Assignments)" (p. 76) as one option. He describes these "products" as the amount, accuracy, and quality of work completed and suggests that student goals should be to increase all three. For quality of work completed, Wright proposes that an increase in teacher ratings on subject area rubrics could serve as an RTI method for monitoring progress.

A large part of this chapter is devoted to issues of validity and reliability of open-ended classroom assessments. If a teacher intends to use such assessments as screening tools for Tier 1 or as progress monitoring tools for Tiers 2 and 3, it is crucial that the assessments be as valid and reliable as possible. Perhaps the most important point in monitoring RTI is to carefully differentiate comprehension of subject matter content from facility in the process used to demonstrate understanding. In other words, comprehension of subject matter and the writing, speaking, or performance processes used to demonstrate comprehension should be kept separate in the rubric. As discussed in this chapter, the purpose of instruction dictates the construction of the rubric. Is the goal for the student to learn about the westward expansion or the parts of a cell? Or does the goal focus on acquisition of comprehension strategies that support learning, such as effective note taking or identification of important ideas and supporting details?

Rubric simplicity is a critical variable, as is rubric uniformity. A teacher using rubrics for RTI evaluation should maintain a uniform scoring system so that progress can be recorded and compared over time. In other words, if you begin using a system that translates to a letter grade, don't switch in midstream to one that describes performance in terms of words or numbers.

Open-ended assessments vary widely within a classroom, with some projects and activities representing more complexity and a higher level of difficulty than others. I do not think it is possible to maintain a similar level of difficulty in order to accommodate the RTI process. A unit on the life cycle of stars will naturally be easier than one on wave motion. Understanding the causes and progress of a war will be easier than dealing with the causes of economic growth and/or decline. A teacher should note such differences on a student's progress report.

I do believe that open-ended assessments can be used as screening tools in Tier 1 under certain circumstances. However, such screening measures should be uniform across a grade level, which may be difficult to implement. It does not make sense to screen some children on an assessment that is more difficult or complex than one used in another classroom at the same level. If RTI is to move into the upper grades, teachers will have to collaborate on the choice, design, and rubric format of the screening assessment used in Tier 1 assessment.

Summary

• Open-ended comprehension assessment can take multiple forms: short-answer and essay questions, as well as performance assessments for projects, experiments, journals, oral reports, and portfolios. Open-ended assessments are generally viewed as drawing on a higher level of comprehension and, like constructed response assessments, can address all three components of the comprehension process.

• To establish the validity of open-ended comprehension assessments, match an assessment to specific instructional objectives. Avoid general statements. Determine important factual knowledge. Clarify the processes that students should acquire. Indicate what students should do with their knowledge.

• Focus on important or significant content and/or processes. Textbooks contain much information that is not germane to a teacher's purpose. Focus on content and processes that match the purpose of your instruction.

• Identify and differentiate the levels of comprehension expected: literal, inferential, and application.

• Acknowledge the possible interference of performance variables such as language ability, writing skill, and group dynamics and separate these from assessment of comprehension.

• Improve the reliability of open-ended comprehension assessments by constructing rubrics that match instructional objectives. A rubric describes and scales student levels of achievement and is made up of three elements: criteria, gradations of quality, and a system for translating quality gradations into a grade.

• Keep rubrics simple and specific and share and construct rubrics with students.

• Teach students the format of open-ended assessments and evaluate proficiency in format separately from comprehension of content.

• Guidelines for open-ended comprehension assessment include the following: identify and code the three components of comprehension represented by the assessment; base assessment on important instructional goals; maintain a focus on simplicity in constructing objectives and rubrics; gather multiple samples of student comprehension; and, whenever possible, collaborate with peers in designing and revising assessments.

• Open-ended assessments can be used in the RTI process if carefully aligned to the purpose of assessment. Rubrics for progress monitoring should be simple and consistent in format. Tier 1 screening assessments should be uniform across a single grade level.

Professional Development Activities for Improving Open-Ended Comprehension Assessment

• Choose an open-ended assessment you have used in the past. Examine the assessment carefully and consider its validity. What were your instructional objectives for the instruction that preceded it? To what degree did the assessment match the objectives?

• Choose an open-ended assessment that you have used in the past. Examine it in relation to the three levels of comprehension. Which level is primarily represented by the activity?

• Construct a rubric for an open-ended assessment that differentiates between literal, inferential, and application levels of comprehension. Score several students using that rubric. Then ask several peers to score the same students, using your rubric. How close were the scores? Discuss the rubric with the teachers. How did they interpret your criteria and quality scales? How can you improve the rubric?

• Investigate websites for rubrics and experiment with rubric templates. You may not find the perfect template, but the exercise can offer suggestions for constructing your own rubrics.

• Try constructing rubrics with your students. Have the students engage in self-assessment, using the rubric. Compare your evaluation with those of the students. Discuss the scoring with the students. What part of the rubric needs to be changed or clarified?

• When you attend a conference, seek out a presentation on rubrics. You may find some you can adapt and use. You may also find some examples of what not to do.

CHAPTER 6

Look Who's Talking

Assessing Comprehension through Student Dialogue

Patterns of Classroom Talk

Dialogue with others plays an extremely important role in our comprehension of the world around us. However, because we engage in it so often and so effectively, we tend to take it somewhat for granted. All of us can generate examples of situations when our understanding was increased or clarified through discussion. We read directions, signs, newspapers, and magazines; we listen to the radio; and we watch television shows and movies. In all these instances, we use dialogue with family, friends, and acquaintances to clarify and enhance comprehension. We describe our thoughts and admit our uncertainties and, as we listen to the positions and interpretations of others, we clarify and modify our perspectives. Why is talking so effective? Talking gives us an opportunity for "immediate feedback and constant readjustments" of our original beliefs and positions (Donahue & Foster, 2004, p. 364).

During dialogue, we continually assess the comprehension of others. We listen carefully, we ask questions, and we agree or disagree with the accuracy or sensitivity of their understanding. And they are doing the same thing, which is evaluating our comprehension of the topic being addressed. Discussion with others positively influences our comprehension, and the same can hold true for students in the classroom (Alvermann et al., 1996; Meloth & Deering, 1994). Bransford et al. (2000) emphasize the importance of discussion for talking about ideas, for making students' thinking explicit, and for applying what has been learned to new situations.

Think about the last time you engaged in a stimulating and collaborative discussion. It is easy to differentiate such a discussion from one dominated by a single individual or by a predetermined and rigid agenda. In your collaborative discussion, all participants took an active part. They all listened carefully and respectfully and questioned sensitively. As participants signaled their desire to speak, their peers included them in the conversation and interruptions were at a minimum. If the direction of the discussion changed, it was because the group agreed to move away from the original topic and focus on another. Effective exchange of ideas and information occurs when speakers and listeners adhere to the guidelines of quantity, quality, relation, and manner (Donahue & Foster, 2004) by offering informative contributions (quantity) that are truthful (quality), relevant (relation), and clear (manner).

Contrast this type of conversation with what passes for discussion in all too many of our classrooms. Few would quarrel with the statement that classroom talk is primarily directed by the teacher. In addition, teachers themselves do most of the talking. Teachers lecture, explain, give directions, ask questions, and offer suggestions for completing activities. They set the stage for what to talk about and how to talk about it, and students soon learn that their role is to listen and respond according to the demands of the teacher. Although classroom dialogue can be whole-group or small-group discussion, its purpose and format primarily originate with and are directed by the teacher.

Classroom dialogue tends to fall into two broad categories: directive scaffolds and supportive scaffolds (Wilkinson & Silliman, 2000). The term *scaffold* refers to the type of assistance a teacher provides to support and assess learning during discussion. Teacher control primarily defines the directive scaffold. The teacher asks questions, chooses students to provide answers, and evaluates their accuracy or worth. Answers are often called right or wrong, with little discussion or explanation as to why, and the focus is primarily on literal understanding of content. Directive scaffolds are the more prevalent type, perhaps because teaching is often conceptualized as transmitting knowledge from the teacher to the student. In fact, directive scaffolds are often referred to as transmission approaches, with the teacher as the transmitter and controller of learning (Wade & Moje, 2000). The teacher knows, and the purpose of discussion is to determine if the students have learned. Wilhelm (2001) describes this as a "teacher/information-centered model" in which "learning is centered on the information possessed by the teacher, which flows one way, from the teacher to the student" (p. 8).

Supportive scaffolds are more learner centered and are more similar to the discussions we engage in every day. They are often referred to as instructional conversations or participatory approaches, and they "function as formats for supporting the development of new conceptual understanding" (Wilkinson & Silliman, 2000, p. 345). Supportive scaffolds go beyond judging an answer as either right or wrong. They provide opportunities for responsive feedback in a classroom conceptualized as a community of learners, of which the teacher is one (Bransford et al., 2000). The teacher models specific strategies for thinking about the text and guides the students in developing and articulating their responses. Instead of asking content-specific questions, the teacher invites student participation by using content-free questions such as "Why do you think that?" and "What else would you like to say?" If misunderstandings occur, the teacher guides the students in repairing comprehension breakdowns. In participatory approaches to discussion, "teachers work with students to decode, comprehend, extract and synthesize information from multiple texts but they also encourage students to generate their own knowledge and to make their own interpretations of text" (Wade & Moje, 2000). Wilhelm (2001) refers to this as a learning-centered model.

What does all this have to do with comprehension assessment? If interactive dialogue enhances comprehension, then observing and noting student behavior during such discussion can provide a window on the comprehension process. Unfortunately, this seldom occurs in the classroom. Most teacher and student dialogue centers on assistance rather than assessment. That is, instead of using dialogue to explore student understanding or provide guidance in reflection, the aim is to help them find a correct answer or successfully complete a task. And when teachers do use discussion as a form of assessment, it is an informal and casual process with little record keeping and an optimistic dependence on memory (Calfee & Hiebert, 1991).

The purpose of this chapter is to demonstrate how interactive classroom discussion can inform comprehension assessment through use of two activities: thoughtful talk and thinking aloud.

Thoughtful Talk as Comprehension Assessment

Outside the classroom, students, like adults, talk about what they have read, heard, or viewed. Such discussion involves thoughtful talk, talk that goes far beyond the typical classroom recitation format of recalling and retelling literal items. Thoughtful talk, also referred to as thoughtful literacy by Allington (2001), primarily involves a focus on students' response to a text as opposed to literal recall. Did the students like or dislike the text? Why? What parts did they find confusing or disturbing? What relevance does it have to their lives? Thoughtful talk centers on drawing and sharing inferences and constructing what Kintsch and Kintsch (2005) call the situation model. There is the application level at which individuals recognize and express the relevance of an experience to their own lives and to new situations. In thoughtful talk, do individuals focus at all on literal aspects? Of course. They may recall or retell literal components in order to set the context for their remarks. For example, they may briefly summarize a movie or television show for those who have not yet seen it in order to provide a basis for the discussion that follows. However, most of the dialogue centers on thoughts and feelings, in short, on personal responses to the text and on efforts to clarify and understand it.

Unfortunately, student talk in the classroom is not generally thoughtful in nature. It focuses not on response but on memory for content. It primarily involves answering teacher questions and retelling explicit content, and students soon learn that this is what is expected. This is clearly evident if you ask students to describe or retell what they read or heard. I have listened to the retellings of many students following their reading or listening to both narrative and expository text. The majority offer all the explicit facts that they can remember and seldom include inference or application comments. If you ask them to respond to the text in a personal manner, they seem genuinely puzzled.

A teacher can assess comprehension of facts through the directive scaffold approach and through literal questions. However, this does not offer an opportunity to assess inferential and application-level comprehension. In order to do this, the teacher must teach students to engage in thoughtful talk. Thoughtful talk moves beyond the ability to remember and recite. Allington (2001) describes it as connecting what we see, read, and hear to ourselves, to other text, and to the world at large. It also involves such comprehension activities as summarizing, analyzing, synthesizing, and evaluating.

How does a teacher lead students into thoughtful talk? In other words, how does a teacher employ a supportive discussion scaffold that allows for assessment of inference and application levels of comprehension? There are two approaches to leading students into thoughtful talk. The teacher can ask inference and application questions that are directly tied to specific content. That is, the teacher can construct inference and application questions based on the text and use these to direct discussion and assess higher levels of student comprehension. An alternative approach involves the use of content-free questions.

Content-Free Questions

Content-free questions are general questions that students can ask about any selection. Beck et al. (1997) call such questions "queries" and state that they are "designed to assist students in grappling with text ideas as they construct meaning" (p. 23). In using queries, the student questions the author in order to construct and expand understanding. Initiating Queries focus on the author's purpose. What is the author describing? What does the author want us to understand? What is the author's message? Follow-up Queries center on integrating ideas. Does the author explain this clearly? What does the author want us to know? How does this connect to what the author has already told us? Why is this important? Content-free questions have more utility than content-specific questions. Only the teacher can craft content-specific questions, but students can use content-free questions to guide their comprehension. In fact, regular use of content-free questions can serve two purposes. It can provide the teacher with an assessment model for discussion, and it can provide the students with a strategy for making sense of what they read, hear, or see.

In order to assess comprehension through thoughtful talk, the teacher must ask content-free questions that foster inference- and application-level comprehension. Then, by listening to and assessing a student's response, the teacher can determine the extent to which the student's comprehension moves beyond the literal level. Using content-free questions to assess inferential and application-level questions does not mean that literal-level questions should be abandoned. Content specialists think it is important that students understand and remember certain factual information, and although teachers can assess this through literal-level questions, they can also find that such understanding is often demonstrated through student response to inferential and application-level discussion. In order to draw inferences and make applications to new contexts, students must also understand at a literal level, so, in a sense, discussion that focuses on thoughtful talk also addresses literal comprehension.

Content-free questions can be used effectively with any age group. I watched a first-grade class of urban children eagerly discuss a book about turtles. Some of the content-free questions that the teacher asked were as follows: What is this book about? What did the author want to teach us? What did you find most interesting? What did you learn that you never knew before? How is this book like the one we read about farm animals? What would you like to say to the author about the book? What would you still like to know about turtles? The children eagerly responded to the questions, and it was evident that they had comprehended the book at both a literal and inferential level and considerably expanded their knowledge base.

The following tables include examples of content-free questions, each labeled as asking for an inferential or application level of comprehension. These are not all-inclusive lists. There are many variations of such questions, and you can easily construct your own after a little practice. The question words from Table 4.2 that signal inferential or application comprehension are italicized. Also note that inference-level content-free questions often involve comprehension of literal elements.

Content-Free Questions for Narrative Material

Inference content-free questions	Application content-free questions
Who is the main character, and *why* do you think so?	*Evaluate* this text in relation to other texts you have read.
Who are other important characters, and *why* are they important?	*Judge* how the events in this text are like events happening today.
Explain the character's problem.	If you were to write to the author, what *opinion* of this narrative would you share?
How is the character trying to solve his (her) problem?	*Predict* how the characters might act in another time period.
Do you agree or disagree with the character's thoughts or actions and *why*?	Is this text true to life? *Defend* your answer.
How is the setting important or unimportant?	*Judge* whether this text would make a good movie or television series. Why or why not?
How did the narrative end, and was it an appropriate ending? *Why*?	*Evaluate* the author's purpose in writing this text and whether it was achieved?
Describe what you don't understand.	*Imagine* if this text were set in a different time or place. Would it have been different? Why or why not?
Summarize this text in order to make it attractive to a reader or viewer.	*Create* a different ending for this text.
Describe individuals for whom this text would be appropriate or inappropriate.	Would you *recommend* this text to others? Why or why not?

Content-free questions serve two purposes. They provide a guide for easing a teacher into scaffolding a supportive discussion. They also provide guidelines for students; that is, they suggest ways of thinking about text and provide questioning strategies that enhance comprehension. Such strategies will not be new to students. They use them in their everyday discussion activities. What may be new is applying them to school text.

Content-Free Questions for Expository Material

Inference content-free questions	Application content-free questions
Describe the topic or main idea of this section.	*How might* this be important to our everyday life?
Explain _____ and tell why it is important.	*Evaluate* the importance of _____.
Compare _____ with _____.	What is your *opinion* of _____?
What is most interesting to you and *why*?	If we did not know _____, *what might happen*?
Describe what you learned that you did not know before.	*Defend* how would you deal with _____.
What did you already know about _____?	*Judge* the importance of _____.
Describe what confuses you or what you don't understand.	*Evaluate* the author's purpose in writing this text and whether it was achieved.
Explain some new terms that you have learned.	*Design* a different way to accomplish this.
What are some words that you do not know the meaning of? *How* does the text give you clues as to their meaning?	What *might be some possible consequences* of _____?
How is _____ different from what you already knew or thought?	How could you *modify* _____?
Interpret _____ in your own words.	*Design* an alternative to _____.

Example of Content-Free Question Usage

The following transcript demonstrates how one middle school social studies teacher used content-free questions to guide a small group of students to engage in thoughtful talk about a segment of their textbook that focused on the aftermath of World War I, specifically the Treaty of Versailles. The supportive scaffold for discussion was not new to the students, as they regularly engaged in thoughtful talk about text. Prior to the discussion, the teacher briefly reviewed the text by listing key topics on the board and asking if any clarifications were needed. I have labeled each example of student comment as demonstrating a literal, inferential, or application level of comprehension based on the content of the text. You may want to refer to Table 4.2 and examine the question words that suggest the three levels of comprehension.

TEACHER: Anyone want to start? What are some big ideas?

STUDENT 1: The Treaty of Versailles and how they really stuck it to the Germans. *(Literal: The treaty name was stated in the chapter heading. Inferential: An evaluation of the treaty demands was not made in the text.)*

STUDENT 2: That's only part of it. It was mainly about why the treaty didn't really work. *(Inferential: The text stated the terms of the treaty but did not indicate that it didn't work.)*

TEACHER: Can you expand on that? Why didn't it work?

STUDENT 2: Well, they asked for more money than Germany could ever pay. *(Literal: The text stated that monetary demands were made. Inferential: the text did not indicate that Germany could never pay.)*

STUDENT 3: Which was dumb. Why ask for something you won't ever get? *(Inferential: The student is asking why something happened.)*

TEACHER: Why do you think the Allies did that?

STUDENT 1: Well, they were the winners and maybe they thought they would eventually get the money. *(Inferential: The student is interpreting the situation.)*

STUDENT 4: To use to rebuild their cities and all. *(Inferential: The student is suggesting why something occurred. The text never mentioned rebuilding cities.)*

TEACHER: Should the Allies have done things differently?

STUDENT 2: Well, they just made Germany angry. I think Germany expected to pay something but not that much. So they stayed enemies when they might have become friends. *(Literal: The text comments on the anger of the German delegation. Inferential: The student is suggesting a reason for the anger. Application: The student is suggesting a possible future consequence.)*

STUDENT 5. The author called it unjust, so I guess it probably was. *(Literal: The student is simply paraphrasing the text.)*

TEACHER: What do you think?

STUDENT 5: I guess I agree. *(Literal: The student is simply agreeing with what was explicitly stated.)*

STUDENT 4: The treaty really cut down the German military. The navy couldn't have submarines and the army was limited. *(Literal: This was stated in the text.)*

STUDENT 5: Germany couldn't have airplanes either. *(Literal: This was explicitly stated in the text.)*

TEACHER: Why was this important?

STUDENT 4: They were preventing Germany from ever going to war again. I mean, they couldn't if they didn't have an army or navy. *(Inferential: The student is explaining the motives of the Allies, which were not explicitly stated in the text.)*

STUDENT 2: Well, they did go to war again, so it was just like asking for all that money that they never got. It just didn't work, so it was dumb and they should have been smarter. *(Application: The student is evaluating the treaty and offering a personal opinion.)*

TEACHER: How about expanding on that?

STUDENT 2: Well, we had World War II, so Germany did build up their military despite the treaty. I don't think there was any way the Allies could have checked up on what they were doing. I mean, you just can't go into another country and stick your noses in to find out what they are doing. If they don't want you to know, they will hide everything. Which is probably what Germany did. *(Application: The student is predicting the future behavior of the Germans and evaluating the actions of the Allies.)*

STUDENT 1: Just saying you have to do something doesn't mean you will. People do that all the time. They don't do what someone tells them to do. Germany could agree and then just do what they wanted to. *(Application: The student is moving to a new context, other people's actions.)*

TEACHER: How would all of you have modified the treaty?

STUDENT 3: Make it reasonable so Germany might be willing to become an ally after a few years. *(Application: The student is moving beyond the text to consider a new alternative.)*

STUDENT 2: I think the Allies were greedy. But they were also mad. After all, a lot of people died. *(Inferential: The student is interpreting the Allies' motives.)*

TEACHER: What was more important? Greed or anger?

STUDENT 2: I think mad, because we read yesterday about how many people died and how long the war went on. *(Literal: The text referred to time and casualties. Inferential: The student is interpreting motives.)*

STUDENT 5: Wilson wasn't greedy and I don't think he was mad either. He wanted those Fourteen Points, which were pretty neat but he had to back down. *(Literal: The text described the Fourteen Points and Wilson's inability to carry them out as he would have liked. Inferential: The student is interpreting Wilson's actions. Application: The student is judging the worth of the Fourteen Points, albeit very briefly.)*

TEACHER: Is this important? I mean, has it affected us?

STUDENT 3: Yes. Maybe if the treaty had been more fair, there would never have been another war. *(Application: The student is predicting future events.)*

TEACHER: Is there anything that you find confusing?

STUDENT 4: All those new countries they formed. Why did people let them get away with it? *(Literal: The text described the new countries that were formed. Inferential: The student questions why the Allies were able to carry out their intentions.)*

STUDENT 2: Well, the winners had all the power, but you would have thought they would have listened to how people felt. *(Inferential: The student is questioning why the Allies acted as they did. Application: The student is applying the action of the Allies to winners in general, a new context.)*

STUDENT 1: They probably never even asked them until it was too late. *(Inferential: The student is explaining how something may have occurred.)*

TEACHER: Is this like anything that happens today?

STUDENT 5: A lot of people make decisions for others without asking them. *(Application: The student is applying understanding of the Allies' actions to a new context, people in general.)*

STUDENT 3: Government does too. And our principal. A lot of rules we have to follow we would never have agreed to. *(Application: The student is applying understanding of the Allies' actions to a new context.)*

TEACHER: Other opinions?

STUDENT 4: It seems to me that France and England were trying to increase their power by those mandates, or whatever they were called, so how were they any different from Germany? *(Inferential: The student is interpreting the motives of France and England as well as comparing them to Germany.)*

STUDENT 1: They were the winners; that's how they were different. *(Application: The student is applying understanding to a new context, winners in general.)*

TEACHER: And what about winning?

STUDENT 3: Well, winners have all the power! *(Application: The student is applying understanding to a new context, winners in general.)*

STUDENT 2: And winners can hurt losers. Remember all the nasty signs when we lost the tournament? *(Application: The student is applying understanding to a new context.)*

STUDENT 5: Part of the fun of winning is sticking it to the guys that lose. I bet the Allies enjoyed themselves. *(Application: The student is applying understanding to a new context.)*

STUDENT 1: It's different with a game; this was a war. *(Application: The student is evaluating the issue.)*

STUDENT 3: I want to go back to being mad. If my dad or brother died, I would have wanted to hurt the Germans. *(Application: The student is imagining a new situation.)*

TEACHER: What can we learn from this?

STUDENT 5: Don't overreact? *(Application: The student is making a judgment.)*

STUDENT 3: That's asking a lot. *(Application: The student is making a judgment.)*

STUDENT 2: I don't know. It was all so long ago. Maybe we can't really know how it was. *(Application: The student is making a judgment.)*

STUDENT 5: They probably thought what they were doing was right. It's easy to criticize, but we weren't there. *(Application: The student is making a judgment.)*

It is easy to see from the transcript that all students were reacting at an inferential or application level. Of course, a transcript like this never really parallels what your students will do or say. It is tempting to say, "My students would never talk like that!" and perhaps they wouldn't. Such a transcript is only an example, not a prescription. Assessing comprehension through discussion can vary greatly, depending on the age of the students and the text that is involved. Underlying concepts in the Treaty of Versailles text were relatively familiar to the students: war, winning, losing, revenge, and so forth. The discussion may not have been so interactive if students were dealing with unfamiliar concepts, such as viral replication. It is also important to realize that inference and application are based on literal understanding; that is, if you do not understand how organisms make RNA from DNA, you will not be able to draw inferences concerning the role of retroviruses. Similarly, if you do not understand the differences between lytic and lysogenic cycles of viral replication, you will not be able to predict the emergence of tumor-producing viruses. The brief review of literal content provided by the teacher set the stage for a discussion that moved far beyond the literal level.

What are the keys to successful implementation of supportive scaffolds for thoughtful discussion? First, share the use of content-free questions with students as a strategy they can use to make sense of text. Second, resist saying that a response is wrong. Instead, ask the student to expand and, if need be, return to the text for clarification. There is nothing wrong with asking students to reread to clarify. Third, relax and focus on changing your discussion structure first before you use it as an assessment tool. Fourth, realize that not every text lends itself to inference and application processing. There will always be situations in which the teacher must promote and assess literal understanding.

Thinking Aloud as Comprehension Assessment

There is another activity that lends itself to comprehension assessment, the strategy of thinking aloud. Readers or listeners stop after short segments of text and say what they are thinking about; that is, they describe the state of their comprehension at that particular moment in time. This technique, often referred to as verbal protocol analysis, has been used extensively in research and has provided valuable information about the cognitive strategies readers use as they attempt to comprehend text (Afflerbach & Johnston, 1984; Myers, 1988; Olson, Duffy, & Mack, 1984; Pressley & Afflerbach, 1995; Pritchard, 1990). Thinking aloud has been used effectively with elementary, middle, and high school students, and it allows the teacher "to examine what the reader does to facilitate comprehension" (Myers & Lytle, 1986, p. 140). Thinking aloud is also an effective classroom instructional tool for fostering comprehension and for teaching comprehension strategies (Oster, 2001; Smith, 2006).

Think-alouds are not exact reproductions of a student's thoughts. Wilhelm (2001) warns that "no one can thoroughly and accurately capture all of what he sees in his mind's eye" (p. 20); however, think-alouds do allow us to infer something of what is going on during the comprehension process. Think-alouds can suggest whether a student comprehends and whether comprehension is literal or inferential in nature. They can also indicate whether the student applies the comprehended material to other contexts (Oster, 2001).

Wilhelm (2001) describes think-alouds as a valuable form of performance-based assessment that moves beyond the usual kinds of comprehension testing. Whereas traditional assessment primarily focuses on the end product of comprehension and is often literal in nature, think-alouds focus on the process of comprehension, what Wilhelm (2001) calls the "meaning-making tools" of students. (p. 162). In the classroom and as part of discussion, think-alouds are perhaps most suitable as formative assessments. The teacher can note whether students comprehend and adjust instruction accordingly. However, written think-alouds can be used as summative assessment tools. Think-alouds also provide a sensitive diagnostic procedure for evaluating the strengths and needs of struggling readers.

Coding or Describing Think-Alouds

Using think-alouds to assess comprehension demands a system for coding or describing the comments. Although there is considerable variation across studies in regard to descriptions of think-aloud comments (Chou-Hare & Smith, 1982; Cote, Goldman, & Saul, 1998; Crain-Thoreson, Lippman, & McClendon-Magnuson, 1997; Myers, Lytle, Palladino, Devenpeck, & Green, 1990; Olshavsky, 1976), all coding systems include both literal paraphrases and inferential statements. Leslie and Caldwell (2001) identified think-aloud comments that were actually offered by middle school students as they read narrative and expository text. Students paraphrased and made inferences. They commented about their understanding or lack of it. They reported their prior knowledge, that is, what they already knew or didn't know about the topic of the text, and they identified personally by describing their feelings, opinions, or judgments. They also asked questions about what they understood as well as about things that confused them. Leslie and Caldwell (2006) found that the most frequent types of think-aloud statements were paraphrasing and inferencing, which parallel the first two components of comprehension.

Trabasso and Magliano (1996a) coded inferences as causal explanations, predictions of future consequences, and associations that provide additional information and enrich or fill in detail. This coding of inferences has been useful in understanding think-aloud statements made during reading of narrative (Trabasso & Magliano, 1996b) and expository text (Caldwell & Leslie, 2007; Graesser & Bertus, 1998). Inferences can also be coded as knowledge-based or text-based; that is, the reader can make an inference using his or her prior knowledge or using information provided in the text (Kintsch & Kintsch, 2005). Although such detailed coding is probably not realistic for the classroom teacher, it does suggest that thinking aloud may provide an interesting window into the comprehension process.

Using Think-Alouds with Groups

Thinking aloud has primarily been used as an individual strategy; that is, the teacher listens to an individual student as he or she thinks aloud. However, the technique can be easily adapted for both small and large groups (Caldwell, 2008; Caldwell & Leslie, 2005; Oster, 2001; Smith 2006; Wilhelm, 2001). Thinking aloud is not unlike thoughtful talk, but instead of guiding the discussion with content-free questions, the teacher simply says, "Tell me what you are thinking about." However, as in thoughtful talk, students must learn to respond in a manner that is far different from the typical classroom discussion format.

Wilhelm (2001) describes several ways to conduct think-alouds. In the beginning, the teacher thinks aloud and students listen. The teacher models what is probably a new process for the students by reading short text segments and sharing his or her thoughts. The teacher then invites the students to share their thoughts, and it has been my experience that they join in quite quickly once they understand that their responses are not being judged as good or bad, as right or wrong. What happens if a student offers an inappropriate think-aloud comment? The teacher accepts and acknowledges it and models a possible alternative.

Once the students understand the think-aloud process, the teacher's role changes to that of observer and facilitator. While the students engage in thinking aloud, the teacher primarily listens, acknowledges the comments, occasionally questions for further clarification, and invites other students to join in.

Think-alouds can be used with individuals, small groups, and large groups. Introducing the think-aloud process works best with a small group. Then, as the teacher and the students become more familiar with the process, it can be extended to large groups. In research settings, thinking aloud has usually involved silent reading and oral response. However, think-alouds can also be used in a listening format, in which the teacher reads to the students. They can also be used in a viewing format by pausing video presentations for think-aloud dialogue. Think-alouds do not have to take the form of oral response. Students can write think-alouds. They can put Post-it notes on a page in a textbook, or they can simply indicate the page number and placement (top, bottom, or middle of the page) and write their think-aloud comments on paper or in a journal. There are advantages to written think-aloud comments. They can be compared with those of peers and they offer the teacher more time to examine them.

Individual think-alouds can provide valuable diagnostic information about a student's comprehension. For this reason, the think-aloud process has been included in an informal reading inventory used to assess the strengths and needs of struggling readers (Leslie & Caldwell, 2006). Individual think-alouds are probably too time-consuming for the classroom teacher, but they do offer valuable insights for the literacy or special education specialist. However, classroom teachers can effectively employ individual think-alouds during reading conferences and sustained silent reading. The teacher simply asks the student to read (orally or silently) a short portion of a chosen book and think aloud.

In order to use think-alouds for assessment, you must have a checklist of some kind to code the think-aloud comments. Caldwell (2008) and Caldwell and Leslie (2007) used six coding elements: Paraphrasing, inferring, questioning, noting understanding or lack of it, connecting to prior knowledge and reacting personally. Wilhelm (2001) suggests similar coding categories: summarizing, using background knowledge, making inferences, predicting, questioning, visualizing, indicating awareness of problems, and using monitoring strategies. These categories are very workable if you are dealing with a single individual, but they can become unwieldy if you are assessing the think-aloud comments of a large group. For group work, it makes good sense to fall back on the three levels of comprehension: literal, inferential, and application.

The following table matches possible think-aloud comments to the three levels of comprehension. I included monitoring as a category because, although it does not indicate comprehension, it does reveal whether students are aware of the difficulties they may or may not be having. A teacher should feel free to delete this and focus on just the three categories: literal, inferential, and application.

Literal think-aloud comments	Inferential think-aloud comments	Application think-aloud comments	Monitoring
Paraphrasing	Inferencing	Reacting personally	Noting understanding or lack of understanding
Summarizing	Predicting	Judging	
Noting the topic of the text	Visualizing	Applying content to a new or different context	
	Questioning based on understanding		

Example of Student Think-Aloud Comments

The best way to understand the power of think-alouds used as an assessment strategy is to examine the think-aloud comments of students. The following represents the comments of four middle school students who read a narrative account of a young boy's involvement in the Vietnam war. While visiting grandparents, his family was captured and imprisoned and the father was eventually taken away. Instead of reproducing the lengthy text, I have provided short summaries of the contents, followed by the think-aloud comments of the students. I coded each comment and provided my rationale for so doing. By examining the think-aloud comments, you can easily note who comprehended the text and at what level.

> *The mother and children are imprisoned in a basement with other captives, and the father is taken elsewhere.*

Betsey	Morris	Antonio	Anna
The women and children were put in a basement with thick walls. They kept hearing gunfire, but it didn't bother them any more because they were used to it. There were about 10 families in the basement. *(Literal)*	They were out in a basement room. *(Literal)* They were probably really scared because the dad is in a different place and they are all by themselves. *(Inference: The text does not refer to how they felt.)*	They're in a basement with other people. It said that prisoners would have to nurse the wounded and gather the dead. *(Literal)* It would be horrible to have to pick up dead bodies. I couldn't do it. I hate to see dead deer by the side of the road, and people would be worse. *(Application: Antonio is reacting personally and applying the text to a new context, animals.)*	They were captured and put in a building. *(Literal)*

The captives talk among themselves about possible rescue. The mother refuses to eat. On the second day, she is called out to see her husband and she warns the boy to look after his sisters while she is gone.

Betsey	Morris	Antonio	Anna
The mother won't eat anything. Then she went to see her husband. *(Literal)* The prisoners thought they would get out pretty fast. *(Literal)*	The mother isn't eating anything. *(Literal)* She is probably scared about what will happen. I wonder if it is a trick to get the mother to come out by saying her husband wants to see her. *(Inference: The text offers no comments about why the mother doesn't eat or the reason for the summons.)*	Everybody is saying that they will be rescued soon *(Literal)*, but I don't think the mother believes it. I think she knows they are in big trouble. *(Inference: The text does not explicitly talk about the mother's feelings or beliefs.)* They let her go to her husband *(Literal)*, and maybe it is to see him for the last time. *(Inference: Antonio is predicting a possible future event.)*	They called the mother out to go somewhere. They were talking a lot. *(Literal)*

The boy watches the soldiers setting up a field hospital. The mother returns and says that they are going to see his father, who will be taken away for a few days of reeducation. The boy asks what reeducation means, and she replies that it is like school.

Betsey	Morris	Antonio	Anna
They set up a little hospital and then the mother came back and said the father has to be reeducated. *(Literal)*	They are going to reeducate the father. *(Literal)* The mother acts like it's really nothing, and she didn't sound excited about going back to see her husband. *(Literal)* I think she is trying to protect the boy and doesn't want to say what is really going to happen. *(Inference: The text does not describe the mother's feelings.)*	They were putting together a pretty pathetic hospital with ponchos and bamboo cots and a bathtub full of water. *(Literal)* It doesn't seem that they are very well equipped. It didn't even have medicine or a doctor. *(Application: Antonio makes a judgment as to the quality of the hospital.)*	I really don't know what was going on. It had something to do with a hospital and a bathtub *(Literal)*, but it didn't make much sense. *(Monitoring: She is aware of her lack of understanding.)*

The soldiers give the prisoners some clay burners, coal, and rice. The mother cooks food for the father with water the soldiers gave her, which came from the hospital bathtub. The water smells of disinfectant that was used to wash the wounded soldiers.

Betsey	Morris	Antonio	Anna
They ate because the soldiers gave them food and a stove. The mother made rice for the father. *(Literal)* But she used dirty water because the soldiers made her use it. *(Inference: Betsey infers that use of the water was forced on the mother.)*	It was pretty generous of the soldiers to give them coal and clay burners, because they were in captivity and the soldiers really didn't have to give them anything. They could just let them starve. *(Inference: The text does not describe the motives of the soldiers.)* I remember a movie where prisoners were starved because they were just forgotten about, and afterwards the soldiers were all tried and punished. *(Application: Morris is applying the content to a new context.)*	Now that is gross! Giving someone water to drink that was full of disinfectant and was probably used to clean wounds. It's disgusting and it's cruel. It's probably all full of germs and it may kill the father. But I guess the soldiers don't care. *(Application: Antonio is making a judgment about the soldiers' actions and is also applying text content to a new context, the effect of germs.)*	The mother is going to take water to the father. She made some tea. *(Literal)*

The boy and his mother take food and clothing to the father. The boy doesn't know what to say and wonders if his father tasted the disinfectant. The father keeps caressing the boy's head but shows little emotion. The father says he will return in a few days.

Betsey	Morris	Antonio	Anna
The father ate the rice and tea, but the boy didn't know if he tasted the disinfectant. The father says he will be back in a little while. *(Literal)*	The boy is worried about his father, who seems to have his mind on other things. *(Inference: The text does not explain the boy's feelings or the father's thoughts.)*	The soldiers said he would be reeducated. *(Literal)* I wonder what that really means. Maybe it means that he will have to learn how to do things their way. *(Inference: The text never describes reeducation.)*	I don't understand why they are going to let the father go back with the other prisoners in the basement. *(Anna has misinterpreted the text, which says nothing about the father rejoining the other prisoners.)*

The boy and his mother return to the basement. Around midnight the soldiers take the father and other men away tied together. It will be 16 years before the boy sees his father again.

Betsey	Morris	Antonio	Anna
I wonder what the father was thinking. I wonder if he knew he would be a prisoner for that long. The boy must have felt terrible. *(Inference: The text does not discuss the father's thoughts or the boy's feelings.)*	How hard it must have been for the boy to have seen that, and then not to see his father for that long. I wonder what his father was like when they finally met and if they even recognized one another. I would like to get this book! *(Inference: Morris is inferring the boy's feelings and predicting future events.)*	I don't think reeducation really means going to school or getting taught. Not if they tied them all up. *(Inference: The text does not specifically say what happened to the father.)* This is a lot like the Japanese imprisonment in World War II in our country. *(Application: Antonio is applying to a different context.)*	They took him away all tied up, and he didn't see him for a long time. *(Literal)*

It is easy to see who truly understood the text and at what level. Betsey's comprehension was predominantly literal in form; she seldom moved beyond the text itself, yet her last think-aloud comments show that she sympathized with the boy's plight. Students often initially respond as Betsey did by emphasizing literal content. I find it helps to acknowledge such comments but then offer prompts that focus on making inferences: "What do you think about this?" "What are your feelings at this point?" It also helps to model an inferential comment. "I wonder why the mother isn't eating. Maybe it is because she is worried. I know when I am worried, really worried, I'm not too hungry." Emphasis on literal recall is often a natural outcome of classroom experiences that focus on and reward such comments. Once students begin to realize that their feelings and opinions are valued, they make more inferential and application think-aloud comments.

Both Morris and Antonio comprehended at inferential and application levels of comprehension. And then there was Anna. Even when she offered literal information, I was never sure that she saw the text events in any connected fashion. I asked Anna to orally read parts of the selection, and she willingly complied. She read fluently and accurately, so I knew that word recognition was not an issue. I asked if she would think aloud through a different selection. And this time I offered a number of specific prompts to move her comprehension to a higher level: "How do you think they felt?" "Why do you think they did that?" "How would you feel if this were happening to you?" She responded to all of my prompts in vague and general terms or resorted to saying, "I don't really know." She never actually seemed to enter into the feelings and concerns of the characters. Anna did very well when asked to answer literal questions about the selection on a traditional measure of comprehension but had difficulty in answering questions that required an inference of some sort.

Guidelines for Using Dialogue to Assess Comprehension

• *Guideline 1. Design a simple way to keep track of student talk.* Whether using thoughtful talk or think-alouds, assessment during discussion can become quite impressionistic. That is, unless the teacher keeps some sort of written record, it is easy to forget specific comments by students. It is even more difficult to remember whether comments reflected the literal, inferential, or application level of comprehension. The teacher needs a simple way of keeping track of who participates in the discussion and the comprehension levels of their comments. The following template can serve such a purpose, I illustrate its utility by recording the thoughtful talk comments of the five students who were discussing the Treaty of Versailles. The teacher, using the template attached to a clipboard, simply placed a checkmark in the appropriate column whenever a student offered a comment. The same simple template can be used to keep track of the think-aloud comments of Betsey, Morris, Antonio, and Anna. Given such a template, the teacher can assess the students' progress in moving beyond the literal level in their understanding of the Treaty of Versailles.

Student	Literal	Inferential	Application
Student 1	✓	✓ ✓ ✓	✓ ✓ ✓
Student 2	✓ ✓ ✓	✓ ✓ ✓ ✓ ✓	✓ ✓ ✓ ✓ ✓
Student 3		✓	✓ ✓ ✓ ✓ ✓ ✓
Student 4	✓ ✓	✓ ✓ ✓	✓
Student 5	✓ ✓ ✓ ✓	✓	✓ ✓ ✓ ✓

• *Guideline 2. Don't agonize about recognizing the different levels of comprehension reflected in thoughtful talk and think-aloud comments.* A discussion moves quickly, and a teacher cannot stop and deliberate at length about his or her coding, nor does a classroom teacher have time to tape-record and transcribe all dialogue in order to code it at a later date. Classroom use of thoughtful talk and think-alouds requires on-the-spot analysis. Code and move on. You can't stop the discussion while you decide whether a comment represents the inferential or application level. Remember that comprehension is a very complex entity, and the identification of comprehension levels for student comments is a rather inexact science. Literal comments are easy to recognize; differentiation of inferential and application levels is not as clear-cut. And there will always be student comments that defy coding. However, as you get better in listening to your students, your coding will become more consistent.

Remember that you are collecting multiple samples over a period of time and you are not making a final decision about a student's comprehension level on the basis of a single discussion. Over time, the mislabeling of comments becomes less problematic. You are looking for patterns; you are not counting the numbers of comments and turning them into a grade. You are using dialogue to answer the overall question, Did the students comprehend and at what level?

Also remember that comprehension varies, depending on the content of the text that is read, listened to, or viewed. The same five students who demonstrated inferential and application levels of comprehension in a social studies account of a treaty may perform very differently with a science text. For example, both Morris and Antonio reverted to literal think-aloud comments when reading a selection about viral replication. Their unfamiliarity with the topic did not allow them to move to an inferential level.

- *Guideline 3. Ease into thoughtful talk and thinking aloud.* Start slowly and gradually extend the length of the discussion and the number of times you use it for assessment. It will take practice on your part and on the part of the students. Trying to change the way in which you talk to students and the way in which you respond to them is not easy. It is a little like learning to use a stick shift after years of driving with an automatic transmission. It will feel different. It may be frustrating. You may be tempted to give it up because you believe you are doing it poorly and the students are not responding as they should. Having purchased a stick shift car (in a weak moment), I wondered if I would ever feel proficient in driving it. Then I suddenly found that I no longer knew exactly how many times I had shifted gears in driving from the university to my house and that I could shift and listen to the radio at the same time. Proficiency and comfort often appear when you least expect them, but they do appear.

Begin by focusing on one or two students during thoughtful talk or think-aloud discussion. That is, just code the responses of those students. Then extend your attention to one or two other students. As you begin to feel more comfortable, you can gradually increase the number of students you include in your coding. You can also begin by just differentiating literal from inferential comments. Then, when you feel comfortable doing this, move to the application level.

- *Guideline 4. Don't expect to remember all the content-free questions the first time you use them.* Allow yourself a "cheat sheet." Place a copy of the questions on your desk where they are easily accessible, tuck them into your textbook, or attach them to your lesson plan. That way, if you momentarily forget what question to ask, you have a ready reference. I have used Post-it notes attached to the text to remind myself of what to say.

Don't try to handle all of the content-free questions at once. Choose a few to begin with, and when you and your students are comfortable with them, add one or two more. It is even better if content-free questions are accessible to students as well. Put them in a conspicuous place, such as in large print on a bulletin board. I know of one teacher who placed them on laminated bookmarks for students to tuck inside their textbooks. Access to content-free questions reminds students of a strategy that can help them comprehend.

- *Guideline 5. Prepare for modeling thoughtful talk or think-aloud comments.* If you are modeling thoughtful talk or think-aloud comments, it helps to prepare by reading the text and deciding beforehand what you might say. I use Post-it notes to remind me of the modeling comments I want to make. After a while, these are no longer necessary.

- *Guideline 6. Keep some record of student performance in your grade book.* It can be too cumbersome to quantify student comments or translate template records into numerical grades. The important concern is not how many comments of one type students make, but that they make them. Remember Betsey?

At first, she primarily made literal think-aloud comments, but at the end she demonstrated comprehension at a strong inferential level.

What can a student record look like? Grade book formats vary tremendously, ranging from the traditional paper-and-pencil book record to various electronic versions. A simple way to proceed is to label a grade book entry as TT (thoughtful talk) or TA (think-aloud). Then record your students' performances as L (literal), I (inferential), or A (application), using a simple system of +, ✓, –, or ?. A plus mark (+) means that literal or inferential comprehension was clearly evident. A checkmark (✓) means that the student demonstrated some inferential comprehension. A minus (–) indicates that a specific level of comprehension was not evident. A question mark (?) indicates that you are not sure; perhaps the student comment cannot be easily coded or the student chose not to participate. A teacher might summarize the performances of Betsey, Morris, Antonio, and Anna in the following way:

Betsey	L +	I ✓	A –
Morris	L +	I +	A ✓
Antonio	L +	I +	A +
Anna	L ✓	I –	A –

Student Dialogue and Response to Intervention

When students engage in discussion based on content-free questions and offer think-aloud comments, they are retelling what they remember and think about the text. In RTI as presently described, a rather limited measure of retelling is sometimes utilized. The student is asked to read a short passage and retell it within a 1-minute time frame. The retelling is scored for the number of words it contains, but no attempt is made to evaluate the accuracy, quality, or completeness of the retelling. This procedure may be appropriate for beginning readers and the primary grades, but it can have limited utility for upper elementary, middle, and high school levels. Basically, content teachers are not interested in the number of words present in a retelling; they are interested in the accuracy and completeness of the student's comprehension.

Can student dialogue be used in the RTI process? I believe it would be most appropriate at the progress-monitoring stage of Tiers 2 and 3. In these tiers, teachers are working with small groups and individuals, and it is much easier to keep track of and code the oral responses of a small number of students, as opposed to an entire classroom. The effectiveness of the monitoring system rests on a simple and uniform coding system like those described in this chapter.

Summary

- Classroom dialogue falls into two broad categories: directive and support-ive. Supportive scaffolds are more learner-centered and support the development of comprehension.
- Observing and noting student behavior during supportive discussions can provide a window on the comprehension process through the use of two activi-ties: thoughtful talk and thinking aloud.
- Thoughtful talk primarily involves a focus on student response to the text, as opposed to literal recall.
- Teachers can lead students into thoughtful talk by generating questions that focus on the inferential and application aspects of comprehension and by the use of content-free questions.
- Content-free questions are questions that students can ask about any text. They provide a guide for easing a teacher into scaffolding a supportive discus-sion, and they offer students ways of thinking about a text and engaging in ques-tioning strategies that enhance comprehension.
- Thinking aloud involves students' stopping after reading short segments of text and saying what they are thinking about, that is, describing the state of their comprehension at that particular moment. Think-alouds allow a form of performance assessment that focuses on the process of comprehension.
- Think-alouds can be coded as literal, inferential, or application in nature.
- Guidelines for using dialogue to assess comprehension include the follow-ing: coding student comments during discussion; collecting multiple samples of think-aloud comments; easing into the use of thoughtful talk and think-aloud comments; keeping a copy of content-free question in an easily accessible place; and maintaining a record of student performance in your grade book.
- Recording and coding student dialogue can be a possible form of Tiers 2 and 3 progress monitoring in RTI.

Professional Development Activities for Assessing Comprehension through Dialogue

- Tape-record a segment of classroom dialogue and listen to it. Count the number of times you talk, as opposed to how often the students talk. Who is doing most of the talking, you or the students? Consider the length of each utterance. Who is talking longer during each exchange, you or the student? Are you providing a directive or a supporting scaffold to students? Are you primarily asking literal-level questions? Are your comments primarily focused on helping students complete a task?

• Choose a selection of text and consider how you would model the use of content-free questions. Write appropriate questions on Post-it notes and place them on the text. Do the same for think-alouds.

• Initiate a thoughtful talk discussion modeling content-free questions and drawing students into the process. Or do this using the think-aloud process. What went well? How can you improve the process?

• Initiate a thoughtful talk or think-aloud discussion and tape-record it. At your leisure, play it back and assess the students' comments.

• Tape-record a thoughtful talk or think-aloud session. Work with another teacher to code the responses.

• Work with an individual student and ask him or her to think aloud. Code the responses. What do they tell you about the student's comprehension?

CHAPTER 7

Words! Words! Words!

How Can We Assess Word Comprehension?

The Nature of Words

Can you imagine a day without words? I can't. We listen to words, we read words, and we speak and write words to express our thoughts and feelings. Much of our experience takes the form of language and words are our primary form of communication. Even if we spend a day alone with no television, radio, or books, words are still part of the experience because when we think, we think in words. The words we know and use are critical in establishing what we can understand. If we do not know the meaning of words, we cannot comprehend, and knowing word meanings makes us better readers and better listeners. In short, words are "the tools we use to access our background knowledge, express ideas, and learn new concepts" (Stahl & Nagy, 2006, p. 4). In addition, the words we know may determine our reading ability in general and our comprehension specifically (Stahl & Fairbanks, 1986).

There is a strong relationship between vocabulary and comprehension. If we know the meanings of the words in a selection, we will be better able to comprehend it. Again and again it has been demonstrated that scores on vocabulary measures are strongly correlated with scores on comprehension measures. Given the importance of vocabulary knowledge to comprehension, it makes good sense that comprehension assessment should involve assessment of word knowledge.

Words are unique entities. First, in any language, it is probably impossible to know how many words there are. Even if we count all the words in an unabridged dictionary, in the time it takes to do this, new words will come into being. Language is a living entity, and each year new words appear and old words fall into disfavor.

Most words represent more than one meaning. Consider the word *court,* as in *tennis court, courtyard, king's court* (both palace and entourage), *court of law, court a girl,* and *court disaster.* On the flip side, there are many words that represent variations of a similar meaning, such as *overweight, fat, corpulent, adipose, pudgy, stout, plump, heavy, thickset, chubby, solid, obese,* and *chunky.* Many words are derived from other words, using an extensive system of prefixes, suffixes, and roots. Given the word *check,* we have *checks, checked, checking, checker, checkers, checkered, checkerboard, checkerboards, recheck, rechecks, rechecked, rechecking, checkbook, checkbooks, checkmate, checkroom, checkrooms, checkout, check off, checkup,* and *check-in.* An individual with a strong vocabulary not only comprehends more words but also understands multiple meanings for the words he or she knows (Stahl & Nagy, 2006).

When we know a word, we understand what it means. Johnson (2001) describes a single word as having two sides: the meaning of the word and its sound. Both are absolutely necessary, but there is little relationship between the sound of the word and its meaning. That is, the component sounds of *candy* have no relationship to the meaning that is attached. However, the sound of a word is important because it is sound that calls up meaning. For example, when we hear or pronounce a word, we use the sound to access the meaning of the word in memory. If there is no entry corresponding to the sound of the word, we cannot attach meaning. In that case, we either ask someone what it means, try to figure it out through context or by some other method, or just let it go.

How many words does an individual know? That is, how many words does an individual have in his or her memory, often referred to as a mental lexicon or mental dictionary? It is impossible to tell. There are several systems for describing the categories of words that a person knows. In one respect, we all have four vocabulary systems. We have a listening vocabulary, composed of all the words whose meaning we recognize when we hear them. We have a speaking vocabulary, that is, the words that we retrieve from memory and use as we talk. A word may be in our listening vocabulary but never or seldom used during speaking. We have a reading vocabulary, made up of all the words we can translate from print to sound to meaning, and, finally, we have a writing vocabulary, words we can spell and commonly use when writing. Similarly, Kamil and Hiebert (2005) describe an individual's vocabulary as productive and receptive. Productive vocabulary are words used when speaking or writing; these tend to be relatively familiar and frequently used. Receptive vocabulary includes words to which a listener or reader can attach meaning, but which are often less well known and seldom used spontaneously. Receptive vocabularies tend to be larger than productive ones. Although all of the aforementioned vocabularies share common words, some contain unique examples. For instance, an individual may attach meaning to words like *capsid* and *prion* when reading a selection on viruses but may never use the words in writing or in speech unless directed to do so in a test format.

Mental lexicons contain more than word knowledge. They also include world knowledge or knowledge about the contexts "in which a word is appropriate and in which it is not" (Johnson, 2001, p. 17). There are four such contexts. One is knowledge of words that frequently occur together, such as *cotton candy* and *blue sky*. The second is understanding of syntax or position in a sentence. For example, we say, *The dog barks at the delivery man,* not *The dog bark at the delivery man*. We say, *Yesterday I jumped,* not *Yesterday I will jump*. We must also have knowledge of semantics, or how words fit together. *John chewed the milk* does not work well; *John drank* or *sipped the milk* does. Finally, we need to understand pragmatic contexts. Saying, *Shut up* to a friend might be acceptable; to a teacher, it generally is not.

How is this mental lexicon or dictionary organized? In other words, when we learn a new word, what do we do with it? Unlike the typical dictionary or glossary, we do not store word meaning alphabetically. We store new words and their meanings in what has been called semantic clusters or networks (Stahl & Nagy, 2006; Johnson, 2001). New word meanings are stored with related words, concepts, facts, and memories. Simply put, we store words according to their similarity in meaning to other words. For example, we group together words that have similar features, such as wheels. So *automobile, car, bicycle,* and *scooter* may all be linked together. We store words in general categories. If we just learned the word *echinacea,* we would probably store it with the category of *flower, plant,* or *perennial*. We may also group it with *daisy,* because of the similarity of the flower structure. Sometimes we group words that often go together, such as *blue sky* or *red rose*. What is so interesting is that we do this unconsciously; we are not generally aware of how we build our vocabulary networks.

When we comprehend a word either through listening or reading, we tend to recall other items in the network as well. For example, suppose you learn the meaning of *ratel*. A ratel is an animal, a carnivore that lives in India and Africa. It looks something like a badger. Now you would probably store your new word knowledge in networks of other animals that eat meat and live outside the United States. If you lived in Wisconsin, you might also store this new information with your knowledge of football, because "the Badgers" is the name of the University of Wisconsin football team and the badger is a familiar Wisconsin animal. When you access word meaning, other associations are also called up because of the interrelatedness of your semantic networks. You can test this grouping arrangement by asking people to free associate, that is, say what first comes into their minds when you pronounce a word. Try saying *mouse* and *pizza.* I predict that the following will be included in people's responses.

> *mouse:* Mickey, cheese, cat, trap, rodent, ears, tail
> *pizza:* cheese, food, crust, hot, sauce, frozen, delivery

Levels of Word Meaning

What does it mean to comprehend a word? It is certainly not an all-or-nothing proposition. There are many things that are either known or not known, with few gradations in between. For example, we either know how to spell *ingenious* or we don't. We know that viruses and cells are different entities, or we don't. We know that periods go at the ends of sentences, or we don't. However, for any word, we can know a little about it or a lot (Beck, McKeown, & Kucan, 2002). We may have absolutely no knowledge of the meaning of a word. We may have a general sense of the word as something good or bad. We may be able to recognize it in a supportive context but be unable to recall it for use in other situations. We may have a rich knowledge of the word that allows us to appreciate its use in metaphors and employ it appropriately in speaking and writing. This becomes more complicated when we consider that our levels of word knowledge apply to only one meaning of a word. As mentioned previously, most words carry multiple meanings. In addition, word learning is an incremental process; that is, we can learn more about a word each time we encounter it (Harmon, Hedrick, Soares, & Gress, 2007).

Many people think that knowing a word means being able to provide a definition or synonym. This is a limited view, because definitions and synonyms can be memorized and, as indicated in Chapter 1, the ability to memorize does not always indicate understanding. In addition, you know many words that you would find hard to define. What happens when someone asks you what a word means? Often, you cannot provide a definition. Occasionally, you can call up a synonym, but most of the time you can't even do that. And so you resort to an explanation in which you put the word in a specific context and describe its meaning in that way. Try providing neat and tidy definitions of the following words: *meander, disoriented, strut,* and *proclaim.* Doesn't it work better to offer an explanation or example? Here are examples from students whose teacher fosters talking about words and placing them within the context of their own lives.

> *Meander* is when you are killing time in the mall and just walking slowly around looking at things. Or when you are in a museum and just going though, just seeing what is coming up next.
> *Disoriented* is how you might feel if you got hit hard on the head or if you

felt very dizzy and thought you might faint. People who drink too much are often disoriented and they don't act like themselves.

Strut is what baton twirlers and band members do during halftime at a football game.

Proclaim is like those commercials on television that say how good their product is and they keep saying it over and over and very loud.

A word stands for a concept, and a concept is much richer than a definition or a synonym. Knowing a concept involves knowing its critical attributes, the category to which it belongs, examples of the concept, and nonexamples. There are three types of concepts that students must learn in school (Stahl & Nagy, 2006). The first type is learning the print match of words already in a student's oral vocabulary. That is, the student knows the meaning of *house, horse,* and *bicycle.* Now he or she must learn to recognize the print counterparts of these words. This type of learning represents a large part of reading instruction in the early grades. Second, a student faces words that he or she has never heard or seen before, but which represent familiar concepts. For example, the student understands the concept of *run* but now faces new words such as *lope, scuttle, scurry,* and *sprint.* A third and more difficult issue is learning unfamiliar words for unfamiliar concepts, such as *nucleic, organelles,* and *nanometer.* Related to this is learning new meanings for familiar words, such as learning *envelope* as the outer covering of a virus and *core* as its acid center. This type of vocabulary learning is very important in the content areas.

Vocabulary and Comprehension

The relationship between vocabulary knowledge and comprehension is not as simple as it may appear (Pearson, Hiebert, & Kamil, 2007; Nagy, 2005). One hypothesis, often termed the instrumentalist hypothesis, is that knowledge of word meanings causes comprehension. Given two readers or listeners, the one who knows more word meanings will be better able to comprehend than the one who knows fewer. A second hypothesis is the knowledge hypothesis, which posits that what causes comprehension is not word knowledge but the background knowledge that readers or listeners may have about a specific topic. That is, an individual comprehends a selection on ancient Egypt, not because he or she knows words such as *papyrus, mummification,* and *obelisk,* but because he or she knows quite a bit about Egyptology. According to this hypothesis, vocabulary knowledge is a sort of proxy for background knowledge. A third hypothesis is the aptitude hypothesis. Some people have strong verbal aptitudes and, as a result, learn more word meanings as well as comprehend more effectively. Nagy (2005) suggests that verbal aptitude may allow readers and listeners to become more adept at manipulating language and determining word meanings from both context and morphological analysis. A final hypothesis is the access hypothesis: It is not enough to know the meanings of many words. One must know them well enough to access them quickly and accurately in multiple contexts. Probably all of these hypotheses are true to some extent.

The relationship between vocabulary and comprehension is a reciprocal one. That is, for whatever reason, knowing many word meanings and effective comprehension go together. If you have an extensive vocabulary, you will comprehend better than if you don't. And if you comprehend effectively, you will probably learn more word meanings through context. Stanovich (1986) describes this reciprocity as the Matthew effect, derived from the biblical passage in Matthew suggesting that the rich get richer and the poor get poorer. The rich (good comprehenders) comprehend what they read and hear, and as a result they learn more words. Because they know more words, their comprehension increases and they read more and pay greater attention to what they hear. In short, they get richer. Poor comprehenders, however, avoid reading and extensive listening, such as to classroom lectures or read alouds, and as a result they do not increase their vocabulary knowledge. Lack of vocabulary knowledge contributes to continued comprehension difficulty, so they avoid reading and listening situations to an even greater extent. As a result, the poor get poorer.

Whatever hypothesis you espouse, few dispute the importance of vocabulary instruction in elementary, middle and high school classrooms. The National Reading Panel (2000) identified vocabulary as one of the five major components of reading and drew specific conclusions about effective practices in vocabulary instruction. It is not a purpose of this book to describe best practices in vocabulary instruction. There are five wonderful books that do that better than I ever could. My focus is how to validly, reliably, and sensitively assess comprehension of vocabulary.

Books on Vocabulary Instruction

Baumann, J. F., & Kame'enui, E. J. (2004). *Vocabulary instruction: Research to practice.* New York: Guilford Press.

Beck, I. L., McKeown, M. G., & Kucan, L. (2002). *Bringing words to life: Robust vocabulary instruction.* New York: Guilford Press.

Hiebert, E. H., & Kamil, M. L. (Eds.). (2005). *Teaching and learning vocabulary: Bringing research to practice.* Mahwah, NJ: Erlbaum.

Johnson, D. D. (2001). *Vocabulary in the elementary and middle school.* Boston: Allyn & Bacon.

Stahl, S. A., & Nagy, W. E. (2006). *Teaching word meanings.* Mahwah, NJ: Erlbaum.

Assessments of Word Comprehension

It is interesting that vocabulary assessment in the classroom is not as popular a topic as vocabulary instruction. It is certainly not mentioned to any great extent in the vocabulary books I recommend here, and a lengthy discussion of vocabulary assessment by Pearson et al. (2007) focuses almost entirely on standardized and large-scale vocabulary assessment as opposed to classroom assessment. By devoting an entire chapter to classroom assessment of word comprehension, in a sense, I am forging into new territory.

Johnson (2001) lists three issues with assessing comprehension of vocabulary. Which words should teachers choose to assess? What will students do to demonstrate their word knowledge? What testing format should be used?

Choosing Words to Assess

In the classroom, words for vocabulary assessment generally come from what the students are reading or learning about. Usually, but not always, they are assumed to be critical to comprehending the selections. Who makes such a decision? Obviously, the final choice of which words to teach and test is up to the teacher, who will probably be guided by a variety of influences. Targeted words are often identified in a teacher's manual, and some school districts have compiled lists of high-frequency words that should be taught and assessed in the early grades. In regard to informational texts in grades 4–8, Harmon, Hedrick, and Fox (2000) found little agreement between words that teachers thought were critical and those listed by the publishers. Publisher recommendations often centered on words that occurred only once or twice in the textbook selection.

Unfortunately, we do not have a comprehensive and agreed-upon list of words that students should know at a certain age (Biemiller, 2004). Hirsch assembled a list of terms and phrases that he believed every American should know and described this knowledge as "cultural literacy" (Hirsch, 1987; Hirsch, Kett, & Trefal, 1993). Eventually Hirsch and his colleagues designated key vocabulary items for each grade level, which involved almost 5,000 terms across grades K–8. Questioning Hirsch's methods for choosing words, Marzano, Kendall, and Gaddy (1999) used state benchmarks and standards to craft their list of essential vocabulary in 14 content areas: mathematics, science, history, language arts, the arts, civics, economics, foreign language, geography, health, physical education, technology, behavioral studies, and life skills. They grouped their almost 7,000 words into four levels: grades K–2, grades 3–5, grades 6–8, and grades 9–12.

Beck et al. (2002) describe words as composing three tiers. The first tier includes basic words such as *walk, mother, animal,* and so on. These rarely require instructional attention. The second tier of words includes high-frequency words that are found across a variety of content areas, such as *compromise, diligent,* and *fortunate.* Because of their utility, they deserve instructional attention. The third tier of words are those limited to specific content areas, such as *capsid, organelles,* and *nanometer.* In order to understand science and social studies topics, among others, the teacher must address these third-tier words.

Words to be taught and assessed should be important and useful. Important words are words that the reader or listener needs to know in order to understand the text. Useful words appear frequently in diverse and multiple contexts (Harmon et al., 2007). "Words that are related to the selection, the content, or to a thematic unit have instructional potential and should be considered high on the list of candidates for explicit instruction" (Kamil & Hiebert, 2005, p. 12).

Demonstrating Word Knowledge

Once the words to be assessed are determined, a second problem arises. How will you know if a student knows a word? Should the student provide a definition, synonym, or antonym? Should the student use the word appropriately in a sentence, categorize the word as like or unlike other words, or provide examples or attributes? Any of these activities can suggest word knowledge, but there is a slight catch. Knowing a word does not mean that a student can do all of these things. A student may be able to provide examples of a word but not offer a definition. A student may be able to use a word appropriately but not provide a synonym. This should not surprise us. It has been noted that students can comprehend in one type of text and in one kind of situation and do poorly in a different text and under different circumstances. Like comprehension of reading, listening, and viewing, comprehension of word meaning varies with the text and the context. A teacher should not assume that if a student fails on one type of vocabulary assessment task, he or she does not know the word. Beck et al. (2002) suggest that word knowledge falls along a continuum, ranging from relatively simple to complex, and different measures assess different points on the continuum. For example, providing a simple association (*devour* as in *devour food*) is probably easier than giving an example (*a lion might devour food* or *a person who is starvingmight devour food*). This, in turn, may be easier than offering a synonym (*demolish, consume*) or a full explanation of the word's meaning (*devour means to eat greedily or gulp down*).

Stahl (1986) and Stahl and Fairbanks (1986) proposed three levels of word knowledge: association, comprehension, and generation. Association means that the student can associate a word with other words even if he or she does not know its meaning, such as associating *devour* with *food* or *immense* with *treasure.* Comprehension means the student knows common meanings of the word, such as *devour* means *eat* and *immense* means *big.* Generation means that the student can provide or use the word in a new or novel context (*He devoured her with his eyes* or *The immense tip of a nickel angered the waiter*). Although all three levels involve comprehension of word meaning, the teacher should focus on comprehension and generation as opposed to association. In addition, the teacher must be very clear about how the students will demonstrate their knowledge at these levels.

Assessment techniques should "reflect the level of word knowledge needed for performing particular tasks" (Harmon et al., 2007, p. 139). Students may need to demonstrate only a general understanding of some words. For other words, they may require more in-depth knowledge because such a word represents a concept that is crucial to understanding the text. This calls for an assessment task that captures a rich comprehension of word meaning, which, of course, leads to the third problem, selecting the testing format.

Selecting the Assessment Format

Once the teacher has chosen the words and specified what the students should do to demonstrate word knowledge, the next step is to determine the assessment format. Assessment of word comprehension is divided into two general categories that have been discussed earlier: selected response and constructed response. Selected response in the form of multiple-choice questions is probably the most widely used assessment of word knowledge and can take several forms. The student reads a word in isolation or in context and indicates understanding by choosing a picture, a definition, a synonym, or an antonym. Although this seems relatively straightforward, there are problems. If a student fails the item, this does not necessarily mean that he or she did not know the word. The problem may lie with the distracters, the wrong items that are provided as choices along with the correct answer. Consider the following example. Suppose a student was asked to provide a meaning for *court* and offered the following distracters: *compel, strike, woo, drink.* In order to arrive at a correct answer (without lucky guessing), the student must know the meanings of the distracters. If the student does not know the meaning of *woo,* he or she will not arrive at the correct answer even if he or she does understand the meaning of *court.* And of course there is another issue. The student may know *court* in a sports context but not in the context of a romantic relationship. So multiple-choice selected response items, although very common, are not always reliable. Large-scale standardized vocabulary tests employ a multiple-choice format almost exclusively, and perhaps the best that can be said about them is that they provide only general information about a student's standing in relation to his or her peers (Beck et al., 2002).

Constructed response items ask a student to supply a missing word in a sentence (the cloze technique), draw a picture, provide a synonym or antonym, offer a definition or explanation of the word meaning, place the word in a category, or use the word in a sentence. Given the complexity inherent in knowing a word, a student may be able to choose the correct synonym in a selected response format but not be able to provide the synonym in a constructed response measure.

The previously listed books contain myriad examples of classroom activities for teaching vocabulary that can also be used for assessment. These are generally constructed response scenarios that fall into four general categories. One category involves explaining word meaning by providing a definition, a synonym, or an antonym. A second category involves comparison. The student compares a word to other words and/or categorizes it some way. A third involves extension; that is, the student extends the meaning of a word by building a visual map or by providing examples and nonexamples of the word. The fourth category is usage, in which the student uses or applies a word to a new context.

In previous chapters, I have characterized levels of comprehension as literal, inferential, and application and suggested that teachers code their comprehension assessments accordingly. I believe we can do the same with vocabulary assessment. Explanation of word meaning falls into the literal level of comprehension. Comparison and extension represent the inferential level, and vocabulary usage corresponds to the application level. By retaining the same three levels across all forms of comprehension assessment, the teacher can note patterns in the comprehension of individual students as well as of the class as a whole.

The chart on the facing page categorizes activities recommended as suitable for both vocabulary instruction and assessment according to constructed response categories and levels of comprehension.

The activities listed in the chart involve constructed responses. I have already discussed constructed response activities in Chapter 5, but it bears repeating that such measures often require some sort of rubric to ensure reliability of scoring. If a vocabulary assessment is summative in nature, that is, used to describe a student's performance and provide a grade, simple rubrics can help to ensure more consistent scoring. The following rubric is easily adaptable to most constructed response vocabulary assessments.

3	2	1	0
Comprehension of word meaning is clearly evident.	Comprehension of word meaning is evident but some vagueness is present.	Comprehension of word meaning is vague and lacks specificity.	There is no indication that word meaning is understood.

Harmon et al. (2007) present a rubric based on a 6-point scale that describes word understanding as exceptional, excellent, proficient, minimal, limited, or missing, with variations based on accuracy of information, presence of significant detail, and adequate support of personal interpretations and insights.

Constructed Response Vocabulary Activities for Instruction and Assessment

Literal level	Inferential level		Application level
Explanation	**Comparison**	**Extension**	**Usage**
Provide a definition of a word (Stahl & Nagy, 2006)	Note differences between a word and related words (Stahl & Nagy, 2006; Beck et al., 2002)	Provide examples of the word (Stahl & Nagy, 2006; Beck et al., 2002)	Create sentences using target word(s) (Stahl & Nagy, 2006)
Provide a synonym for a word (Stahl & Nagy, 2006)	Create compare-and-contrast diagrams (Stahl, 2005; Stahl & Nagy, 2006)	Provide nonexamples of the word (Stahl, 2005; Stahl & Nagy, 2006; Beck et al., 2002)	Connect a word to personal contexts/ experiences (Beck et al., 2002; Johnson, 2001)
Provide an antonym for a word (Stahl & Nagy, 2006)	Sort and categorize words (Stahl, 2005; Stahl & Nagy, 2006; Johnson, 2001)	Create word maps or word webs (Stahl, 2005; Stahl & Nagy, 2006; Johnson, 2001)	
Rewrite a definition in your own words (Stahl & Nagy, 2006)			

Comparison and expansion instructional activities at the inferential level primarily involve group work, with students sharing and collaborating to construct word maps, sort words, and generate examples and attributes. In fact, much of the instructional value of these activities comes from such interaction. For this reason, if they are to be used for assessment, the assessment should be primarily formative in nature and used to guide the teacher in modifying instruction. The teacher can observe the students as they collaborate and use a simple template to record the words that pose difficulties and those that are known. For example, suppose that the target words were *dread, fraud, orator, attire, audition, director, strut,* and *mimic.* The following template can be used as a formative guide for the teacher as he or she moves among the classroom groups. Whenever he or she notes group understanding of a word, the teacher places a checkmark in the Known column. If confusion is evident, a checkmark is placed in the Not known column. A third column is reserved for those instances when the teacher is unsure about the group's word knowledge. This allows the teacher to identify words that may require additional instruction.

Word	Known	Not known	?
dread	✓ ✓ ✓ ✓ ✓	✓	
fraud	✓ ✓ ✓ ✓ ✓		✓
orator	✓ ✓	✓ ✓ ✓	✓
attire	✓ ✓ ✓ ✓	✓ ✓	
audition		✓ ✓ ✓ ✓ ✓	✓
director	✓ ✓ ✓ ✓ ✓		
strut	✓ ✓		✓ ✓ ✓
mimic	✓ ✓	✓ ✓ ✓ ✓	

Using Words in Sentences

Having students create sentences using the target words is a common method of assessing vocabulary and represents an application level of word knowledge. Unfortunately, it is used so poorly as to be of little value. When I was in school (and you don't need to know how long ago that was), vocabulary assessment, generally in the form of a homework assignment, meant looking up the meanings of words in a dictionary and using them in sentences. In turn, I taught as I was taught and asked my students to do the same. And I see this practice repeated again and again in today's classrooms. Teachers realize that if a student can do this, it shows a high level of vocabulary knowledge, which Stahl (1986) and Stahl and Fairbanks (1986) described as a generation level. But there is a problem. We do not teach students how to write such sentences and so we seldom get sentences that tell us much of anything.

I well remember assigning *extrovert* as a word for my middle school students to define and use in a sentence, and receiving the following sentences:

I saw an extrovert. This told me that the student recognized *extrovert* as a noun, but nothing more.

I extroverted down the hall on my birthday. The student seems to have some idea of the meaning of extrovert but does not understand that it is a noun, not a verb.

An extrovert is a happy person. An extrovert may or may not be happy, and the student's understanding of the word's meaning is ambiguous.

And so it went, no matter how many times I assigned the task. The majority of responses were grammatically correct but seldom indicated whether the students really understood the word. Finally, I added the following requirement:

"Use the word in a sentence that shows me you understand the meaning." This did not improve matters, although several enterprising students included a dictionary definition in their sentences: *The extrovert is concerned with things outside himself.* I have never forgotten these examples because I found the whole process of using words in sentences extremely frustrating. I basically knew that correct word usage signaled understanding, but I did not know how to bring it about.

Using vocabulary words in a sentence requires the same sort of teacher modeling as thoughtful talk and think-alouds. You have to teach students how to use a word to demonstrate their understanding of it. Once they catch on, their sentences begin to make sense, as well as to indicate whether they comprehend the word.

First, identify each word as a noun, verb, or adjective. If you are working with younger children or wish to avoid grammatical terms, use the following alternatives: thing word, action word, and describing word. Before using sentence writing for an assessment, show students how to use the following directions to create meaningful sentences. Model this for them and help them to create their own sentences. Talk about their sentences and explain how they reflect word meaning and how they might be improved.

If the word is a noun, write a sentence describing what it does or does not do, what it might or might not do.
- ✓ *Extroverts* will probably share their feelings and be interested in the feelings of others.
- ✓ When there is an *emergency,* usually the police are called and people move really fast.
- ✓ The *merchant* sold old clothes and shoes and funny hats in order to make money.

If the word is a noun, write one or two sentences describing it.
- ✓ An *extrovert* is friendly and chatty. An *extrovert* likes to be with people.
- ✓ When the hurricane hit, it was an *emergency* and a lot of people were hurt and needed help right away.
- ✓ *Merchants* have to know how to be nice to customers and how to choose the right things to sell.

If the word is a verb, write one or two sentences that tell who or what would perform the action and how they might do it.
- ✓ My mother always *insists* that I do my homework before I watch television. She just won't let me turn on the set.
- ✓ A thief might *covet* some fancy jewelry because he wants to get money for it. So he tries to steal it.
- ✓ Friends *banter* with each other all the time. They kid each other and even insult each other, but it's all in fun.

If the word is an adjective, write one or two sentences telling who or what this word describes.

> ✓ My brother is very *reluctant* when it's his turn to take out the garbage. He waits as long as he can until my mother yells at him.
> ✓ The sun was so *dazzling* that I couldn't look at it without my eyes hurting.
> ✓ The show was *tolerable*. I only watched it because I had nothing else to do.

What about adverbs? Adverbs are basically adjectives with -*ly* added on. If a student understands the meaning of an adjective, he or she can readily transfer this to adverb form.

Once students have learned how to write sentences that demonstrate their knowledge of a word, such an activity becomes an effective target for assessment. It has been my experience that students enjoy this form of sentence construction, and they often incorporate their own experiences in the sentence composition. It is wonderful if they do so, because people build new knowledge on the basis of what they already know (Bransford et al., 2000). Therefore, tying a new word to personal experience and to the contents of one's mental lexicon helps students learn and remember it. Harmon et al. (2007) suggest a similar assessment activity, which asks students to categorize words in three ways: words that describe persons, things, actions, or feelings; words that name objects, things, or actions; and words that show what people and things can do.

Connecting Words to Personal Experiences

In assessing word comprehension, an effective alternative to asking students to use words in sentences is to be a little more free-form and ask them to put the words in the context of their own lives, which represents the generation or application level of comprehension (Stahl & Fairbanks, 1986). In other words, if the word is a noun, when did they see or meet this item? In their families? Did they encounter it on television or in their neighborhood? If the word is a verb, who or what in their lives did this? If the word is an adjective, what in their lives does it describe? Begin with this as an instructional activity before using it as an assessment measure. This activity is very motivating for students of all ages who enjoy matching word meaning to their own personal experiences. Here are a few examples from fourth graders who were actively engaged in what they called "putting words in my life."

> ✓ I was *fortunate* when Grandma gave me my new scooter because I didn't have enough money for it and now I can ride it to school. Yea Grandma!
> ✓ I watched a movie on television that was really *sinister* about someone who

came back from the dead. It scared my little sister so much that she had bad dreams all night.

✓ My older sister is always making *comments* about how great she is and how popular she is. I don't like to hear them. She is just so conceited.

✓ Going camping in the summer is like going on an *expedition.* We have to pack up everything and take food and it's a lot of work but it's also fun.

✓ Mom *altered* our whole kitchen. She put up new curtains and painted all the cabinets and even hung a picture over the sink.

✓ My little brother *blurts* out stuff that gets him in trouble. Once he hurt his finger and *blurted* out a certain word that I can't write. Boy, was Dad mad!

Guidelines for Assessing Word Comprehension

• *Guideline 1. Carefully choose words to assess.* There is always a temptation to assess all of the words suggested by the teachers manual or listed in the textbooks as key words that students should know. Use your professional knowledge and your knowledge of the content you are teaching to emphasize those that will be most useful to your students. Of course, we want our students to know all the words, but that is both improbable and impossible. Choose words that are truly critical to the comprehension of a chosen selection or to the students' developing knowledge of a content field.

• *Guideline 2. Share with your students the words that you intend to include in the assessment.* This does not "give away the store," that is, place the students in the position of not having to study. Instead, knowing which words will be on the test focuses their attention and prompts them to study what you want them to know. Tell the students how you will test their word knowledge, because it can make a difference when they study. As mentioned earlier in this chapter, providing a definition requires a very different approach than offering a synonym. Preparing for a selected response measure involves different skills than getting ready for a constructed response task.

• *Guideline 3. Design your assessment to parallel your classroom instruction.* If you ask students to use words in sentences as part of instruction, have them do this as part of assessment. If you ask students to categorize words, ask them to do it on the summative examination as well. It just makes good sense to match instructional and assessment formats whenever possible, because it ensures that student performance in an assessment is not negatively affected by lack of understanding of the task itself. For example, if an assessment measure asks students to categorize words by placing them in columns and this is a new and unfamiliar task, a student may fail simply because of the unfamiliar format. Remember that in Chapter 5, I cautioned that students should be taught how to construct open-ended measures such as essay questions before they are used as summative assessments. The same holds true for vocabulary assessment.

• *Guideline 4. Adapt the assessment format to the age of the child.* Observation is probably a better format in the early grades. A teacher and students can have rich discussions about word meaning, and the teacher can use a simple template to keep track of which students understand a word and which seem to be experiencing difficulty. I watched an enthusiastic discussion by first graders that centered on the meaning of the word *buoyant.* I do not know how or why this word was singled out for emphasis, but when I arrived the children were eagerly talking about which things were buoyant and which were not. They obviously loved the sound of the word, because each of the children used it repeatedly as they described items in the classroom and in their houses that were or were not buoyant. It was relatively easy for the teacher to recognize which students knew the meaning of *buoyant* and which did not. Paper-and-pencil vocabulary assessment is appropriate from third grade up, but the teacher should always make certain that the students understand the format of the test before using it to assess word knowledge.

• *Guideline 5. Don't assume that the literal level of vocabulary knowledge is easier than the inferential or application level.* The three categories represent different forms of comprehension, which may vary in difficulty depending on the circumstances. For example, in some cases it may be easier to apply word meaning to one's own life than to provide a synonym or antonym. Consider *extrovert.* All of us can describe extroverts we have known and loved, but can you quickly provide a synonym? Other than *introvert,* can you offer an antonym? The point is to choose assessment activities according to their match with your instruction and not according to their supposed level of difficulty.

• *Guideline 6. Code vocabulary comprehension levels according to what students do with the words.* How can you code comprehension levels when a vocabulary assessment may include a variety of words of different types? Wouldn't it be an incredibly complex task? Not really. Remember that you are coding according to *how* the students demonstrate their word knowledge, not according to the difficulty or richness of the concept represented by the word itself. We are used to thinking of words as having different levels of difficulty, and to a degree, they do. In a selection on viruses, *infect* is easier to understand and remember than *proteins.* And *proteins* may be less difficult to learn and remember than *retrovirus* or *lysogenic.* You are not coding comprehension according to the difficulty level of the words but according to what the students do with them. If you ask students to provide or choose a definition for all four words, you would code that activity at a literal level of comprehension. If you ask students to categorize these words in some way or provide examples, you would code that at an inference level. And if your assessment involves application of the underlying concept to a situation other than that described in the text, you would code that at the application level. Remember, coding follows the form of the assessment, not the meaning of the individual word.

Word Comprehension and Response to Intervention

Knowing the meaning of words means knowing concepts. Known concepts represent our prior knowledge and, as discussed in Chapters 1 and 3, an individual's conceptual base strongly influences the comprehension process. If we have prior knowledge about a topic, comprehension occurs faster and more easily than if we lack such background. Increasing the richness and depth of a student's conceptual base can well be an important instructional component in RTI Tiers 2 and 3.

Many students do not have a rich conceptual base or one that is aligned with the language of schools. I remember a teacher lamenting the fact that immigrant children from Asia did not even know what a merry-go-round was. My response was that if she felt such knowledge was important, she should teach it. I also gently reminded her that the children probably had knowledge of many other concepts related to their culture and home experiences that might well be unfamiliar to us. Many students experience problems with comprehension because of a mismatch between their cultural background and the topics and language stressed in our schools. I do not suggest that they have a learning disability, but they may well profit from Tier 2 lessons focused on expanding the depth of their background knowledge through vocabulary instruction. Remember, in the RTI process, only response to Tier 3 instruction allows a student to be designated as learning disabled. Guidelines in this chapter for choosing words and assessing word knowledge provide viable suggestions for both Tier 2 and Tier 3 instruction and progress monitoring.

Summary

• There is a strong relationship between vocabulary and comprehension. If we know the meanings of the words in a selection, we will be better able to comprehend it.

• Most words have more than one meaning and many are derived from other words through a system of prefixes, suffixes, and roots.

• An individual's word knowledge (or mental lexicon) has been described as involving four components: a listening vocabulary, a speaking vocabulary, a reading vocabulary, and a writing vocabulary. Mental lexicons contain knowledge of words that frequently go together, understanding of word position in a sentence, understanding of how words fit together, and knowledge of pragmatic contexts or when it is appropriate to use a word. Words are stored in the mental lexicon in semantic clusters or networks.

• For any word, we may know a little about it or a lot, and we learn more about a word each time we encounter it. Students need to learn the print match of words already in their oral vocabularies, unfamiliar words that represent familiar concepts, and unfamiliar words for unfamiliar concepts.

- Although scores on vocabulary measures are strongly correlated with scores on comprehension tests, the relationship between vocabulary and comprehension is complex. However, it is also reciprocal; that is, if you have an extensive vocabulary, you will comprehend better. And good comprehension leads to increased word knowledge.

- Assessing word knowledge involves choosing which words to assess. These should be useful and important words.

- Demonstrating word knowledge can involve a variety of tasks: providing a definition, synonym, or antonym; categorizing the word; providing examples or attributes; or using it in some way.

- A selected response format is very common in vocabulary assessment; however, a student may miss a question because of lack of knowledge of the multiple-choice distracters.

- Constructed response formats can be divided into explanation, comparison, extension, and usage. Explanation represents the literal level of comprehension. Comparison and extension are examples of the inferential level, and usage reflects the application level.

- If students are asked to use words in sentences for an assessment of vocabulary knowledge, they should be taught how to do this.

- Connecting words to personal experiences reflects the application level of word comprehension.

- Guidelines for assessing vocabulary comprehension involve the following: carefully choosing words to teach and assess; sharing with students the words that will be on the assessment, as well as the format of the assessment; designing assessment to parallel classroom instruction; adapting assessment to the age of the student; not assuming that the literal level of word knowledge is easier than the inferential and application levels; and coding comprehension levels according to what the students do to demonstrate their comprehension.

- A focus on expanding knowledge of word meanings may be appropriate for Tier 2 and Tier 3 instruction and progress monitoring.

Professional Development Activities for Assessing Word Comprehension

- Examine your textbooks and note how they suggest word comprehension should be taught. Do they focus primarily on the literal, inferential, or application level of comprehension?

- Examine how you teach vocabulary. Is there a match between your instructional practices and how you assess vocabulary knowledge? If not, consider how you can adapt either instruction or assessment to form a closer match.

- Talk with your peers. How do they assess word knowledge? Are they satisfied with their methods? Would they be interested in collaborating with you to make some changes?

• Locate the vocabulary instruction books that are listed in this chapter and try some of the suggested activities, first as instruction and then as assessment.

• Teach students how to write sentences that demonstrate their knowledge of word meaning. Once they get the idea, use this as an assessment activity.

• Teach students how to tie word comprehension to their own lives. Once they have understood the concept, use this as an assessment activity.

CHAPTER 8

Comprehension Assessment Proxies
Stand-Ins, Not Stars

The Value of Proxies

The word *proxy* has numerous synonyms, such as *substitute, stand-in, understudy,* and *replacement,* and we have many examples of the utility of a proxy in our everyday life. A familiar theme in old Hollywood movies was the aspiring understudy waiting eagerly for his or her chance to become a star. And, of course, because this was Hollywood, it always happened. The star would become sick, be detained on the way to the theater, or suffer some form of accident. The stand-in would take his or her place and a new star would be born!

We have examples of less successful stand-ins. We have all been to conferences where the replacement for a cancelled keynote speaker fell far short of our expectations. And what about the substitute for a movie that was sold out by the time we reached the theater? It may or may not have been as entertaining as our original choice. There is hardly any area of our life that does not allow for the substitution of some form of proxy. Consider what happens when you are half-way through a recipe and discover you do not have a key ingredient. You apply a substitute and hope for the best. You can't find your usual brand of dishwashing liquid in the store, so you choose another one and, of course, hope it will work as well as your preferred brand.

The success of a proxy depends on its similarity to what it substitutes for. If the cancelled keynote speaker is informative, entertaining, and relevant, then a successful proxy should be informative, entertaining, and relevant. If the missing ingredient has a tomato base, then a successful proxy should also have one. If the dishwashing liquid removes scum without a lot of scrubbing, then the proxy should also do this.

Why do we choose proxies? In some cases, we do so because we have no choice. The speaker has cancelled so we need to select another one. The recipe is half mixed and there is no time to go to the store. At other times we choose proxies because they seem easier. They offer a shortcut or save time and money. So a sweater bought at a discount store becomes a proxy for one with a designer label. A frozen dinner replaces a home-cooked meal, and a formica countertop substitutes for granite. Sometimes proxies work very well and sometimes they are disastrous.

In education we also have proxies, methods that claim to be viable substitutes for longer and more complex comprehension assessments. As discussed in previous chapters, choosing or constructing and scoring a valid and reliable comprehension assessment is not easy. It is tempting to think that there may be something faster and simpler that will work just as well. Several possibilities have surfaced as proxies for assessment of comprehension. One is assessment of fluency, that is, the speed and accuracy with which a student orally reads a passage. A second is the cloze technique, in which a student reads or listens to a passage and fills in words that are missing in the text. The third is the sentence verification technique, in which a student verifies that a sentence is actually present in the text. All three of these techniques appear very different from answering questions, writing essay tests, designing open-ended projects, or engaging in thoughtful conversation. What does reading quickly, supplying a missing word, or recognizing a previously read sentence have to do with that complex entity called comprehension? What is the basis for believing that they measure comprehension? It all rests with a statistic called correlation; scores on these proxy measures correlate moderately or strongly with scores on more traditional tests of comprehension.

Understanding Correlation

Before examining fluency, cloze, and sentence verification measures as possible proxies for comprehension assessment, it is necessary to understand what correlation tells us and what it doesn't. Correlation indicates the degree to which two or more sets of scores are related. It is "the mathematical extent to which two sets of numbers are related to each other" (Trice, 2000, p. 58). Correlation tells us two things. First, is the relationship a strong one? The strength of the relationship is indicated by a number that ranges from 0 to 1. A correlation is always expressed as a decimal, and the higher the number, the stronger the relationship. Correlations between .40 and .60 are considered moderate; correlations between .60 and .80 are regarded as substantial (Ravid, 2000). Correlation also tells us the direction of the relationship. A correlation can be positive or negative. In a positive relationship, both sets of scores increase or decrease. In a negative relationship, one score set increases while the other decreases or vice versa.

It can be helpful to examine some common examples of correlation. There is a correlation between height and weight in elementary school children. Taller children tend to weigh more. Of course, there are some short children who weigh more than their taller peers, but, generally speaking, the taller children are heavier. There is a correlation between intelligence and grade point average. This does not mean that all people with high IQs have high grade point averages, but many do. There is a correlation between the number of calories consumed and pounds gained. The more you eat, the more weight you will amass. There is a correlation between reading achievement and spelling achievement. Good readers tend to be the better spellers.

If you take a set of students' scores on a measure of reading fluency and correlate it with their scores on a traditional comprehension test (usually a standardized measure), you will find, depending on the study, that the scores are moderately or highly correlated. The same occurs if you correlate cloze scores and sentence verification scores with traditional comprehension measures. Because of these substantial correlations, they are considered viable proxies for comprehension assessment. And, of course, they are faster and easier to administer and score than more traditional measures of comprehension.

Basically, all that such correlation tells is that fluency and comprehension are related in some way as are cloze and comprehension and sentence verification and comprehension. However, people often misinterpret correlation as indicating causality, and then they get into all sorts of trouble. Correlation indicates only the existence of a relationship, not the nature of the relationship. To put it another way, correlation suggests that one set of scores can predict another, but not that one set necessarily causes the other. However, because so many correlations are actually causal in nature, individuals find this confusing and tend to regard all correlations as causal.

Let's examine a few examples. As mentioned previously, there is a moderate to high correlation between the number of calories consumed and weight gain. We also know that excessive calorie consumption causes weight gain so, in this case, the relationship has a strong causal component. However, consider college entrance examination scores on the SAT, ACT, and GRE. There is a high correlation between students' scores on these measures and their grade point averages in college or graduate school. Does this mean that the test scores cause achievement? That makes no sense. What correlation says is that the same components that lead to a high test score also contribute to high achievement in higher education—that is, student intelligence, reading ability, motivation, test-taking skills, subject matter knowledge, and the like. In this case, correlation is predictive, not causal.

Consider another example. If, over the months of July and August, we kept track of the number of bee stings that were reported at our local urgent care medical facility and the number of bags of ice sold in area convenience stores, we would probably find a moderate or even strong correlation. Does this mean that ice sales cause bee stings or vice versa? Hardly. What is common to both situations? It is the weather. In warm weather there are more bees flying around and encountering people. In warm weather, more people buy bags of ice to supplement their home supply. So the correlation is predictive, not causal.

We need to keep the difference between prediction and causality in mind when interpreting proxy scores. A proxy score may predict comprehension without causing it. This is important, because educators who confuse prediction with causality often make a grave error. That is, if fluency is poor, they work on increasing fluency, assuming that comprehension will rise as well. It may or it may not. Training a student to recognize a missing word may increase a cloze score, but it may not cause an accompanying increase in comprehension. It is important to keep these issues firmly in mind in examining comprehension assessment proxies.

Fluency Assessment as a Proxy for Comprehension Assessment

The National Reading Panel (2000) defined fluency as reading with accuracy, speed, and intonation and doing so without conscious attention on the part of the reader. Fluent readers are accurate; that is, they pronounce words correctly. This includes familiar words as well as words they have never seen before. They can do this because they are adept at matching letter and sound patterns, which allows them to accurately pronounce unfamiliar words. Fluent readers read at a relatively fast rate; they do not slowly plod through the text word by word. This suggests that such a reader is automatically identifying words either from memory or as a consequence of efficient letter–sound matching. Because the reader does not have to direct conscious attention to identifying words, he or she can focus on the meaning of the text. This in turn allows the reader to read with expression, using appropriate intonation and a rhythm that parallels natural speech. In order to be fluent, a reader must have a large store of what we often call sight vocabulary words or words whose pronunciation is already committed to memory. The reader must also possess effective strategies for pronouncing new words.

Similarity of Fluency and Comprehension

The success of a proxy basically depends on its similarity to what it substitutes for. How are fluency and comprehension alike? In other words, why would fluency even be considered as a proxy for comprehension? First, efficient word recognition is necessary for comprehension. We cannot comprehend if we are unable to recognize words. We recognize words by their sounds; the sound of a word allows us to retrieve its meaning from memory (Johnson, 2001). In Chapter 1, I described the active processing that occurs when individuals comprehend what they have read, heard, or viewed by assembling and building a microstructure, macrostructure, text base, and situation model. If readers' attention is focused on word recognition, they do not have the cognitive resources to do this. They are so involved in pronouncing words that they are not able to comprehend idea units and use these to construct the text base and situation model. We have limited cognitive capacity (LaBerge & Samuels, 1974), and if this capacity is directed at recognizing words, little will be left over for comprehension. This also occurs in listening when we are not fluent in a certain language and must direct most of our attention to the pronunciation and meaning of individual words and, as a result, miss much of the speaker's message.

Fluency is a necessary component for comprehension; without fluency there will always be some limitations or constraints on comprehension (Adams, 1990). However, "fluent word recognition is not a sufficient condition" (RAND, Reading Study Group, 2002, p. 22) for successful comprehension, which is influenced by those complex processes described in Chapter 1. So, in a sense, fluency allows comprehension to occur, but it is not the same as comprehension. Perhaps an analogy can help. If you want to start a fire, you need a match or fire starter of some sort. For comprehension to occur, you need fluency. However, a single match is very different from the fire it ignites. If you want to unlock a door to a room, you need a key, but the key is very different from the contents of the room, just as fluency is very different from the comprehension process.

Fluency Assessment

How is fluency assessed? It is usually assessed through computation of reading rate: number of words read per minute (WPM) or number of correct words read per minute (CWPM). In each case, the student orally reads a selection and the teacher or examiner records the time it takes to do this. The examiner then counts the number of words in the text, multiplies by 60, and divides by the number of seconds it took to read the selection. This yields the WPM score.

Computing a CWPM score is done approximately the same way, except that the examiner counts only the words that were read correctly, omitting any mispronounced or omitted words.

Reading rate is quite variable. Although there are tables that suggest rate ranges for different grade levels, these should be interpreted with caution. Most readers vary their reading rate according to their purpose and according to the type of text they read. Narrative texts on familiar topics are probably read faster than expository texts on unfamiliar topics For example, we probably read a newspaper account of a football game at a much faster rate than we read conditions for a home loan. We generally read a mystery novel faster than a chapter in a science or statistics textbook. An English teacher may find that students take much longer to read a Shakespearian play than other forms of literature because of the unfamiliar structure and language. Content teachers are often dismayed at the time it takes students to read textbook chapters, forgetting that although the chapter contents are familiar to them, the teachers, such material is unfamiliar to their students, who, as a consequence, read it more slowly. Unfortunately, tables of reading rate ranges seldom address such variables as type and familiarity of text.

Fluency: A Popular Proxy

Fluency or reading rate is a popular proxy for reading comprehension for several reasons. First, there is a strong correlation between reading rate scores and comprehension scores. That is, if you correlate students' fluency scores with scores on some measure of comprehension, you usually find a moderate to strong correlation. However, this correlation is predictive, not causal; that is, the presence of fluency predicts a comprehension score but does not cause it. If you are fluent and do not have to direct most of your attention to recognizing words, you can focus on meaning and will probably comprehend more. In other words, the presence of fluency suggests that a reader, listener, or viewer has cognitive capacity for comprehension. If other components are in place, such as vocabulary knowledge, linguistic knowledge, inference ability, motivation, understanding of cognitive strategies, and topic knowledge, the reader, listener, or viewer can use that cognitive capacity to comprehend. Fluency is also a popular proxy because it is fast and easy to measure. It is much easier to time a segment of reading and count words than it is to assess comprehension by asking students to answer questions or summarize their reading. A test of fluency is also easier to score than open-ended measures that require rubrics or standardized assessments that must be sent to a publisher to be machine scored.

The use of fluency as a proxy for comprehension is perhaps most prevalent in the primary grades. Over the last 10 or 15 years, educators have realized the critical importance of early literacy development. Literacy scores in third grade predict literacy achievement in later grades with amazing accuracy (Snow, Burns,

& Griffin, 1998), and a plethora of early literacy programs and assessments have come on the market. Almost all employ some form of fluency assessment (Southwest Educational Development Laboratory, 2007; Meisels & Piker, 2001) and use fluency scores to identify children who are at risk of developing reading difficulties. Fluency as a comprehension proxy is also used to measure reading at grade level through a process called curriculum-based measurement. Students read from grade-level texts, and their fluency rates are used to suggest those reading below, at, or above grade level (Hasbrouk & Tindal, 2006; Fuchs, Fuchs, Hosp, & Jenkins, 2001; Davidson & Myhre, 2000; Fuchs & Fuchs, 1999; Hasbrouck & Tindal, 1992).

Fluency: A Problematic Proxy

There is nothing wrong with assessing fluency and using it to suggest that a student may be at risk for comprehension failure. But proxies, by their very nature, carry a danger, that of becoming the very item they substitute for. If we assess only fluency and never directly address comprehension itself, we run the very grave risk of misinterpreting the extent of a student's understanding. Similarly, if we emphasize fluency development and neglect comprehension, we may deny students what they most need, instruction in strategies for comprehension. Unfortunately, I see too many classrooms where scores on fluency assessments drive teachers to devote large amounts of time to fluency development. This is not bad in itself. We know that fluency can be increased through instruction (Rasinski, 2003; Rasinski, Padak, Linek & Sturdevant, 1994; Stahl & Heubach, 1993), but often this is done at the expense of comprehension instruction and in the naive belief that, as fluency increases, so will comprehension. If we stopped for just a minute and thought about it, we could see how problematic this is.

Although fluency suggests that there is cognitive capacity for paying attention to comprehension, it does not indicate if or how that freed capacity is actually being used. In Chapter 1, I described the conscious and controllable processes and strategies that readers, listeners, and viewers employ to comprehend and remember text. If a student does not know how to use these, fluency alone will not guarantee comprehension. We know that fluency is important and should be developed in students but, as a proxy, it can never substitute for careful instruction and assessment of comprehension itself.

The Cloze Technique as a Proxy
for Comprehension Assessment

A cloze passage is a passage with words systematically omitted, usually every fifth, seventh, or ninth word. The reader or listener supplies the missing words, and the higher the number of words correctly identified, the higher the comprehension score. A related technique is the maze technique, in which three choices are provided for a missing word and the student chooses one. Thus, cloze is a constructed response task and maze is a selected response measure. Developed in the 1950s as an alternative to the traditional standardized reading tests (Pearson & Hamm, 2005), cloze has been adapted in a variety of ways. Originally, a student's response was correct only if the exact word was produced; that is, no synonyms were allowed. Over time, cloze was modified to allow for reasonable synonyms. The original deletion of every fifth word soon expanded to the deletion of every seventh or ninth word. Whereas cloze passages at first deleted every fifth word, no matter what it might be, later adaptations deleted only every fifth, seventh, or ninth content word, as opposed to function words such as articles, prepositions, and the like. Some cloze versions delete only words at ends of sentences, presumably to give the reader or listener the benefit of the entire sentence in choosing the missing item.

Perhaps the best way to understand cloze is to experience it. In the following selection, every ninth word has been deleted and replaced by a line of equal length. Read the selection and insert the words you think are missing. Please resist the temptation to look at the answer key as you do so.

A New Friend from Europe

Mrs. Wagner was reading a story to her _____ grade class. While Joseph listened carefully, he also _____ the new boy. Ivan looked sad and confused. _____ Joseph could understand why. Mrs. Wagner had introduced _____ to the class about a week ago. Ivan _____ from a country in Europe. It had a _____ long name that Joseph found hard to pronounce. _____ parents were both dead and he had spent _____ of his life in an orphanage. Then Mr. _____ Mrs. Mayer adopted him and brought him to _____. Mrs. Wagner explained that Ivan did not speak _____ but she was sure he would learn it _____ soon. No wonder Ivan looked sad and confused. _____ would feel that way if he could not _____ the story that Mrs. Wagner was reading. Joseph _____ to make friends with Ivan but he didn't _____ how to do this if Ivan could not _____ English. That night, Joseph asked his parents what _____ should do. Father thought a bit and then _____ answered, "You know, Joseph, words are not the _____ way to communicate with people. You can let _____ know you want to be friends by the _____ on your face and the gestures you make. _____ can share things with Ivan such as a _____ treat from your lunch or perhaps a toy."

Answer Key
A New Friend from Europe

Mrs. Wagner was reading a story to her 5th grade class. While Joseph listened carefully, he also watched the new boy. Ivan looked sad and confused. And Joseph could understand why. Mrs. Wagner had introduced Ivan to the class about a week ago. Ivan was from a country in Europe. It had a very long name that Joseph found hard to pronounce. Ivan's parents were both dead and he had spent most of his life in an orphanage. Then Mr. and Mrs. Mayer adopted him and brought him to America. Mrs. Wagner explained that Ivan did not speak English but she was sure he would learn it very soon. No wonder Ivan looked sad and confused. Joseph would feel that way if he could not understand the story that Mrs. Wagner was reading. Joseph wanted to make friends with Ivan but he didn't know how to do this if Ivan could not understand English. That night, Joseph asked his parents what he should do. Father thought a bit and then he answered, "You know, Joseph, words are not the only way to communicate with people. You can let Ivan know you want to be friends by the look on your face and the gestures you make. You can share things with Ivan such as a special treat from your lunch or perhaps a toy."

How did you do? As you can see, some of the missing words were function words such as *and, was,* and *you.* Some were content words such as *understand, America, wanted,* and *watched.* Did you insert synonyms such as *his* for *Ivan's, all* for *most,* or *speak* for *understand?* Did you pay attention to periods at the end of sentences? Cloze tests are often scored according to the informal reading inventory tradition of independent, instructional, and frustration levels. The Joseph and Ivan story has a readability level of fifth grade. If you want to determine your score, take your number of right answers and divide by the total number of missing words (24) to arrive at a percentage score. A score of 0–38% signals the frustration level; a score of 40–56% represents the instructional level; and if you achieved a score of 58% or above, you are at an independent level for fifth-grade text (Trice, 2000).

Similarity of Cloze and Comprehension

Filling in missing words in a cloze passage does not seem very similar to the comprehension process. In a sense, cloze is similar to fluency and seems to measure how well an individual can identify words. However, when we read or listen, we do not encounter difficulties on a regular basis—that is, at every fifth, seventh, or ninth word. Just as fluency and expressive reading suggest a capacity for comprehension, so does the ability to successfully identify missing words probably suggest that some comprehension is in place. However, like a measure of fluency, a cloze measure does not describe the nature or extent of that comprehension nor does it identify comprehension as literal, inferential, or application in nature.

Cloze: A Once Popular Proxy

Cloze is not as popular a proxy for comprehension as fluency, but at one time it engendered a fair amount of enthusiasm. It is still widely used as a reading assessment for English language learners (Bachman, 2000) and is part of several published reading tests, including the Degrees of Reading Power, the Stanford Diagnostic Reading Test, and several early reading assessments (Southwest Educational Development Laboratory, 2007; Meisels & Piker, 2001).

At one time teachers were encouraged to make cloze tests using representative classroom materials as a way of determining student reading levels. On the surface, this seemed like a simple thing to do. However, it was quite time-consuming to retype the passages in order to ensure that missing words were indicated by spaces of the same length. If one accepted only the exact word, not a synonym, counting and scoring was relatively straightforward. However, many teachers thought that synonyms were reasonable choices, and determining the acceptability of each possible synonym lengthened the scoring time. The percentages for determining frustration, instructional, and independent levels were also problematic. Teachers found it difficult to accept that scores of 40% and 58% represented acceptable performance. Teachers soon returned to other methods of assessment.

Cloze: A Problematic Proxy

What do cloze tests actually measure? Are they "measures of individual differences in comprehension or measures of the linguistic predictability of the passages to which they are applied?" (Pearson & Hamm, 2005, p. 24). The Ivan passage was relatively simple. Consider the next cloze example, again with every ninth word deleted. It is not as linguistically predictable.

Cloze Example

There are several assumptions for use of ANOVA _____ a statistic. Your groups are independent of each _____. You are measuring the dependent variable on an _____ or ratio scale. The dependent variable is normally _____ in the population and the scores are random _____. Finally, the variances of the populations from which _____ samples come are equal (homogeneity of variances).

Answer Key

There are several assumptions for use of ANOVA <u>as</u> a statistic. Your groups are independent of each <u>other</u>. You are measuring the dependent variable on an <u>interval</u> or ratio scale. The dependent variable is normally <u>distributed</u> in the population and the scores are random <u>samples</u>. Finally, the variances of the populations from which <u>the</u> samples come are equal (homogeneity of variances).

In addition, cloze measures do not seem to be sensitive to comprehension across sentences or in passage integration (Bernhardt, 2000). That is, readers fill in a blank based only on the sentence in which it occurs. If the sentences in the Joseph and Ivan story were scrambled, cloze scores would probably not differ from those obtained in reading the coherent passage (Pearson & Hamm, 2005). Success in cloze seems primarily to reflect sensitivity to grammatical and semantic constraints within a single sentence. "Like multiple choice questions, cloze tests are not ideal if one wants to assess understanding and recall of ideas and information in natural passages" (Carlisle & Rice, 2004, p. 535).

The Sentence Verification Technique as a Proxy for Comprehension Assessment

The sentence verification technique (SVT) measures comprehension by asking students to choose which of four sentences was actually present in a passage. Because students are not answering content questions but are simply saying if a sentence was or was not present, SVT limits the influence of external factors such as prior knowledge or intelligence (Pearson & Hamm, 2005). The technique was developed by Royer and colleagues (Royer, 2001; Rasool & Royer, 2001; Royer, Greene, & Sinatra, 1987; Royer, Lynch, Hambleton & Bulgareli, 1984; Royer, Hastings, & Hook, 1979) who describe it as a practical procedure for assessing comprehension. Like the cloze technique, it is recommended for teacher use and can be applied to most classroom texts for the purpose of determining student reading level as well as comprehension of material presented in class.

After reading or listening to a passage, a student is presented with a list of sentences that can take one of four forms: an original sentence from the passage; a paraphrase sentence in which the words are different but the meaning remains intact; a meaning change sentence in which substitutions of one or two words substantially alter passage meaning; and a distracter sentence. A distracter sentence is consistent with the theme and is similar in syntax to the original sentence; however, it is unrelated to the passage. The student indicates "yes" if the sentence was present. Original and paraphrase sentences are "yes" sentences. If the sentence was not present in the text, the student replies "no," as would be appropriate for the meaning change or distracter sentences. Royer (2001) and Royer et al. (1987) offer examples of such items and give detailed instructions on how to construct a sentence verification task.

Consider, as an example, a sentence in the Joseph and Ivan passage that was used to examine cloze.

Ivan's parents were both dead and he had spent most of his life in an orphanage.

Original sentence: Ivan's parents were both dead and he had spent most of his life in an orphanage.

Paraphrase sentence: Ivan's parents had died and he lived in an orphanage.

Meaning change sentence: Ivan's parents were not dead even though he had spent most of his life in an orphanage.

Distracter sentence: Ivan wrote to his parents and told them he was leaving the orphanage.

Constructing an SVT involves writing one of the four kinds of sentences for each sentence in the passage. Passages composed of 12 or 16 sentences are ideal because they allow for an equal number of each sentence type. If the passage is appropriate for the students, good comprehenders score in the range of 80% and above. Average comprehenders score at about 75%, and poor comprehenders at 70% or lower (Royer, 2001).

Similarity of the Sentence Verification Task and Comprehension Assessment

When we comprehend text, we remember the meaning but not the exact words. The "purpose of the SVT is to establish whether or not a reader has represented the meaning of a text in memory" (Rasool & Royer, 2001). Saying whether or not a sentence was present is akin to accessing our memory for what we read or heard. That is, if you read the Joseph selection and someone asked you, "Did the story say anything about Ivan's parents?" you would retrieve from memory the meaning represented in the sentence about Ivan's dead parents and his residence in an orphanage. Although the sentence verification task does not look like typical comprehension assessment, it does seem to nicely parallel the memory retrieval process. Of course, it says nothing about how we comprehended the sentence, that is, the strategies we used to draw meaning form the text. But it does seem to bear more resemblance to comprehension than supplying missing words or reading fluently.

Sentence Verification Task: A Promising Proxy

Royer and his associates have applied the SVT to a variety of populations and diverse subject matter areas: technical text (Royer et al., 1984), third through sixth graders (Royer et al., 1979), college students (Royer, Abronovic, & Sinatra, 1987), and limited English proficient students (Royer & Carlo, 1991). The SVT is sensitive to reading skill differences (Royer et al., 1979), can be used to measure both reading and listening comprehension, and correlates with other measures of comprehension. (Royer et al., 1984).

Although it is not difficult to construct an SVT, it is somewhat time-consuming, at least until you gain some practice. However, in all fairness, it probably does not take any more time than it does to construct the typical multiple-choice tests so prevalent in many of our classrooms. One drawback may be the short 12- or 16-sentence passages, which may make it less appealing for high school content teachers who often assess comprehension of larger amounts of text.

Despite a large number of studies investigating the SVT, it is not used much in the classroom. Pearson and Hamm (2005) suggest this may be because "it just does not have the look and feel of what we mean by 'comprehension assessment.' After all there is no retelling and no question answering. This lack of interest is unfortunate because the technique or at least some of its features could be useful in building new, conceptually sound, efficient and replicable assessment procedures" (p. 39).

Guidelines for Using Comprehension Assessment Proxies

I wonder if it has crossed your mind that, in a sense, all classroom assessments are proxies for the real comprehension process. The complexity of comprehension and the fact that we still do not completely understand it suggests that any comprehension assessment is actually an understudy for the real thing. However, at this point in time, it is all we have, and some comprehension assessments seem more like what we do when we read, listen, or view than the proxies described in this chapter. Still, proxies can be useful, but only if we heed certain guidelines.

• *Guideline 1. Always interpret a comprehension assessment proxy in terms of the text.* Of course, we should do this with all comprehension assessment. It makes a great deal of difference whether students are reading narrative or expository text. It makes a great deal of difference whether they are reading or listening to familiar or unfamiliar content. A student can be fluent in reading one passage and halting and slow with another. A student may be able to supply missing words in a story about a familiar topic, yet fail totally with unfamiliar text. For example, how well did you do on the statistics example?

• *Guideline 2. Always interpret proxy utility by knowing exactly what the measure is correlated with.* Is it a group-administered standardized measure? Is it an individually administered standardized instrument? Is it an informal assessment of some sort? Your belief in the importance and validity of the instrument as a valid measure of comprehension should determine the extent to which you value the proxy. One of the attractive aspects of fluency assessment is correlation to standardized measures that school districts employ to meet the demands of the No Child Left Behind Act.

• *Guideline 3. Don't assume that the correlations between the proxy measure and a standardized instrument hold true for all grade levels.* Although fluency is strongly correlated in the lower grades, it is less so for older students. Therefore, it may be a less appealing proxy for some students.

• *Guideline 4. Do not assume that training in the proxy will automatically transfer to improved comprehension.* It may or it may not. When I first began teaching, cloze was a very popular technique and teachers were encouraged to use it. I remember working with students to improve their performance on cloze by providing practice in choosing alternatives for the missing words. I did this in the naive assumption that I was helping them to comprehend. I may have been doing that, but I may not have. Although they may have gotten better in cloze (and of course many did), I cannot recall that I noted any significant growth in their ability to comprehend the stories and novels we read.

• *Guideline 5. Never confuse a proxy with the real thing.* Fluency, word insertion, and sentence recognition are very different from the complex entity that we call comprehension. If you choose to use a proxy or if your district requires it, regard it as only one sample of comprehension.

Comprehension Assessment Proxies and Response to Intervention

The use of reading fluency measures as classroom screening tools is extremely popular in RTI. Fluency probes are administered three times a year to identify students who are not progressing as they should. In one sense, there is nothing wrong with this practice. We know that fluency is highly correlated with later reading comprehension. However, there is a danger that fluency assessment will become the only screening measure, and this can present an incomplete picture of student performance (Gersten & Dimino, 2006). Fluency is fast and easy to assess; however, the comprehension process does not lend itself well to speed of assessment. And to the extent that fluency assessment remains the only screening tool, there is a very real risk that some students will not be identified as needing help. Not all fluent readers are good comprehenders. A fluency probe may not identify those students who lack some of the basic comprehension strategies identified in Chapter 1 as being so necessary for effective comprehension.

The structure of RTI involving classroom screening, additional tiers of instruction, and frequent progress monitoring can be an effective model for helping students who struggle academically. However, its success rests on the close match between identification of student need, instruction to address that need, and the assessment measure that monitors student progress. A measure of fluency may be not an appropriate choice for assessing basic comprehension strategies. A student may be able to read fluently and expressively and still be unable to summarize, question, infer, or take useful notes. Measures of fluency have their place, but in regard to comprehension, educators should not assume that acceptable fluency will always carry over into successful comprehension or that the instruction of comprehension strategies can be effectively assessed by fluency probes.

Summary

• A proxy is a substitute, and the success of a proxy depends on its similarity to what it substitutes for.

• The basis for education proxies is a statistic called correlation, which is a measure of the degree to which two sets of scores are related.

• Three possibilities for comprehension assessment proxies are fluency assessment, the cloze technique, and the sentence verification technique. Each is moderately or strongly correlated with comprehension scores.

• Correlation does not suggest causality. It suggests that one score can predict the other. Training students to do well in a proxy may or may not lead to increased comprehension.

• Fluency is necessary for comprehension. If we cannot quickly and automatically identify words, comprehension will suffer. Without fluency there will always be some constraints on comprehension.

• Fluency is assessed by determining the number of words read per minute (WPM) or the number of correct words read per minute (CWPM).

• Fluency is a popular proxy for comprehension, especially in the primary grades. It is a problematic proxy because extensive attention on increasing fluency can limit the amount of time directed to comprehension.

• In the cloze technique, students supply words missing in a selection. A variety of adaptations to the original cloze format have evolved over the years.

• Cloze does not seem similar to the comprehension process and is more sentence- than passage-based. It is a problematic proxy because it does not seem sensitive to comprehension across sentences or to passage integration.

• The sentence verification technique measures comprehension by asking students to choose which of four sentences were present in a passage: an actual sentence, a paraphrase sentence, a meaning change sentence, or a distracter sentence.

• The sentence verification task is similar to comprehension assessment in that we tend to remember meaning but not exact words; as such it parallels the memory retrieval process. It is a promising proxy, has been applied to a variety of populations and subject areas, and is sensitive to reading skill differences. However, it is not used much, perhaps because it does not look like traditional comprehension assessment measures.

• Guidelines for using comprehension assessment proxies include the following: interpreting proxies in terms of the text, knowing what measures a proxy is correlated with, realizing that proxy correlations may not hold true for all grade levels, not assuming that training in a proxy will transfer to improved comprehension, and not confusing a proxy with the real thing.

Professional Development Activities for Examining Comprehension Assessment Proxies

• If you are presently administering fluency measures to younger students, examine the test manual accompanying your instrument. What comprehension measures are correlated with it?

• Take a class list and categorize your students as above, at, or below reading level according to your perceptions of their classroom performance and progress in comprehension. Do your evaluations parallel their fluency scores?

• Construct a short cloze passage and ask your students to fill in the missing words. How does their performance match their classroom performance on other assessments?

• Construct an SVT from a passage in your reading or content-area textbook. Does the performance of your students parallel your perceptions of their classroom performance?

CHAPTER 9

Grading Practices

Taking a New Look
at Grading Comprehension

Overview

The recognized purpose of grades is to provide descriptions of the extent to which students comprehended, learned, and applied classroom content. Teachers may assign grades for math, social studies, or science, but what they are actually doing is evaluating a student's comprehension of these subjects. In a sense, academic achievement is a synonym for comprehension; it is impossible to imagine any form of academic success without comprehension.

Comprehension assessment is closely tied to grading practices because grades are an integral part of every elementary, middle, and high school classroom. Grades offer shortcut tools for describing a student's comprehension (Marzano, 2000; Olson, 1995) in the form of letters (e.g., A, B, or C), numbers (e.g., 93% or 75%), or words (e.g., Above average, Average, or Below average). Teachers assign grades to various classroom projects and tests. They also give report card grades that are assumed to accurately represent student learning over an extended period of time. Whether grades are tied to a single class activity or to a district report card, teachers, students, parents, and the general public all regard grades as valid and reliable measures of student learning. "Americans have a basic trust in the message that grades convey—so much so that grades have gone without challenge and are, in fact, highly resistant to any challenge" (Marzano, 2000, p. 1).

Are classroom grades as valid and reliable as the educational establishment and the public seem to think? In Chapter 2, I defined a valid assessment as one that measures what it was designed to measure. If the purpose of grading is to describe student comprehension and learning, then several levels of validity must be present. The assessment tool (project, test, assignment, etc.) must measure comprehension or learning as accurately as possible, and the resulting grade must correctly describe it. In addition, the grade assigned to a student's cumulative work over a grading period must truly reflect progress and achievement. In short, classroom assessments and the grading process should "accurately reflect and communicate the academic achievement of the student" (Allen, 2005, p. 219).

A grade attached to a classroom project or a report card summary should also be reliable or, in other words, consistent. An objective test consisting of 35 items marked correct or incorrect is very reliable. That is, given a clear and accurate answer key, any number of individuals can score this measure and arrive at the same score. But what about essay tests and classroom projects? Would two different teachers arrive at the same grade for a single essay? Do teachers apply similar criteria for scoring classroom projects across a single grade level or content area? Do they employ rubrics? Do the rubrics adequately describe the assessment?

Reliability also refers to the consistency of the report card grading process itself. Given a series of grades in a grade book, would several teachers arrive at the same cumulative grade? Would they weight each single grade the same way? Would they choose to use all of the grades, or would they decide to omit some from the final computation?

Despite the public's belief in the validity and reliability of our present grading system, critics question its effectiveness. Marzano (2000) summarizes such criticism as focusing on three issues. First, despite the belief that grades are intended to reflect academic achievement, teachers consider other factors, such as effort and behavior, when they assign grades. Second, when assigning report card grades, teachers weight assessments differently and use different grading criteria for arriving at a single grade. A third issue is that letter and number grades are "shortcut" labels. A single grade designation is basically a primitive tool (Cizek, 2000), in that it does not reflect the multifaceted nature of student comprehension and learning on a single assignment or over a period of time.

Assessment, as described in Chapter 2, is a four-step process. We decide what we intend to assess, we collect evidence, we analyze the evidence, and we make a decision. In Chapters 4 through 8, I examined collecting and analyzing evidence of student comprehension and learning using a variety of tools. In this chapter, I focus on the final step of deciding that comprehension and learning has or has not occurred and communicating that decision to students, parents, and the education establishment.

Validity and Reliability
of Classroom Grading Practices

What is the basic purpose of assigning grades? Allen (2005) suggests that grades serve several purposes. Grades are meant to communicate information about student comprehension and learning. Grades also provide a public record of student achievement and offer guidelines for making informed decisions about promotion, class placement, and/or college acceptance. It is assumed that grades accurately reflect students' academic achievement and their comprehension of classroom instruction. As such, grades carry much weight. Transcripts of student grades are important evidence in promotion, placement, and acceptance decisions that can positively or negatively affect a student's future. Report card grades can result in a positive family experience or one fraught with anxiety. Students use grades as measures of their ability, and grades foster positive or negative perceptions of their academic skills. Grades can act as motivation to avoid or seek out certain fields of study. Low grades in science, for example, may influence a student to avoid the medical profession. Students often describe themselves, in terms of grades, as A students or C students. Given the power attached to grades, it is important that they be as valid and reliable as possible.

Unfortunately, the basic validity and reliability of grading practices are suspect (Cizek, 2000), and grades have been described as "so imprecise that they are almost meaningless" (Marzano, 2000, p. 1). Several issues weaken the validity of current grading procedures. First, there is confusion surrounding the primary purpose of grades. Should grades communicate information about student comprehension and learning, or should they also address student attitude and motivation? Various studies have determined that, when calculating grades, teachers use nonacademic criteria such as student motivation, behavior, and attitude to raise or lower grades (Allen, 2005; Brookhart, 2003; McMillan, Myran, & Workman, 2002; Cizek, 2000). This raises a concern regarding grading validity and reliability. Evaluating effort, motivation, and attitude tends to be very subjective and is often based on teacher impressions that can easily vary across individuals (Allen, 2005). As a result, some students are scored more leniently or more strictly than others. For example, a student who tries very hard and expends continual effort is often rewarded with a higher grade than is actually deserved, given the student's performance. And there is another scenario, the brilliant student who never seems to extend him- or herself who is penalized with a lower grade than his or her performance would warrant.

When calculating grades, teachers tend to use "a hodgepodge of inputs" (McMillan, 2003) involving academic and nonacademic variables. Academic variables include test grades, homework, quizzes, classroom projects, missing or incomplete work, student class participation, and attendance. The relative influence of a single factor varies across teachers. Grading policies often reflect a teacher's individual philosophy of education (Cizek, Fitzgerald, & Rachor, 1996). For example, some teachers believe it is very important that all students succeed, so they employ extra credit options as means of raising poor grades; other teachers do not. Some teachers include homework completion in a report card grade; others do not. In summary, what is included in a grade and its relative importance are extremely idiosyncratic. Because of this, a grade of B in one classroom may represent something very different from a B in the classroom across the hall. Similarly, a grade of B may not accurately reflect a student's comprehension and learning but represent instead a vague amalgamation of a variety of constructs.

Lack of consistency across teachers, often in the same school or at the same grade level, weakens the validity and reliability of the grading process. In calculating grades, one teacher may factor in missing assignments or homework to lower a grade; another teacher may not use these as determinants. Some teachers may include all quiz grades in the final grade calculation; others do not. Even if two teachers at the same grade level and in the same school include perceived motivation or effort in their grades, they may weight its influence very differently. One teacher may employ perceived effort as a factor that raises or lowers a total grade level, that is, dropping an A to a B or raising a C to a B. Another may use perceived effort to raise or lower grades, but only within a single level, that is, moving from B to B+ or C to C–. As a result, a grade is not always an indication of student comprehension and learning but may be a fusion of many variables. This poses a problem for the reader of the grade, whether it is a student, a parent, a school administrator, or a college admissions officer. How can the reader know what factors the teacher included in the grade and the weight assigned to each?

Another issue that weakens the validity and reliability of the grading process is the perspective used by the teacher to evaluate performance and assign grades. Is the grade an indication of a student's comprehension performance "irrespective of the other students in the class," or is it indicative of performance as compared with that of peers (Smith, 2003, p. 28)? To put it another way, do grades emphasize competition or personal improvement (Black, Harrison, Lee, Marshall, & Wiliam, 2004)? The infamous practice of grading on a curve, in which only a certain number of A grades are given, suggests a focus on competition. There are only so many A's to be earned and each student is in competition with his or her peers to get one. However, if grades are based on a standard of comprehension performance, then each student has an opportunity to meet that goal and receive an A.

There is an unfortunate tendency for teachers to grade as they were graded, and it is admittedly difficult to "change the invalid 'grading' schema that has become embedded in our minds" (Allen, 2005, pp. 218–219). Many districts require a single report card grade, and the majority of teachers assign one grade to a classroom test or project. Grading reflects "a mixture of attitude, effort and achievement" combined with "idiosyncratic approaches to combining information to form a grade" (Smith, 2003, p. 28). It is perhaps unrealistic to think that a single letter, number, or word can adequately communicate multiple pieces of information such as different levels of comprehension, various skills involved in a project, and the motivation or attitude of a student. Unfortunately, it remains the accepted practice in the majority of our schools.

Guidelines for Increasing the Validity and Reliability of Grading Practices

• *Guideline 1: Clearly differentiate the relative influence of performance and effort factors in assigning grades.* If effort, attitude, and behavior are to be noted on a report card or on a classroom project, they should be reported separately. Simply put, a teacher's impression of student effort or behavior should not be included as part of a grade for academic performance or comprehension. The sole purpose of grades is to accurately communicate to others a student's level of comprehension achievement. If only one grade can be reported, then that grade should represent academic achievement (Allen, 2005). Including effort as part of a grade sends a mixed message and allows students who are not competent, and their parents, to believe that they have performed adequately in achieving required knowledge and skills (McMillan et al., 2002). A school district in Wisconsin, after 2 years of study, recommended removing evaluation of student effort and participation from academic achievement in determining a report card grade (Hetzner, 2007).

This recommendation is not difficult for teachers to put into practice in classroom assessments, because classroom grading practices are rarely controlled by district policies. A teacher can easily assign two grades, one for performance and one for effort, and thus maintain some aspect of grading validity. However, this may not be possible for report card grades, as some districts mandate a single grade on the report card.

What are the options for increasing grading validity by focusing grades on student academic performance as opposed to effort? There are several. First, the school or district can change the report card format to reflect two grades: one for performance and one for perceived effort. If this is not possible (and, of course, it is, but people often just don't want to change), then the teacher can assign a grade for academic performance and mention effort in the teacher comments section. Another option is to record a two-number grade such as B/A, which translates into B for performance and A for effort. If the school uses an electronic grading system, this works well because most systems allow for at least two spaces.

If none of these options is possible, then teachers in a school or across a single grade level or content field can agree to use a uniform formula for determining the relative weight of performance and effort, that is, three-quarters of the grade represents performance and one-quarter represents effort. A school in my area attempted to set up such a uniform procedure, but teachers found it so difficult to arrive at any agreement regarding the percentage of achievement versus effort that they redesigned their report card system to allow for two grades for each subject, one for performance and one for effort. Interestingly, this was something they had adamantly declared impossible prior to their attempts to agree on the different contributions of performance and effort to a single grade.

• *Guideline 2. Before determining report card grades for academic achievement, decide what factors will be included as indicators of student performance and the weight of each.* Teachers accumulate a variety of grades over the course of a single grading period. These include grades for homework, quizzes, major tests, class activities such as worksheets and in-class assignments, and major classroom projects. Do all these count equally? Are homework assignments as important as performance on summative tests? Unfortunately, there is no consistency within a school district or grade level in regard to which factors are used for grade calculation and how they are weighted (McMillan et al., 2002). "Individual teachers develop their own grading practices, typically in isolation, to serve their own instructional, professional and personal purposes" (Smith, 2003, p. 27). Grading practices are seldom written down, which means that teachers can change guidelines over different grading periods. Teachers should carefully determine exactly what they will factor into a grade and how they will do this. The ideal would be for teachers across a school, a grade level, or a content area to spend some quality time discussing the issue and set an evaluative policy as to what components should be included in a report card grade and the relative importance of each.

• *Guideline 3. Decide whether the report card grade reflects performance over time or performance at the end of the grading period.* Some students begin the year or grading period doing poorly but by the end are doing quite well. Should the teacher put more weight on later work or factor in all work equally across the period? Although this seems like a relatively easy decision, like most issues involving grading practices, it is fraught with difficulties. If the grade reflects performance over time, poor grades early in the grading period will lower a student's grade and, in a sense, a student may be penalized for learning at a slower rate than his or her peers. Yet assigning a grade based on performance at the end of the grading period may not be reflective of all classroom activities. There are no easy answers; however, validity and reliability demand, at the very least, some discussion by teachers. The ideal would be for a school or grade level to address the issue, discuss concerns, consider options, and reach some consensus.

• *Guideline 4. Determine a uniform system for combining grades into a single report card designation.* A common option is to average all the grades to arrive at a numeric percentage. Many schools have criteria for translating this percentage into a letter grade, with 93–100% representing an A, 92–85% representing a B, and so on. Letter grades are also translated into numbers: an A involves 4 points, a B counts for 3 points, a C represents 2 points, and so on. Suppose you have the following grades: A, A, B, C, A. Given these values and using a numerical average, the total of the letter grades would be 17. With this total divided by 5, the student would receive a 3.4 or a B. However, there are problems with averaging grades. First, averaging is based on the assumption that all scores have equal importance. This may or may not be true. Second, one very high or one very low score can skew a grade up or down and make it less reflective of overall performance.

Given the difficulty of averages, using the median or the midpoint may be more meaningful and better represent overall class performance (Hetzner, 2007). If the median is used, the grades are arranged in order of value: A, A, A, B, C. The midpoint of the five grades is A, so the student's grade would be A. What happens if there is an even number of grades, such as A, A, A, B, C, C. The two middle points are A and B. If an A represents 4 points and a B represents 3, these are added for a point total of 7 and divided by 2 for a grade of 3.5, or a B. Electronic grade books make such computations quite easy. However, remember that such a system assumes that all the grades contribute equally to the total score.

• *Guideline 5. There will always be a measure of subjectivity to grading, even given the use of rubrics and the most careful attention to grading validity.* Often subjectivity results from lack of precision regarding assessment purposes. In preceding chapters, I made two recommendations for increasing the validity of classroom comprehension assessment and grading. First, it is important to know which component of comprehension is being assessed: literal, inferential, or application. Assessment validity can be weakened by using a single score to represent performance on very different skills and abilities. Marzano (2000) offers the example of a math test with items that address four distinct numerical skills. A single score on the test would be ambiguous; two students may have the same number of correct answers but demonstrate very different patterns of mathematical learning. A test that does not differentiate literal, inferential, and application levels of comprehension would be similarly ambiguous. Second, assessments should adequately reflect classroom instruction. If an assessment mirrors what was demonstrated and studied in the classroom, it has validity. Assessment should match the teacher's instructional objectives and the instruction, which Brookhart (2003) calls "defining the construct" (p. 10). In simple terms, items on the test should correspond to what was covered in class.

• *Guideline 6. Grades in grade books, like individual assessments, should be coded as representing literal, inferential, or application components of comprehension.* If a teacher is to describe comprehension and learning in a more exact and defined manner, these three aspects should be grouped and reported separately. In calculating a single report card grade, each should figure into the total score according to a predetermined system. They each can count for one-third of the total grade or one component can carry more weight, depending on the purpose of the assessment. Ideally, teachers across a school, grade level, of content area should agree as to the weighting and it should remain consistent across the entire school year.

• *Guideline 7. Don't confuse formative and summative assessments in assigning a report card grade.* Report cards grades are a form of summative assessment. The final grade assigned to a class project is also summative in nature. Homework assignments, many class activities, and short quizzes are more formative in nature. They suggest whether the teacher needs to reteach or refocus the instruction. They constitute a form of feedback to both the teacher and the student and, as such, serve very different purposes than summative measures. Many teachers do not distinguish between formative and summative assessments during grade computation. A formative assessment is analogous to practice. In sports, we make a clear distinction between a scrimmage and an actual game, between the preseason and the actual season. Unsuccessful scrimmages or scores in the preseason do not count toward the season won/lost record. Similarly, unsuccessful formative "scrimmages" should not count toward the final grade.

Merging Comprehension Coding and Grading

Throughout this book I have strongly recommended that teachers code comprehension as involving three distinct components: literal, inferential, and application. I have also suggested that teachers clearly differentiate selected response assessment activities from constructed response assessment activities on the assumption that they target very different forms of comprehension. Comprehension assessment is described as a process based on sampling and categorization. The teacher collects multiple samples of comprehension and categorizes them in order to determine a pattern across a class or in regard to an individual student. The grade book is the vehicle for recording student performances on samples and for categorizing them in such a way that patterns can be easily noted. Is the student and/or class equally adept in the literal, inferential, and application components of comprehension? Are there differences in selected response versus constructed response assessment measures?

Grade books come in many forms, ranging from the old-fashioned paper version to the newer electronic types. It would be an impossible task to specifically address all the differences in the many versions that are present in our schools. However, they are all similar in one way. They are based on the format of columns and rows and represent different versions of a spreadsheet.

In setting up your grade book to allow for categorization and pattern recognition, use the following template. Of course, you can abbreviate the headings in the table as CRF, SRF, L, I, and A. Your grade book will probably be longer or involve more pages, but it will allow you to differentiate comprehension in a more specific way.

	Description of assessment					
	Constructed response format			Selected response format		
	Literal	Inferential	Application	Literal	Inferential	Application
Name						
Name						

How can a teacher address type of text if, as in English and reading classrooms, different genres are assessed? The type of text goes in the description. Teachers may want to keep separate pages for narrative and expository genres; however, this is not necessary. When determining progress grades, simply review all narrative assignments and determine a grade and then move on to expository assignments. What about reading teachers who often present texts on unfamiliar topics? Student performance on unfamiliar topics is usually noted by assessment specialists who are attempting to determine why a student is struggling academically. However, if a classroom teacher realizes that unfamiliarity of a topic is an issue (remember the Chapter 3 example of urban second graders listening to a story about a farm?), this can also be noted under the heading "Description."

Grading Practices and Response to Intervention

At first glance, it may seem that classroom grades have little connection with RTI initiatives. However, suppose a student is designated as not responding to Tier 1 classroom instruction. What can happen? The student would presumably move into small-group Tier 2 instruction, perhaps in a pull-out format. However, this would seldom involve all subjects. In other words, the student would receive some small-group specialized instruction with progress monitoring, but would continue to be part of classroom instruction in other subjects. The same would probably happen if the student moved into Tier 3 individualized instruction. Thus, classroom grading practices do play a role in RTI as describing the progress of Tier 2 and 3 students in the classroom setting.

A student with academic difficulties, or one described as "learning disabled" through the RTI process, would still participate in some classroom activities. It is hoped that the teacher would assign grades on class projects and tests using many of the suggestions offered in this book in regard to differentiating levels of comprehension, separating assessment formats, and using rubrics. However, for students identified by RTI, the common practice of blending effort and performance into a single report card grade has important ramifications. If the teacher includes effort and behavior as part of the grade, the student may receive a grade that contradicts his or her placement in Tier 2 or Tier 3 instruction. I have often seen students with special needs receive grades that suggest a level of performance at odds with their learning disability status. Many of these students work very hard and deserve to be rewarded for their efforts; however, if they are not performing well academically for any reason, this needs to be noted by separating actual academic performance from effort and behavior. There is an important difference between the student who is not progressing academically but is expending a lot of effort, and the student who is not progressing and is making little if any effort to do so.

Separating academic learning from effort and behavior allows the teacher to note progress. Many academic difficulties, including a learning disability, are not lifelong conditions; they can be improved. With careful assessment and skilled instruction, many students with special needs learn to perform at acceptable and even high levels. Undergraduate students often confide to me that they had a learning problem in elementary school; however, they obviously overcame it because their performance in college classes suggests competent learners. If a classroom teacher combines performance and effort/behavior in assigning grades, that improving competence is often masked.

Summary

- Comprehension assessment is closely tied to grading practices. Grades offer shortcut tools for describing a student's comprehension and are regarded by the educational establishment and the general public as valid and reliable measures of student learning.
- Critics question the validity and reliability of typical grading practices. When calculating grades, teachers may factor in nonacademic criteria such as moti-

vation, behavior, and attitude, which weakens the validity of a grade as a measure of academic performance. The relative influence of academic and nonacademic variables varies across teachers, and lack of consistency, often between classes in the same school or at a particular grade level, also weakens validity and reliability.

• Guidelines for increasing the validity and reliability of grading practices include differentiating between the relative influences of comprehension performance and student effort.

• It is important to decide prior to determining a grade what will be included as indicators of student performance and the relative weight of each.

• Teachers should consider whether an overall grade represents performance over time or performance toward the end of the grading period.

• It is important to determine a uniform system for combining multiple grades into a single report card entry, and using the median may be more workable than using the average.

• Subjectivity in grading can be reduced by precision of purpose, that is, knowing what component of comprehension is being assessed. It can also be reduced if assessment is closely tied to classroom practice.

• Formative and summative grades are two different things. Report card grades are summative in nature; formative grades are not.

• Grade books, whether electronic or paper, can be organized to allow for differentiation of assessment formats and comprehension components.

• For students involved in RTI Tier 1 or 2 instruction, it is important to differentiate progress from effort in assigning report card grades.

Professional Development Activities for Improving Open-Ended Comprehension Assessment

• Examine your present grading practices. Carefully describe how you compute your report card grades by answering the following questions. It can help if you actually write your answers. What changes could you make immediately to improve your grading system?

✓ Do you include effort and behavior as part of the report card grade?
✓ What grades do you include in your grade computation?
✓ Do you weight all grade book entries equally?
✓ Do you average grades or do you use the median?
✓ Do you place more weight on later grades than grades attained earlier in the grading period?
✓ Do you distinguish between formative and summative grades?
✓ Do you differentiate between literal, inferential, and application components of comprehension?

Make some gradual changes in your grading practices and evaluate each one. Don't try to do too much too soon. Changing traditional grading practices is a difficult endeavor.

• Talk with one or two teachers at your grade level or in your content area. How are their grading practices similar to or different from yours? Would they be willing to engage in some discussion regarding possible changes? For many teachers, grading guidelines represent a personal issue of professional autonomy. However, discussion with compatible peers can be nonthreatening and you can learn from them as they can learn from you.

• Set up your grade book using the recommended template and give it a try. At first, it can seem awkward and time-consuming (but that can be true of all new endeavors), but if you persevere, you may see a big difference in how you evaluate your students. You may also have a more fine-tuned system for making decisions about teaching and assessing comprehension in the classroom.

CHAPTER 10

Measuring Comprehension through Standardized Tests

An Oxymoron?

Overview

Once upon a time, standardized tests were a normal and nonthreatening part of the educational environment. They were administered on a regular cycle, students were encouraged to do their best, and schools regularly absented students with special needs from participating. The completed tests were sent out to be scored and usually forgotten until the results were returned months later, too late to have any real effect on classroom instruction. Results were communicated to parents, and administrators rejoiced or wept. After a brief flurry of interest, test outcomes were filed in a drawer and things returned to normal. In 2002, the No Child Left Behind (NCLB) Act was signed into law and everything changed. Standardized achievement testing became high-stakes testing.

States are now mandated to test students in reading and math every year in grades 3 through 8 and at least once in grades 10 through 12. As of 2007–2008, science assessments must also be in place. Testing results are reported as a yearly report card, with scores broken out according to economic background, race, ethnicity, English proficiency, and disability. The overall purpose is to use standardized achievement scores to identify schools that are doing well and those that are not.

At the heart of the NCLB legislation is the concept of adequate yearly progress (AYP). The definition of AYP rests with each state but must be approved by the U.S. Department of Education. Basically, this involves delineating "separate measurable annual objectives for continuous and substantial improvement" for economically disadvantaged students, for those with disabilities or limited English proficiency, and for students from major racial and ethnic groups (Norlin, 2005, p. 1). The law states that 100% proficiency must be reached by 2013–2014 and that schools must demonstrate forward progress each year for all students. Such progress is, of course, defined by standardized achievement scores.

If a school does not meet the state-constructed guidelines for AYP, it will be designated as in need of school improvement and a 2-year improvement plan will be constructed. In addition, parents must be notified of the school's status and they have the option to withdraw their children. If no improvement is noted after the second year, the school will be designated for corrective action by the district or state, which may involve such actions as replacement of school staff, implementation of new curricula, extension of the school day, and/or reorganization of the school's structure.

High-stakes standardized tests have always been with us in some form, such as college entrance exams, tests for determining promotion or graduation, and measures for entrance into curricular options such as gifted or honors programs. A majority of states require passing scores on standardized measures of content or pedagogy for teacher certification. But at no time in our history have high-stakes tests taken such a prominent place, which is likely to continue in the foreseeable future. High-stakes tests have their supporters and their critics and both are similarly passionate.

Debate centers on several issues. Chief among these is the belief that high-stakes testing can be harmful for students (Afflerbach, 2004; Kohn, 2000, 2001; Smith & Rottenburg, 1991) and may negatively impact student motivation and teacher support. In contrast to this perspective, Phelps (2005) claims that such testing has resulted in positive effects on achievement.

Critics suggest that high-stakes tests constrict the curriculum and cause educators to focus on lower-order activities and skills that are perceived to match test content. Supporters point out that NCLB requires that the curriculum be driven by academic standards set by individual states and that standardized tests must be aligned to these standards (U.S. Department of Education, 2005). However, the "quality of the alignment between state-approved content standards and state-approved achievement tests has been very weak" (Popham, 2003, p. 31). States tend to choose off-the-shelf achievement tests without a careful perusal of their match to state standards.

Another criticism focuses on the time and money spent on high-stakes testing (Afflerbach, 2004). Goodman and Hambleton (2005), however, suggest that high-stakes measures do not involve an undue amount of time and money and that expenditure should be weighed against the value of the test information.

At the heart of the testing debate is the extent to which standardized tests actually measure comprehension. Afflerbach (2004) states that a single score provides only a limited snapshot of student performance and should never be used as the sole determinant of student achievement, a position supported by the U.S. Department of Education, which describes a single annual measure as "inadequate" for evaluating student performance (U.S. Department of Education, 2005). Goodman and Hambleton (2005) affirm that "it is not possible for one assessment to measure all the important skills and concepts that are taught over one or more years of instruction, and some processes may be better assessed in the context of the classroom" (pp. 92–93). Unfortunately, parents and administrators often focus on the single score to the exclusion of classroom data, and AYP and school effectiveness are tied to the administration of a single standardized achievement test.

However you feel about standardized high-stakes testing, it is not going away. Such tests are mandated by law and substantial federal funding for states is attached to compliance. In addition, the public generally supports such testing and has done so for more than 40 years (Phelps, 2005). Although there is a general belief that such tests are fair and scientific, public acceptance may also be tied to familiarity inasmuch as most adults have taken such tests during their own academic careers (Afflerbach, 2004).

So where does that leave us? It leaves us with the necessity of understanding what standardized tests measure and what they don't. This means that we must be familiar with how they are constructed and what the scores on standardized assessments represent.

Demystifying Standardized Test Scores

Standardized achievement tests are batteries of tests that assess a variety of content areas: reading, language arts, math, social studies, and science. Standardized tests are so called because they are administered and scored in a uniform or standardized manner. They usually employ multiple-choice questions. The student chooses one of four or five possible answers and records this choice on a separate answer sheet, which is scored by a computer.

Standardized achievement tests used to fulfill NCLB legislation are norm-referenced. When norm-referenced tests are developed, they are field-tested on a large sample of students who are representative of the general population. This is called the norm group. Suppose fifth graders in a norm group were field-tested across the country in November. They had an average score of 48 correct in math reasoning. Because these fifth graders were in their third month of fifth grade, the score of 48 was set as 5.3 (fifth grade, third month). When your student, Justin, gets 48 correct, he is also assigned a score of 5.3. This is a relatively simple example of how grade equivalents are determined, but norm-referenced tests offer a variety of other scoring options, which are discussed later. The main issue is that a norm-referenced score compares an individual's score to the scores of students in the norm group.

Validity and Reliability of Standardized Tests

It is tempting to say that standardized measures are not valid because they do not adequately measure the school curriculum or even state-approved standards. However, standardized measures do have other forms of validity, such as construct validity. *Construct validity* refers to the extent to which a test measures something that cannot be observed directly but must be inferred from patterns of behavior. A pattern of behavior is called a construct. Motivation, anxiety, aggression, racial bias, and the like, are all constructs. Comprehension, because it cannot be directly observed, is also a construct. Construct validity is perhaps best understood in the context of intelligence testing. A variety of abilities or behaviors make up what we think of as intelligence: knowledge of word meanings, facility in mental math, recognition of similarities and differences, understanding of sequence, ability in visual–spatial manipulation, and so forth. We cannot see intelligence; we can see only its effects as demonstrated by test items that tap such abilities. Establishing construct validity is extremely complicated; however, it may be helpful to consider a very simplified version of the process. A researcher identifies a group of intelligent individuals. Then the researcher administers a test containing items that are supposed to measure intelligence. If the intelligent subjects score high on the newly designed intelligence test, then it possesses construct validity. In other words, the extent to which items on intelligence tests actually measure intelligence is called construct validity. Standardized measures of comprehension are constructed using the same basic process. If good comprehenders score high on test items, then the measure has construct validity. Construct validity in regard to standardized comprehension assessment is as problematic as comprehension assessment in the classroom. As noted in Chapter 3, because we cannot actually see comprehension occurring, any assessment measure is "inherently imperfect" in some way (Francis, Fletcher, Catts, & Tomblin, 2005, p. 376)

Another form of validity is criterion validity. To what extent is performance on one instrument or activity related to performance on other measures (the criterion)? There are two kinds of criterion validity: concurrent and predictive. Concurrent validity indicates that performance on one instrument is related to performance on another similar measure. Test makers use a statistic called correlation to establish the relationship. Correlation indicates a relationship between two or more sets of scores. If two standardized achievement tests are highly correlated, this indicates that they are measuring the same thing and thus have concurrent validity. Does the test predict future student performance? If so, it has predictive validity. College entrance exams have this type of validity in that they strongly predict grade point averages for traditional age college freshmen. Test manuals usually report concurrent and predictive validity as part of their rationale for the effectiveness of a measure.

A further form of validity is face validity. Does the test *appear* to measure what it is intended to measure? If so, it has face validity. If individuals involved in the testing process accept the validity of the instrument, then it has face validity. Standardized achievement tests are accepted as valid by some educators, parents, and the general public and thus have face validity. The fact that school effectiveness is judged on the basis of a standardized achievement test makes a strong case for face validity. Unfortunately, face validity "is likely to be assessed on a superficial inspection of a test" (Ravid, 2000, p. 268) or, what is more dangerous, on the basis of established practice. Certainly, the usage of standardized achievement tests over many years contributes to their face validity. Face validity is no guarantee of the actual validity of a test, and it is no guarantee that the test actually measures what it claims to measure. When educators question the widespread use of standardized tests as high-stakes instruments, they are criticizing the face validity of the instruments.

Standardized tests address reliability or consistency in several ways. Test–retest reliability means that a test is administered twice to the same group of people and scores from the two administrations are compared. If the test is consistent, the two sets of scores will be related. Some standardized tests have alternate forms that are considered equivalent. Students are administered both forms, and scores from one form are correlated with scores from the other to determine consistency. Split-half reliability is established by correlating or comparing test questions to determine if the difficulty level is relatively consistent across the test. For example, scores on even-numbered items are usually compared with scores on odd-numbered items.

The Meaning of Test Scores

There are a variety of scoring options that accompany standardized achievement tests. Educators must understand what these scores mean so they can accurately interpret student performance. They also need to describe student performance to concerned parents. As a nation, we seem to be in love with numbers. Student performance expressed in numbers is often regarded more highly than the same performance expressed in words. This is unfortunate, because both have a place. In some cases, words are more appropriate and in others, numbers say it best. But this is only if we understand what the words and numbers mean.

We often assume that we understand the words that describe student performance. However, words can be as slippery as numbers. For example, if I describe a student's performance as above average, what do I mean? Am I comparing the student to his or her classroom peers or to a standard of performance set by the school, district or state? The student may have performed much better than his or her classmates but demonstrated only average attainment of district or state standards. Consider the student in a high-achieving district. Above-average performance on state standards may well be average for his or her classroom.

We use many words to describe student performance: good, poor, above average, below average, high, low, pass, fail, and the like. It is important to qualify such words by indicating how the performance was judged. Was the student's performance compared to a norm group or a cutoff score? Was a set of expectations or a rubric used to judge the performance? Did the teacher "grade on the curve," that is, evenly distribute grades from A to F across the students? What was the criterion for a passing grade? Parents may not be knowledgeable enough to ask such questions. It is up to the educator to describe performance as clearly and extensively as possible.

Unfortunately, many educators are not comfortable with numbers related to standardized tests. In my graduate classes, I spend a fair amount of time on scoring concepts such as percentile, normal curve equivalent, standard score, and so on. I always find that many educators have very fuzzy and often downright inaccurate ideas of what these mean and what they tell us about student performance. You may be tempted to skim or even skip this discussion, but please stay with me. In these times, when increasing emphasis is being placed on standardized test performance, it is crucial that educators understand exactly what these scores mean.

Standard Scores

Suppose that your student, Janet, took two tests, one in math and one in spelling. She received a score of 60 on the math test and a score of 75 on the spelling measure. On the face of it, it looks as if Janet is a better speller than mathematician, but is this a correct analysis? We do not know, for instance, how many items were on each test. We do not know if one test was more difficult than the other. Neither do we know how well Janet's classmates did on the same test. So we really cannot compare the two grades.

Standard scores allow us to make that comparison. We can convert Janet's score into a standard score based on the average of the class and the difference of each score from this average. There are a variety of standard scores, and perhaps they are best understood in terms of IQ. When a student takes an intelligence test, he or she achieves a certain number of correct items, called a raw score. But the raw score tells us very little about a student's intelligence in relation to the norm group. So this raw score is converted to a standard score that has an average of 100, with a give-or-take of 15 points (statisticians call this give-or-take a standard deviation). Any converted score that falls between 85 and 115 represents an average IQ. Any score above 115 is considered above average; any score below 85 is described as below average. All standardized tests convert raw scores to standard scores, but the average and the give-or-take may be different for different tests. For example, the SAT college entrance examination has an average score of 500 with a give-or-take of 100. Colleges or universities that will not accept any student with a score lower than 400 are saying that they want average performers. More selective institutions may accept only students with a score of 600 or above. An educator needs to determine what numbers represent the average and the give-or-take on a standardized test in order to correctly interpret standard scores.

Normal Curve Equivalent

Normal curve equivalents (NCEs) are a form of standard score with a mean of 50 and a give-or-take of 21.06. Normal curve equivalent scores range from 1 to 99 and are particularly suited for comparative purposes. The intervals between scores are equal, which means that NCE scores can be averaged to compare groups of students, classrooms, or schools. NCE scores allow educators to compare a student's score on different sections within a test. For example, if a student receives NCE scores of 33 on the mathematics section and 57 on the reading section, you can correctly say that the reading score is 24 points higher than the math score. NCE scores also allow educators to study gains over time, with a score of 50 indicating an average year's growth.

Scale Scores

Scale scores are another form of standard scores. They generally range from 001 to 999, but some tests have different ranges of scale scores with different minimum and maximum values. Scale scores are difficult to interpret to parents and are mainly used for comparison purposes at a school or district level. Scale scores are most useful for comparing the performance of different groups of students and, especially, for comparing student growth over time.

Percentile Scores

A percentile score can range from 1 to 99 and "indicates the percentage of students you did better than" (Trice, 2000, p. 108). If a student scores at the 42nd percentile, this means he or she did better than 42% of the students in the norm group. Similarly, if a student scores at the 67th percentile, he or she did better than 67% of the norm group sample. A percentile score does not refer to the percentage of questions answered correctly by the test taker. It simply indicates the test taker's standing in relation to the norm group.

Parents and some educators often confuse percentile scores with classroom percentage scores. In the classroom, 70% is usually considered a passing grade, whereas a score of 50% indicates very poor performance and a failing grade. However, a percentile score of 50 indicates average performance; the student did better than 50% of the norm group. A percentile score of 70 suggests above-average performance; the student did better than 70 % of the norm group.

Sixty-eight percent of the norm group scores tend to fall between percentile scores of 15 and 84; these scores are considered to indicate average performance. Admittedly, it is difficult to explain to a parent that a percentile score of 35 is not necessarily an indication of poor performance. In addition, unlike the intervals between NCE scores, the intervals between percentile ranks are not equal, so you cannot average the scores of two classrooms or schools in order to compare them. The intervals are much closer between the ranks of 40 to 60. This means that it is easier for a student in this middle range to improve than for a student in the bottom or top range, which makes percentiles less useful for estimating or monitoring growth. Moreover, the difference between raw scores that convert to a percentile of 65 and a percentile of 75 may be very small. Although percentiles are useful for determining areas of relative strength or weakness, it is best to think of them as broad indicators.

Stanines

Stanine scores range from 1 to 9, with scores from 4 to 6 indicating average performance. Like percentiles, stanines tell us where a student scored in relation to the norm group. Basically, stanines represent groupings of percentile ranks. For this reason, they are less precise indicators of student achievement than percentiles, because one cannot tell if a student's score is at the top or bottom of the stanine grouping. For example, stanine 4 encompasses the percentile rankings of 23–39. A student who ranks in the 39th percentile is certainly performing better than one in the 23rd percentile. Because of the global nature of stanines, they should not be used to measure student growth over time.

Grade Equivalents

Grade equivalent scores describe student performance in terms of the performance of an average student at a given grade level. A grade-level score is a decimal that describes performance in terms of grade and month, with a grade equivalent of 5.7 representing the seventh month of the fifth-grade year. Grade equivalents are based on the raw score averages of the norm group. Thus, a student who receives a grade equivalent of 5.7 achieved the same actual or estimated raw score as average members of the norm group who took the test in the seventh month of their fifth-grade year.

On the surface, grade equivalents seem easy to understand, but, unfortunately, they are very often misinterpreted. Educators and parents often think of grade equivalent scores as similar to school grade levels, but they are actually very different. First, there is no such thing as a standard or identical level of achievement at a certain grade level. Reading, math, and other academic levels vary from school to school, depending on the designated curriculum and the textbooks that are used. Fifth-grade students in a low-performing school may be reading or doing math at a level below their actual chronological grade level. Similarly, if a student is in a high-performing district, the grade equivalent of 5.7 may woefully underestimate performance in the fifth-grade classroom. A grade equivalent score simply indicates that a student's score is similar to the norm group's score at that grade level and on that test level. Thus, student scores must always be interpreted in terms of the test content and the norm group.

Sometimes parents and educators interpret a grade equivalent score of 5.7 as indicating that the student can read or do math at a middle fifth-grade level. Nothing could be farther from the truth! Supposing a third-grade student took the standardized test intended for third graders and attained a score of 5.7. This means only that the third grader obtained the same score that one would expect average fifth graders in April to obtain if they took the third-grade test. Grade equivalents represent only general estimates of achievement. They are best interpreted as rough estimates and never as absolute indicators of classroom performance.

How can educators explain all this to parents? It sometimes helps to explain grade equivalents as representing "ballpark figures." For a fifth grader, a grade equivalent of 5.7 indicates that he or she is performing as an average fifth grader, but only in relation to the content of the test, not necessarily the curriculum of the school or classroom. A third grader with a score of 5.7 is not performing as a fifth grader but is doing extremely well for a third grader, again as based on the content of the test. Of course, if the school or district carefully reviews the content of the test and believes that it is a good representation of its curriculum, then educators can say that performance is average or above average in relation to classroom expectations.

What Standardized Tests Tell Us about Comprehension

The preceding section discusses what a standardized achievement test is and how it is scored. It is now time to address the burning question: Just what does a standardized achievement test measure? To put it more succinctly, does it measure comprehension? Chapter 3 addressed the what, how, and why of assessment related to comprehension, so it makes good sense to discuss the same elements in regard to standardized testing. Let's begin with the easy part, the how.

How Do Standardized Achievement Tests Measure Comprehension?

Standardized achievement tests employ a selected response format, usually multiple-choice questions, and thus represent a lower level of difficulty than those with constructed response formats. Selected response formats measure recognition as opposed to recall; however, the ability to answer a multiple-choice item depends on an understanding of the question distracters. A student may actually know quite a bit about the topic of the question but answer incorrectly because some parts of the distracter items were unknown.

Standardized tests are also timed, and this may pose a problem for some students. In my state, admission to a teacher education program depends on passing scores on standardized measures of reading, writing, and mathematics. Bilingual students whose first language is not English evince great difficulty in passing these tests. As one student put it, "I read it in English, but then I changed it to Spanish to think about it and figure out the answer. And I didn't finish in time!" Even when the students asked for and were granted extra time, passing the test was still problematic, owing in large part to the language issue. A timed test can also increase anxiety, which, in turn can affect test performance. Some individuals are just not comfortable in a timed situation.

In a sense, standardized achievement tests mirror some forms of classroom assessment. Many published materials employ a multiple-choice format, and teachers use these tests to assess comprehension and learning. Classroom tests are also timed, with only a certain amount of time allowed for completion. Classroom testing can be just as "high stakes" as district standardized assessment. Students are clearly aware that their report card grade depends on doing well on a test, and a poor report card grade often has more immediate consequences for them than the standardized score that administrators and teachers worry about. Of course, there are two important differences. First, unlike the grade for an annual standardized achievement test, a report card grade is not dependent on a single test sample. Students have multiple opportunities to demonstrate their competence. And second, a classroom test is, it is hoped, based on the curriculum of the school or district and the classroom instruction that preceded the test.

What Do Standardized Tests Measure?

Popham (2001) makes a convincing argument that standardized tests measure three things: what a student comprehended and learned in school, the student's socioeconomic status (SES), and the student's inherited academic aptitude. Let's examine each in turn. Of course, student comprehension and learning contributes to a test score. If a student knows a lot about science, he or she will probably do better than one who does not know as much. Good readers will do better than struggling readers. Teachers are rarely surprised by standardized scores; they tend to mirror the profile of the classroom, with the better students scoring higher than the poorer ones. The multiple-choice questions that assess comprehension and learning involve both literal and inferential components of comprehension. It seems fair to say that, given the selected response format used, application is rarely involved.

In my state, teacher certification is attached to passing scores on a test of content that encompasses four sections: language arts, math, science, and social studies. Because some students have evinced difficulty in obtaining passing grades, faculty members, in an attempt to design some form of test preparation, have actually taken the test. It is quite clear: What you have comprehended and learned does play a part. The faculty members reported ease in taking some sections of the test and frustration in others, depending on what they had comprehended and learned about the four content areas.

Items on standardized tests are also sensitive to elements connected to students' SES. Certain items are more likely to be answered correctly by children from affluent or middle-class families who "grow up in a home environment rich in the sorts of materials and experiences that will substantially benefit them when it comes time to do battle with a standardized achievement test" (Popham, 2001, p. 57). Such things include access to and familiarity with reading materials, writing materials, cable television, and computer programs. I am reminded of my eldest grandson, whose parents made a point of regularly watching the History Channel and the Discovery Channel with him. Also included are travel experiences such as trips to Disney World and other parts of the country. I wonder how much my youngest grandson learned when his parents took him to Chicago for a day. They visited the aquarium and the Museum of Science and Industry, and he returned enthralled with komodo dragons and submarines. Experiences like these, quite common to affluent or middle-class families, contribute a lot to a student's knowledge base. There is another component that we must consider in regard to SES. Standard American English is more likely to be spoken in the homes of educated parents, and this is the language of standardized instruments. "Children of these parents grow up routinely hearing the words and phrases that form the items on standardized achievement tests" (Popham, 2001, p. 57).

We must also consider the student's inherited academic aptitude. Students differ in their verbal, quantitative, and spatial potential, and their strength or weakness in each of these can affect test performance. Popham (2001) estimated that 40% of the items on a reading achievement test could well be influenced by inherited verbal ability and would be correctly answered by "kids who are born word-smart" (p. 68).

Other factors can affect standardized test scores. Test-taking skills play a part, and because standardized measures are timed, student pacing is important. Staying with one test item too long can interfere with completion of the test, and unanswered items can mean a lower score. Of course, a student can just experience a bad testing day. A student with a headache, or one taunted by his or her peers at recess, can perform poorly on a test for reasons other than lack of knowledge or test-taking skills. The same thing can happen in the classroom, but the teacher can easily reevaluate student performance at another point in time. This is not an option with standardized tests. The student gets one chance, and one chance only, to demonstrate his or her ability.

Do standardized tests match the curriculum? I remember a student in one of my graduate classes who was quite irate because the district standardized test included an item on the life cycle of the butterfly, a topic that would not be covered until the following grade. As a result, the district was seriously considering changing its curriculum. I pointed out that this might not be a workable solution. Test items are regularly changed in order to protect the security of the instrument, and the butterfly question might or might not be part of the next year's battery.

In order to address curricular match, it is necessary to consider how the content of standardized achievement tests is chosen. In choosing standardized test items, test authors face the fact that there is no national curriculum in the United States. There is also wide variability across states, districts, and teachers in regard to what is emphasized in the classroom. In spite of state standards and thick curriculum guides, teachers basically decide what to cover and at what depth, and there is little uniformity even in the same building (Schmoker, 2006; Manzo, 2003; Schmoker & Marzano, 1999). Many state standards are extremely broad and focus on general topics, not the specific content represented by a multiple-choice question. Curriculum is often based on textbooks chosen by the school and district, and test authors attempt to design items that focus on topic similarity across different publishers. However, they meet with marginal success. Popham (2001) claims that "half or more of what's tested wasn't even supposed to be taught in a particular district or state" (p. 43). Part of the problem is also due to the fact that test authors have to limit how many items they can include in a single test.

Standardized tests offer little useful information to teachers about a student's comprehension and learning in the classroom and are not able to offer fine-grained information about an individual student's mastery of curriculum. In fact, "the current generation of high stakes tests is incapable of delivering on the promise of providing high-quality information that teachers can use for individualizing instruction for any particular student" (Cizek, 2005, p. 47).

In summary, standardized achievement tests measure literal and inferential comprehension of selected response items. They measure what students have comprehended and learned in school and out of school, and they measure verbal aptitude. They do not specifically measure district, school, or classroom curriculum, nor do they offer valid information about an individual. This naturally leads to the next issue, the purpose of standardized achievement tests.

What Is the Purpose of Standardized Tests?

Standardized achievement tests are group tests. They are not designed to be individually diagnostic and are too short to provide any in-depth information about an individual. They suggest a general level of comprehension proficiency. For example, on the basis of standardized achievement test results, one might conclude that Suzanne is relatively proficient in reading comprehension, but not that she can generate a main idea or make a valid inference about an unfamiliar topic (Popham, 2001). It is not the purpose of standardized measures to provide "instructional relevance for individual students or specific guidance for teachers" (Cizek, 2005, p. 48).

Standardized tests function best as general indicators of systemic educational health. They provide useful information on large groups such as schools and districts, but less valuable or nonexistent information either on individuals or classrooms. They paint a broad picture of achievement, are useful for comparing scores to national norms, and are appropriate for "reporting to the public . . . and monitoring general effects of curricula" (Lewandowski & Martens, 1990, p. 384).

It is not difficult to cite the misuses of standardized achievement tests. They are misused when standardized scores are considered more accurate, representative, and important than classroom assessment measures. They are misused when they become the only or most important index of student performance and school effectiveness. They are misused when classroom scores from one year are compared with classroom scores in the following year. Because such scores are based on two totally different groups of children, comparison is inherently flawed.

Standardized tests are used wisely when they are regarded as only one measure of student performance or school effectiveness and when scores are considered as estimates of achievement, not as absolute indicators. "It should also be remembered that the long-standing primary purpose of large-scale testing has been to provide a general assessment as to how groups of students are progressing in a school district. Such information, if it does not become the focus of instruction, can be one piece of information used to contribute to a broad base of information for planning, supporting, and evaluating school- and system-wide curricula and instruction" (Farr, 1999, p. 52).

Guidelines for Dealing with Standardized Tests

• *Guideline 1. Recognize that standardized tests paint a broad picture and are not necessarily reflective of the curriculum that you are delivering.* Your classroom assessment, formative as well as summative, tells you what you need to know in order to adjust instruction and address the needs of individual students. Why is it that the public gives more credence to tests administered over a few days than the assessment that teachers engage in throughout the year? Well-thought-out and well-designed classroom assessment tells a teacher much more about student performance than any standardized measure. Comprehension assessment that is specifically tied to instruction and carefully differentiated as literal, inferential, or application can provide a valid chronicle of student progress.

• *Guideline 2. Understand standardized test scores and how to explain them to parents.* My suggestion is to focus on understanding standard scores and use them when talking to parents. Grade equivalents and percentiles are too easily misinterpreted. Always explain standardized test scores as related to the performance of the norm group and as reflective of performance on a specific test, not performance in your classroom or in relation to district curriculum.

The table below and on the next page shows two students' scores on a standardized achievement test taken in fourth grade by fourth graders. Following the table are representative comments that a teacher could use in describing what the scores mean to parents.

Student	Score	Reading	Language	Math	Science	Social Studies
Student A	Percentile	52	43	48	40	31
	Stanine	5	5	5	4	4
	Grade equivalent	4.7	4.2	4.6	4.2	3.7
	Normal curve equivalent	51	46	49	45	39

Student B	Percentile	20	21	44	21	20
	Stanine	3	3	5	3	3
	Grade equivalent	2.6	2.9	4.4	3.3	3.1
	Normal curve equivalent	32	33	47	33	32

Student A

A's percentile scores on all subtests were in the average range. In reading, she did better than 52 % of the students who were part of the norm group sample. Her lowest score was in social studies, but it still fell in the average range for percentile scores.

A's stanine scores were all in the average range.

On four subtests, A's grade equivalent scores indicate that she is performing as an average fourth grader in relation to the content and difficulty level of the test. She is performing at a high third-grade level for social studies in relation to the content and difficulty level of the test.

A's normal curve equivalent scores indicate average performance across all subtests.

Student B

B's percentile scores on four of the five subtests are at the extreme lower range for average performance. B's performance in math represents average performance; he did better than 44% of students in the norm group sample.

B's stanine scores indicate average performance in math and below average performance on all other subtests.

B's grade equivalent scores indicate that he is performing as an average fourth grader in math in relation to the content and difficulty level of the test. In reading and language, B is performing as a second grader would if given the same test. In science and social studies, he is performing as a third grader would if given the same test.

B's normal curve equivalent score for math is in the average range. His scores on the other four subtests are at the extreme lower range for average performance.

- *Guideline 3. Teach test-taking skills, but not at the expense of content.* In fact, merge test-taking skills with your formative assessment. Construct selected response items, and use thinking aloud and thoughtful talk as devices for teaching students how to deal with them. This is not teaching to the test. Teaching to the test involves practice with items that are identical to the content of the test. Teaching test-taking skills involves practice with the genre and format of the test, not the content.

- *Guideline 4. Design classroom assessment to function as a counterpart to standardized assessment.* As educators, we have not sufficiently promoted the importance of classroom measures, nor have we actively dignified classroom assessment options and used them to verify or question standardized results. In short, we must take an additional step and collect, organize, and present classroom assessment data to the public in ways to showcase classroom data as equal and equivalent counterparts to standardized results. Chapter 11, the final chapter of the book, continues the discussion of this subject.

Summary

- Standardized tests are tests in which the conditions of administration are the same for all test takers. Standardized tests are tests in which students' scores are compared to a standard, the scores of the norm group.

- The No Child Left behind Act of 2002 has moved standardized achievement tests to the rank of high-stakes testing.

- Critics and supporters of high-stakes standardized tests focus on the harmful or positive effects of such tests on individuals and curriculum, and the time and money spent on such instruments. Critics and supporters agree that such tests provide a limited index for measuring student performance.

- Standardized tests yield different kinds of scores: grade equivalent scores, percentile scores, stanine scores, and standard scores. All standardized test scores compare the student's score to the scores of the norm group.

- Standard scores are based on an average and the give-or-take of that average across students. In order to interpret average performance in relation to the norm group, a teacher or tutor must know the average and the give-or-take of the standardized measure.

- Percentile scores range from 1 to 100 and indicate how many students in the norm sample scored above a certain student. They are not the same as percentage scores. A percentile score of 50 represents average performance. A score of 50% usually represents a nonpassing grade.

- Stanine scores range from 1 to 9, with scores of 4–6 representing average performance.

- A grade equivalent score means the student received the same raw score as the average student in the norm sample for that grade, month, and test level. A grade equivalent score cannot be equated with a classroom grade level.

- A variety of factors affect test scores: what students learn in school, factors associated with SES, inherited aptitude, test-taking skills, and external factors such as general health.

- Standardized tests have limitations. They do not provide fine-grained information about individuals, nor do they offer much in the way of specific guidance for teachers. They provide useful information for large groups and function as general indicators of systemic educational health.

- Standardized tests can be misused if more importance is given to standardized scores than to classroom performance or if they are used as the only index of school, teacher, and student competence.

- Standardized test scores can be used wisely if they are regarded as only one measure of effectiveness and as a rough estimate of achievement, rather than an absolute indicator.

- Guidelines for dealing with standardized measures include the following: recognizing that such measures paint a broad picture; understanding how to communicate standardized test scores to parents; teaching test-taking skills, but not at the expense of content; and designing classroom assessment to act as a counterpart to standardized assessment.

Professional Development Activities to Increase Understanding of Standardized Tests

- Pretend you are planning for a conference with parents. Choose one form of score (grade equivalent, percentile, stanine, or standard score) and plan what you will say to the parents about a high score and a low score.

- Interview several teachers regarding their perceptions of standardized tests. To what degree do they feel the tests accurately reflect the performance of their students?

- Interview several individuals who are not in the education profession. What are their perceptions of standardized tests?

- Interview several students regarding their perceptions of standardized tests. How do they feel about taking them?

- Discuss standardized achievement testing with a group of your peers, and formulate a position statement that clarifies your stance on the use of standardized achievement tests as measures of student comprehension and learning.

CHAPTER 11

Using Classroom Comprehension Assessment as a Counterpart to Standardized Assessment

A Possibility or a Pipedream?

Overview

In 1966 a new television series made its debut. It was called *Star Trek* and promised to boldly go where no one had gone before. Set in the future, it became the genesis and inspiration for additional *Star Trek* series and numerous movies. Why was it popular? No doubt, there are many possible reasons, but I suspect that one was the picture it painted of the future. Part of the enjoyment lay in watching the characters use machines and tools that viewers found engaging even while they admitted their impossibility. But how impossible were they?

In the original series, doors opened and closed when the characters approached them; that is, there was no need to push a door or turn a knob. Today we have such doors and take them quite for granted. Do you remember the ship doctor called "Bones"? He had a wonderful handheld device that, when passed over an injured or sick patient, revealed exactly what was the matter. Granted, we do not yet have such an item, but we do have MRIs and CAT scans, technologies that were not present in 1966. And what about the computer that directed so many activities of the ship and the communication devices the size of a large button pinned to the crew members' shirts? Today's computers, cell phones and iPods are amazingly similar! If there is any moral to the story, it is that the far distant future can become quite close in a shorter period of time than one might imagine.

Why begin this final chapter with an account of *Star Trek*? Because a view of the future can often act as a gentle nudge for change. I am not saying that the inventors of automatic doors and the MRI were motivated by *Star Trek*, but that visions of a different and improved future can help us enhance the present.

Consider an example that is a bit closer to everyday life. After moving to the country and facing several acres of weeds, barbed wire, and rocks, I knew I wanted a nice lawn and garden but had little idea of how it could look. I toured some local homes on a community-sponsored garden tour. These homes sat on lots similar in size to mine, and they became my vision for the future. I saw garden plots involving amazing combinations of bushes, flowers, grasses, and decorative rocks. Today, some 13 years later, I would not claim that my garden and yard are the equal of what I saw that day, but there are similarities. Perhaps most important, those gardens motivated me to make substantial changes in my original plans, which had been to lay sod, clear out the rocks, and plant a few annuals around the porch.

The aim of this chapter is to present a possible future for classroom comprehension assessment. This future may seem as impossible as *Star Trek*'s communication devices; however, bits and pieces are already present in some schools and districts. They are also present in the minds of teachers and administrators who recognize a need for change, even if unsure about the form it should take.

Rationale for a Counterpart to Standardized Assessment

The general public, lawmakers, and, unfortunately, some educators accept standardized achievement tests as the gold standard for evaluating school effectiveness and student comprehension performance. Chapter 10 demonstrated why such instruments present only one picture of student learning, and a rather general one at that. However, they do have a large amount of face validity; that is, they are accepted as valid by many individuals. In addition, there is an absence of any counterpart or complement to the results of the standardized achievement tests. If such tests paint a dismal picture, a school or district has no evidence to offer as a counterargument. Similarly, if the test results are cause for rejoicing, there is no way to validate this. Given the absence of assessment alternatives, it is easy to see why standardized results have become the defining statement of school and student effectiveness. Nothing else has been provided by the educational establishment.

Could classroom assessment act as a counterpart to standardized results? At present, standardized assessment and classroom assessment are on parallel tracks. In a sense, classroom assessment does not even have a visible track. Classroom assessment is not described or summarized in any valid way that could be distributed to the general public. What about report card grades? They certainly have face validity and are regarded as valid indicators of student comprehension and learning. Chapter 9, I hope, made it obvious how shaky that assumption is. There needs to be some form of counterpart to standardized assessment, something other than imprecise and inconsistent report card grades. Classroom assessment as measured by well-designed instruments across a school year is a logical choice. However, this requires change at the classroom level and, as we all know, change does not occur easily.

Teachers and administrators must work together to effect change. Change does not come from the outside, and it is not a top-down scenario. Lasting change begins with those it will most immediately involve. Unfortunately, education has embraced the concept of change as emanating from professional development as an external entity. Experts from different fields are hired to show teachers what to change and how to do it. In one sense, this is not a bad idea. We can all learn from others. What is problematic, however, is the extent of such professional development. Seldom are teachers given time to implement their new learning, to assess its effect, and to make improvements. Seldom, if ever, are they given time to work with their peers to discuss curriculum, design assessments, and evaluate their effectiveness. "What teachers 'know'—what they have learned—isn't developed or refined on the job on the basis of collaborative empirical processes" (Schmoker, 2006, p. 24). Teachers are isolated. They enter their classrooms, close their doors, and teach as they choose, not because they want to but because the educational structure leaves them no other option. Although teaching is uniformly regarded as a profession, teachers are denied the most important component of being a professional: working together with other professionals to accomplish goals (Wise, 2004). If change in comprehension assessment is to occur, it must begin with teachers and administrators sitting around a table and working together to identify problems and design solutions.

Designing a system for providing a counterpart to standardized assessment is a monumental endeavor in one sense. We have never done it or even conceptualized the need. But perhaps it is our only defense against high-stakes standardized achievement tests. Until educators can offer viable alternatives to these instruments, such tests will continue to dominate and direct the educational scene.

Designing a counterpart to standardized measures cannot be a top-down endeavor; it must be collaboratively crafted by teachers and administrators. It will not be a quick fix, but will take years—yes, years. This is unfortunate, because we often hesitate to embark on long-term projects. Why? We live in and are comfortable with a world of fast solutions. We don't like the television show, so we change the channel. We are bored with a toy; we buy another. We don't feel well, so we ask for a fast-acting pill. However, lasting change takes time and demands a clear vision of the future. If you know where you are going, you will eventually get there. We are all familiar with the story of Odysseus, who left Troy to head for home. Time and time again he was diverted from his path, but he never lost track of his final goal, and, of course, he eventually arrived home to his wife, Penelope. Educators need to set long-range goals and stick to them. There may be detours, but detours become manageable if one knows the final destination.

Few would argue that we need alternatives to the standardized measures, which are increasing in importance every day. We need to dignify the role of teachers and the classroom assessment process and, in so doing, contribute to the recognition of their professional status. Darling-Hammond and Goodwin (cited by Schmoker, 1996) believe that the key to professional status is accountability involving the relationship between teachers and students and teachers and the society at large. Reporting classroom data would be a giant step in this direction.

What should be the goals of teachers and administrators who are desirous of providing a counterpart for high-stakes standardized assessment, a counterpart that depicts student comprehension performance in more specific terms than standardized scores? Instead of listing guidelines, I describe how some hypothetical schools or districts might go about reviewing and revising their assessment system. Basically, I am painting a broad picture of a possible future. Your first impression will probably be "That's impossible! It would never happen in my school or district." Resist this temptation. Remember this is the "Star Trek" of educational assessment.

Going Where No One Has Gone Before

Prioritizing Standards

The first step is to ascertain the match between state-approved standards and classroom curriculum. There is a definite "discrepancy between the intended curriculum and the implemented curriculum" (Marzano, 2003, p. 23). State-approved standards are the intended curriculum and, before these standards were established, district curriculum guides were the intended curriculum. The implemented curriculum is what individual teachers actually teach and assess, and it is often dictated by the textbooks used or the personal choices of the teachers.

In our hypothetical school of the future, teachers and administrators first examined their state standards and identified a major concern, the sheer number of state-approved standards at any level or in any content field. Were they all equally important? The teachers and administrators soon realized that the standards were, in a sense, an unrealistic wish list, "far too numerous to teach and far, far too numerous to test" (Popham, 2003, p. 33). Therefore, the first order of business was to prioritize the standards in terms of essential, highly desirable, and desirable (Popham, 2003). Once the essential standards were identified, teachers and administrators ranked them from most important to least important.

Grouping and ranking the standards took time, discussion, and compromise on the part of everyone. Teachers first worked in grade-level groups; for instance, all fourth-grade teachers, or all middle school English teachers, or all high school science teachers met regularly twice a month for at least 45 minutes (Schmoker, 2006). These meetings represented the whole of professional development for the teachers, that is, the time scheduled for the monthly meetings was in lieu of regularly scheduled district or whole-school professional development activities. After teachers worked in grade-level groups, the meetings were expanded to include other levels, that is, third- and fourth-grade teachers shared their standard groupings and rankings, and middle school and high school science teachers met together. In a spirit of true compromise, some modifications were made. Everyone recognized the dangerous tendency to regard all standards as equally important, and no one wanted to discard a single standard. However, everyone also recognized that it was not possible to teach to every standard, and all acknowledged that there was considerable overlap between them. When the grouping and ranking process was complete, teachers and administrators had basically established "a common, concise set of essential curricular standards" that the teachers agreed to teach to "on a roughly common schedule" (Schmoker, 2006, p. 106).

Were all teachers and administrators equally enthusiastic about the process? No. Some felt it to be a waste of time. Others thought that the twice-monthly meetings could be better used as personal prep time. But the majority of the participants recognized the validity of the endeavor, and their commitment and perseverance won over many of their less enthusiastic peers.

Operationalizing Standards

Grouping the standards led to the next issue. How should the standards be taught or assessed? Standards tend to be "stated so generally that it's tough to get an accurate sense of what the curricular aim really signifies" (Popham, 2003, p. 19). So the next step was to operationalize each standard. Basically, this came down to deciding exactly what the teachers should teach and assess in order to meet a particular standard. For example, consider the following state-approved standard: "Fifth–twelfth grade students studying United States history will learn about colonial history and settlement, 1607–1763" (Wisconsin Department of

Public Instruction, 1998). This standard covered more than 150 years of history and probably three to four textbook chapters. What exactly should teachers emphasize? What exactly should students learn? How does this differ across elementary, middle, and high school? Another standard was equally ambiguous. Students will "analyze primary and secondary sources related to a historical question to evaluate their relevance, make comparisons, integrate new information with prior knowledge, and come to a reasoned conclusion" (Wisconsin Department of Instruction, 1998). And exactly how will a fourth- or fifth-grade teacher accomplish this? What classroom project might be involved? What about middle and high school students? How will they demonstrate their comprehension and learning? Teachers and administrators working first in grade-level and content-area groups wrestled with decisions regarding the specific curricular content to be taught and tested in order to address each standard that had been deemed as essential or highly desirable.

Some teachers thought that deciding as a group what to teach and assess was an invasion of their professional autonomy. Others welcomed the chance to specifically tie classroom instruction and assessment to the standards. Discussion was often heated; however, over time, participants began to see the value of the activity and gradually reached consensus. Compromise prevailed. Everyone got something he or she wanted, but no one got everything he or she wanted.

As they did when grouping the standards, participants shared their initial decisions across grade levels and made adjustments. Eventually, teachers and administrators identified and agreed upon what was important to teach and assess. In essence, they identified a specific curriculum for each grade level and content area on the basis of what students should comprehend and learn.

Assessing Standards

The next step focused on how student comprehension and learning should be assessed. Working in grade-level and content-area groups and meeting at least twice a month, teachers shared their assessment practices. Because they had agreed to teach the same curricular content on a similar timeline, they were able, each month, to share how they were designing instruction and how they assessed literal, inferential, and application forms of comprehension. Basically, they had become what has been described as professional learning communities, "small, instructionally focused teacher teams" (Schmoker, 2006) concentrating on improvement of instruction, assessment, and student learning. At each meeting, they addressed the following questions: How did I teach and assess? What forms of comprehension learning were evident: literal, inferential, or application? What went well? What could be improved? They began to see how collaboration could actually improve their practice. If the teachers needed help or reached a stalemate, they asked outside personnel to join their group. They also asked outside personnel to review their decisions and offer suggestions. Individuals from other schools and districts and from local colleges and universities became part of the learning community and, instead of offering top-down advice, functioned as invited members of the group.

As teachers shared their instructional and assessment practices, described the performance of their students, and learned from each other, this led to the next step: a recognition and a decision that certain assessments should be administered uniformly across the grades and content areas. Such assessments involved published instruments as well as instruments collaboratively designed by the teachers. For example, elementary teachers decided to administer an informal reading inventory twice a year to assess reading performance across the grades. Elementary, middle, and high school teachers agreed on common writing assessments and worked together to choose and/or design writing prompts and rubrics. Content teachers examined their curricula and, working together, chose certain classroom unit tests and/or projects as pivotal to analysis of student comprehension and learning. They agreed that all would use such assessments and analyze them in a similar fashion by differentiating literal, inferential, and application forms of comprehension.

Assessments designed, chosen, or agreed upon by teachers have qualities that standardized tests do not have. First, they tend to be more "user friendly" and may not produce the anxiety that often accompanies standardized assessment. Second, they may more accurately reflect the real comprehension/learning process by asking students to engage in authentic tasks. Third, if well designed, they provide much more information about an individual student's strengths and needs. Fourth, they can truly impact instruction in ways that a standardized measure cannot.

But don't common assessments destroy the creativity and autonomy of teachers? Having wrestled with this question as they operationalized the standards, the learning teams thought that common assessments was a logical first step. There are many ways to design instruction and many strategies for fostering student comprehension and learning. Teaching is an intensely personal act, and each teacher is free to exercise his or her individuality in presenting lessons, utilizing formative assessments, and modifying instructional strategies as needed. There is much room for individual creativity within the framework of a required curriculum tied to standards. Culminating assessments that are discussed, designed, and/or modified by collaborative teacher teams can be the same across all classrooms without limiting the inventiveness and originality of individual teachers.

Once the common assessments were agreed upon (and remember this took a lot of time and continual focused effort in regularly scheduled meetings), the stage was set for providing a counterpart to standardized achievement test scores.

Classroom data could be reported to the general public in much the same way as standardized test scores.

Reporting Assessment Data

First, in reporting assessment data, administrators and teachers decided how they would report student performance. Most of the data collected and analyzed by teachers is individualized in nature, and teachers "tend to evaluate students individually and reflect on how to improve class performance less frequently" (Schmoker, 1996, p. 37). That is, teachers focus primarily on individual student performance, rather than the performance of the classroom group. Our professional learning community of the future decided not to give up an emphasis on the individual, but to broaden the focus to include grouped data that could be reported to the community. Reporting individual scores to the community would be a serious breach of student privacy, but individual scores could be grouped and, as such, reported anonymously.

There were risks to such reporting. If the majority of students at a certain grade level or in a certain content area received high grades, it would be easy to report such data, as it would indicate that students were making progress toward meeting the standards. But what if the majority of students received low scores? The group agreed that to provide an effective and honest counterpart to standardized achievement tests, these scores should be reported as well. Reporting disappointing data, accompanied by an explanation of how one intends to remedy the situation, is as attractive to parents and the general public as reporting high scores across all students. Recognizing a need in students and being able to address it with specific instructional interventions is the mark of a professional.

As learning teams pursued the idea of providing a counterpart to standardized assessment, they soon realized that data can be threatening to teachers as well, so the teams adopted guidelines for choosing and reporting classroom data. Classroom data should be collected and analyzed collaboratively and anonymously by grade level or school, never by classroom, and classroom data should never be used as an indictment of teachers (Schmoker, 1996). The only purpose of reporting such data is to show that students in a school or at a specific grade level are meeting the standards. If the data are reported by classroom, it would be very easy for someone to compare classroom data and come to the erroneous conclusion that some teachers are less effective than others. Unfortunately, teachers themselves could come to the same conclusion. Therefore, it is important that classroom data be grouped anonymously, or teachers will resist reporting it. And who can blame them? Classrooms vary widely within a school, and factors other than instruction can affect student performance. The identification of poor teachers is not the purpose of reporting classroom data, nor is it job of the community. But what if there is only one chemistry teacher or one fourth-grade class? In such cases, data would be grouped across several grade levels or content areas.

The teams agreed that data should be differentiated according to the three components of comprehension: literal, inferential, and application, but the key, in reporting the data, was simplicity. Complex tables of numbers and intricate charts and graphs do not work. The majority of people do not have the background needed to interpret them nor the time or desire to do so. The learning teams set the following guidelines for data reporting. First, focus on the accomplishments of the students; they are of primary interest to parents and the general public. Showcase student achievement in simple but direct terms by reporting the exact number of students who achieved a specific grade or by using the percentage of students who did so. Avoid averages, as one very high or one very low score can skew the results. Use simple graphs such as a bar chart or pie chart. (Calhoun, 2004, provides a variety of templates for data reporting.) Accompany data with a brief explanation or a description of the assessment and how it is tied to a specific standard. After presenting the scores, explain simply and clearly what decisions and changes will be made as a result.

Each year the school district reported its standardized test scores. At the same time, it issued its classroom assessment report. Initially, the media ignored the classroom report, but parents didn't. They eagerly awaited its distribution and, eventually, in small segments, local media began to report student progress as measured by classroom assessment. Is this the end of the story? Of course not. Nothing is ever truly finalized. Administrators and teachers continued to meet regularly. They continued to adjust instruction and assessment on the basis of student performance. Teachers brought new ideas to their twice-a-month meetings. They shared what they learned through professional reading, graduate classes, and conference attendance. Some assessments remained relatively stable. Some were dropped in favor of more sensitive measures. Some were adjusted on the basis of student performance. And, over time, in our hypothetical district of the future, classroom assessments attained an importance equal in standing to standardized measures.

Is this a possibility or a pipedream? If you believe it is a possibility, the first step may be to share the idea with others. Perhaps you can use this chapter as an impetus for change. Perhaps you might surreptitiously place it on your principal's or curriculum director's desk and mark Chapter 11 with a brightly colored Post-it note.

However, if you think it is a pipedream, all you have to do is close this book.

Or . . .

You might think about the possibilities of learning teams focused on a counterpart to standardized test scores and return to the book at a later date.

I hope you do!

Summary

- A vision of the future can act as a gentle nudge for change.
- There is no existing counterpart or complement to standardized achievement tests, which are regarded as the gold standard for evaluating school effectiveness and student comprehension performance.
- Classroom comprehension assessment as measured by well-chosen instruments could act as such a counterpart.
- Classroom assessment could become a counterpart to standardized assessment if teachers and administrators form professional learning communities and meet regularly to effect change. This will not be a quick fix. It will take time, discussion, and compromise.
- Designing a counterpart involves prioritizing standards as essential, highly desirable, and desirable and operationalizing them in specific curricular terms. It involves choosing or designing classroom assessments that are administered uniformly across the grades and content areas.
- Data from such assessments should be regularly reported as grouped data and in simple terms.

Glossary

Adequate yearly progress (AYP). Mandated by NCLB. Districts must delineate annual progress objectives for economically disadvantaged students, students with disabilities or limited English proficiency, and students from major racial and ethnic groups. One hundred percent proficiency must be reached by 2013–2014.

Application comprehension. The student moves beyond the text and applies his or her comprehension to a new situation or context.

Assessment. Involves four steps: Identify what to assess. Collect information or evidence. Analyze the evidence. Make a decision.

Bloom's taxonomy. A familiar form of question categorization involving six levels: knowledge, comprehension, application, analysis, synthesis, and evaluation.

Categories of knowledge. Linguistic knowledge, unschooled or informal knowledge, schooled or formal knowledge, subject matter knowledge, and performance procedures or strategic knowledge.

Cloze. A passage with words systematically omitted, usually every fifth, seventh, or ninth word. The reader or listener supplies the missing words, and the greater the number of words correctly identified, the higher the comprehension score.

Comprehension strategies. Conscious and controllable processes or strategies that are employed to comprehend and remember. Examples include overviewing, paraphrasing, summarizing, rereading, using imagery, taking notes, constructing diagrams, questioning, hypothesizing, forming analogies, revising prior knowledge, and monitoring comprehension.

Concurrent validity. Performance on one instrument is related to performance on another similar measure.

Construct validity. The extent to which a test measures something that cannot be observed directly but must be inferred from patterns of behavior.

Constructed response assessment. Often referred to as open-ended or subjective assessment. The student is required to construct something such as a written answer, an oral summary, or a project of some sort.

Content validity. Is present if there is a match between the assessment and classroom instruction.

Content-free questions. General questions that students can ask about any selection. They can provide the teacher with an assessment model for discussion and the students with a strategy for making sense of what they read, hear, or see.

Convergent thinking questions. Begin with *why, how,* and *in what way.* Students answer such questions by explaining, stating relationships, and comparing and contrasting. Answering such questions requires understanding of the content.

Correlation. A statistic that establishes a relationship between two or more sets of scores.

Cultural literacy. As defined by Hirsch (1987; Hirsch, Kett, & Trefil, 1998), a list of terms and phrases every American should know.

Directive scaffold. Teacher control primarily defines the directive scaffold. Often referred to as a transmission approach, with the teacher as the transmitter and controller of learning.

Divergent thinking questions. Begin with *imagine, suppose, predict, if . . . then . . . , how might . . . , can you create,* and *what are some possible consequences.* Students predict, hypothesize, infer, and reconstruct.

Dual coding theory. Comprehension involves a verbal system and a nonverbal or visual system. The visual system handles graphics and text; the verbal or auditory system handles sound and speech.

Educational assessment. Used to evaluate individuals and programs, to hold particular groups accountable for a set of outcomes, to inform instruction, and to determine who gains access to particular programs or privileges.

Evaluative thinking questions. Begin with *defend, judge, justify, what do you think,* and *what is your opinion.* Students value, judge, defend, and justify choices and move beyond the text to apply or transfer what they have understood to new situations.

Expository text structure. Expository text is usually organized in five patterns: description, sequence or time order, cause and effect, problem and solution, and compare and contrast.

Face validity. A test is said to have face validity if it *appears* to measure what it is intended to measure.

Fluency. Reading with accuracy, speed, and intonation and doing so without conscious attention on the part of the reader. Usually assessed through computation of reading rate: number of words read per minute (WPM) or number of correct words read per minute (CWPM).

Formal assessment. Assessment through commercially produced and published instruments that have specific procedures for administration and scoring. Standardized tests are examples of formal assessment measures.

Formative assessment. Assessment to evaluate instructional effectiveness and to provide feedback to students.

Grade equivalents. Describe student performance in terms of the performance of an average student at a given grade level.

Grades. Shortcut tools for communicating information about student comprehension and learning. They provide a public record of student achievement and offer guidelines for making informed decisions about promotion, class placement, and/or college acceptance.

Inferential comprehension. Comprehension that is the result of an inference on the part of the reader, listener, or viewer.

Informal assessment. Assessment through flexible measures that educators can modify and adapt to the needs of specific students or classroom situations.

Learning. Constructing "a situation model that will be remembered and can be used effectively when the information provided by the text used is needed in some way at a later time" (Kintsch & Kintsch, 2005, p. 76). Learning involves three components: comprehension, memory, and application.

Levels of word knowledge. Association, comprehension, and generation. The student can associate a word with other words even if he or she does not know its meaning. The student comprehends common meanings of words. The student can generate or use a word in a new or novel context.

Literal comprehension. Comprehension of material that is explicitly stated by the speaker, or present in written text/multimedia.

Macrostructure. The passage gist, often conceptualized as the main idea of a passage.

Memory questions. Begin with *who, what, where* or *when*. Students answer a memory question by naming, defining, identifying, or offering a yes or no response. Memory questions assess recall of content but may not indicate understanding of content.

Mental lexicon or dictionary. Word pronunciation and word meaning stored in memory.

Microstructure. A network of interrelated idea units; often conceptualized as passage details.

Multimedia. A medium that consists of multiple information sources such as printed words, spoken words, pictures, diagrams, animation, and forms of simulation. Verbal information enters the verbal system; pictures, animation, and simulation enter the visual system; and the learner builds connections between the two.

Narrative text structure. A predictable pattern involving setting, character, problem, goal, and solution.

No Child Left Behind (NCLB). Legislation mandating states to test students in reading and math every year in grades 3 through 8 and at least once in grades 10 through 12. By 2007–2008, science assessments must also be in place. Testing results are reported as a yearly report card, with scores broken out according to economic background, race, ethnicity, English proficiency, and disability.

Normal curve equivalent (NCE). A form of standard score with a mean of 50 and a give-or-take of 21.06; particularly suited for comparative purposes.

Norm-referenced tests. Compare an individual's score with the scores of students in the norm group.

Open-ended assessment. Often referred to as project or performance assessment, it calls upon the student to apply knowledge and skills to create a product or solve a problem and demands some organization on the part of the student.

Percentile. Ranges from 1 to 99; indicates the test taker's standing in relation to the norm group, the percentage of students the test taker did better than.

Productive vocabulary. Words used when speaking or writing; these tend to be relatively familiar and frequently used.

Professional learning communities. Teacher teams focused on improvement of instruction, assessment, and student learning.

Proxy. A substitute, stand-in, or replacement.

Question–Answer Relationships (QARs). A form of question categorization. Answers to questions can be found in two places: In the Book and In My Head. There are two forms of In the Book questions: Right There questions and Think and Search questions. There are two In My Head questions: Author and Me and On My Own.

Readability formula. A formula that describes text difficulty in terms of the number of words in a sentence, the number of syllables in a word, and the number of relatively unfamiliar words.

Reading comprehension. "The process of simultaneously extracting and constructing meaning through interaction and involvement with written language" (RAND Reading Study Group, 2002, p. 11). This definition can apply ⊛ listening comprehension and comprehension of visual stimuli if "involvement with written language" is changed to "involvement with oral language" or "involvement with visual stimuli."

Recall. Calling up an answer from memory; a measure of what has been understood and committed to memory.

Receptive vocabulary. Words to which a listener or reader can attach meaning; such words are less well known and seldom used spontaneously.

Recognition. Recognizing an answer from a list of possible choices.

Response to intervention (RTI). If a student's response to instruction is dramatically inferior to that of his peers, the student may be determined to have a learning disability.

Rubric. A system for assessing complex responses by providing criteria for describing performance at different levels of proficiency.

Scale scores. A form of standard scores, generally ranging from 001 to 999; mainly used for comparison purposes at a school or district level.

Selected response assessment. Often referred to as objective assessment. The student is presented with several possible choices for an answer and chooses one. Most standardized instruments are selected response in nature.

Sentence verification technique (SVT). Measures comprehension by asking students to choose which of four sentences was actually present in a passage.

Situation model. Composed of the text base and inferences drawn from information present in the text and the reader's prior knowledge.

Split-half reliability. Correlating or comparing test questions to determine if the difficulty level is relatively consistent across the test. For example, scores on even-numbered items are compared with scores on odd-numbered items.

Standard score. A raw score converted to a score with a mean and standard deviation, based on the average of the group and the difference of each score from this average.

Standardized tests. Tests that are administered and scored in a uniform or standardized manner.

Stanine. A score ranging from 1 to 9, with scores from 4 to 6 indicating average performance.

Summative assessment. Assessment used to provide a grade or progress report of some kind.

Supportive scaffold. Learner centered with opportunity for responsive feedback; often referred to as an instructional conversation or participatory approach. The teacher provides feedback specifically related to the needs of the learner and models effective comprehension strategies.

Test reliability. A reliable test is consistent; that is, it yields similar results over time with similar students under similar situations.

Test validity. A valid test measures and accurately reflects what it was designed to measure. Validity is related to knowing the exact purpose of an assessment and designing an instrument that meets that purpose.

Test–retest reliability. To determine reliability, a test is administered twice to the same group of people, and scores from the two administrations are compared.

Text base. "The mental representation that the reader constructs of the text" (Kintsch & Kintsch, 2005, p. 73); composed of the microstructure and the macrostructure.

Text coherence. The top-level structure and overall organization of the text. Includes the physical appearance of the text, how new or important topics are signaled, and how text structure is indicated.

Text factors that influence comprehension. Text structure (narrative and expository), text difficulty (familiar versus unfamiliar), vocabulary load, text syntax, text coherence, and readability.

Text-level processes. Prior knowledge, use of comprehension strategies, motivation, interest, purpose or goal, and anxiety.

Thinking aloud. Readers or listeners stop after short segments of text and say what they are thinking about. Often referred to as verbal protocol analysis; think-aloud comments focus on the process of comprehension as opposed to the product.

Thoughtful talk. Also referred to as thoughtful literacy; involves a focus on student response as opposed to literal recall and moves beyond the ability to remember and recite.

Vocabulary knowledge. One of the five major components of reading.

Word-level skills. Pronunciation, pronunciation fluency, and comprehension of word meaning.

Guidelines

Defining Assessment: A Four-Step Process

1. Define the purpose of assessment as clearly and specifically as possible.
2. Tie assessment activities and instruments to classroom objectives and instruction.
3. Describe the assessment to the students.
4. Use multiple methods and assessment experiences to evaluate a student's performance.
5. Keep assessment simple.

Questions: Promises and Pitfalls

1. Differentiate between literal, inferential, and application questions.
2. Differentiate between selected response and constructed response questions.
3. Tie questions to the objectives of the instruction.
4. Differentiate between formative and summative assessment questions.
5. Do not assume that a wrong answer always means that the student did not comprehend the content.
6. When asking subjective open-ended questions, know exactly what you are looking for.
7. Consider using look-backs to assess comprehension.
8. Organize your questions in a user-friendly way.

Open-Ended Assessments: Powerful but Problematic

1. To establish the validity of open-ended comprehension assessments:
   Match the open-ended assessment to specific instructional objectives.
   Focus on important or significant content and processes.

Differentiate the levels of comprehension expected: literal, inferential, application.

Acknowledge the possible interference of performance variables.

2. To establish the reliability of open-ended comprehension assessment:

    Construct rubrics to match instructional objectives.

    Keep rubrics simple and specific.

    Share or construct rubrics with students.

    Teach students the format of open-ended assessments.

3. Identify and code the components of comprehension that are represented by the open-ended assessment.

4. Base assessments on important instructional goals.

5. Maintain a focus on simplicity.

6. Remember that any assessment is only a sample of student performance.

7. Collaborate with others.

Look Who's Talking: Assessing Comprehension through Student Dialogue

1. Design a simple way to keep track of student talk.

2. Don't agonize about recognizing the different levels of comprehension reflected in thoughtful talk and think-aloud comments.

3. Ease into thoughtful talk and thinking aloud.

4. Don't expect to remember all the content-free questions the first time you use them.

5. Prepare for modeling thoughtful talk or think-aloud comments.

6. Keep some record of student performance in your grade book.

Words! Words! Words!: How Can We Assess Word Comprehension?

1. Carefully choose words to assess.

2. Share with your students the words that you intend to include in the assessment.

3. Design your assessment to parallel your classroom instruction.

4. Adapt the assessment format to the age of the child.

5. Don't assume that the literal level of vocabulary knowledge is easier than the inferential or application level.

6. Code vocabulary comprehension levels according to what students do with the words.

Comprehension Assessment Proxies: Stand-Ins, Not Stars

1. Always interpret a comprehension assessment proxy in terms of the text.
2. Always interpret proxy utility by knowing exactly what the measure is correlated with.
3. Don't assume that the correlations between the proxy measure and a standardized instrument hold true for all grade levels.
4. Do not assume that training in the proxy will automatically transfer to improved comprehension.
5. Never confuse a proxy with the real thing.

Grading Practices: Taking a New Look at Grading Comprehension

1. Clearly differentiate the relative influence of performance and effort factors in assigning grades.
2. Before determining report card grades for academic achievement, decide what factors will be included as indicators of student performance and the weight of each.
3. Decide whether the report card grade reflects performance over time or performance at the end of the grading period.
4. Determine a uniform system for combining grades into a single report card designation.
5. There will always be a measure of subjectivity to grading, even given the use of rubrics and the most careful attention to grading validity.
6. Grades in grade books, like individual assessments, should be coded as representing literal, inferential, or application components of comprehension.
7. Don't confuse formative and summative assessments in assigning a report card grade.

Measuring Comprehension through Standardized Tests: An Oxymoron?

1. Recognize that standardized tests paint a broad picture and are not necessarily reflective of the curriculum that you are delivering.
2. Understand standardized test scores and how to explain them to parents.
3. Teach test-taking skills, but not at the expense of content.
4. Design classroom assessment to function as a counterpart to standardized assessment.

References

Adams, M. J. (1990). *Beginning to read: Thinking and learning about print.* Cambridge, MA: MIT Press.

Afflerbach, P. (2004). *National Reading Conference policy brief: High stakes testing and reading assessment.* Oak Creek, WI: National Reading Conference.

Afflerbach, P., & Johnston, P. (1984). Research methodology on the use of verbal reports in reading. *Journal of Reading Behavior, 16,* 307–322.

Alexander, P. A., & Jetton, T. L. (2000). Learning from texts: A multidimensional perspective. In M. K. Kamil, P. B. Mosenthal, P. D. Pearson, & R. Barr (Eds.), *Handbook of reading research* (Vol. 3, pp. 285–310). Mahwah, NJ: Erlbaum.

Allen, J. D. (2005). Grades as valid measures of academic achievement of classroom learning. *Clearing House, 78,* 218–224.

Allington, R. L. (2001). *What really matters for struggling readers: Designing research-based programs.* New York: Longman.

Alvermann, D., Young, J., Weaver, D., Hinchman, K., Moore, D., Phelps, S., et al. (1996). Middle and high school students' perceptions of how they experience text-based discussions: A multicase study. *Reading Research Quarterly, 31,* 244–267.

Alvermann, D. E., Smith, L. C., & Readance, J. E. (1985). Prior knowledge activation and the comprehension of compatible and incompatible text. *Reading Research Quarterly, 20,* 420–436.

Applegate, M. D., Quinn, K. B., & Applegate, A. (2002). Levels of thinking required by comprehension questions in informal reading inventories. *Reading Teacher, 56,* 174–180.

Assessment Reform Group. (2002). *Testing, motivation and learning.* Retrieved from *www.assessment-reform-group.org.uk.*

Bachman, L. F. (2000). Modern language testing at the turn of the century: Assuring that what we count counts. *Language Testing, 17,* 1–42.

Baumann, J. F., & Kame'enui, E. J. (Eds.). (2004). *Vocabulary instruction: Research to practice.* New York: Guilford Press.

Beck, I. L., McKeown, M. G., Hamilton, R. L., & Kucan, L. (1997). *Questioning the author: An approach for enhancing student engagement with text.* Newark, DE: International Reading Association.

Beck, I. L., McKeown, M. G., & Kucan, L. (2002). *Bringing words to life: Robust vocabulary instruction.* New York: Guilford Press.

Bender, W. N., & Shores, C. (2007). *Response to intervention: A practical guide for every teacher.* Thousand Oaks, CA: Corwin Press.

Bernhardt, E. B. (2000). Second-language reading as a case study of reading scholarship in the 20th century. In M. L. Kamil, P. B. Mosenthal, P. D. Pearson, & R. Barr (Eds.), *Handbook of reading research* (Vol. 3, pp. 791–812). Mahwah, NJ: Erlbaum.

Biemiller, A. (2004). Teaching vocabulary in the primary grades: Vocabulary instruction needed. In J. F. Baumann & E. J. Kame'enui (Eds.), *Vocabulary instruction: Research to practice* (pp. 28–40). New York: Guilford Press.

Billmeyer, R. (2001). *Capturing ALL of the reader through the reading assessment system.* Omaha, NE: Dayspring.

Black, P., Harrison, C., Lee, C., Marshall, B., & Wiliam, D. (2004). Working inside the black box: Assessment for learning in the classroom. *Phi Delta Kappan, 86,* 9–22.

Black, P., & Wiliam, D. (1998). Assessment and classroom learning. *Assessment in education: Principles, policy and practices, 5,* 7–75.

Bloom, B., & Krathwohl, D. (1956). *Taxonomy of educational objectives: The classification of educational goals.* New York: Longmans Green.

Bovair, S., & Kieras, D. E. (1991). Toward a model of acquiring procedures from text. In R. Barr, M. L. Kamil, P. B. Mosenthal, & P. D. Pearson (Eds.), *Handbook of reading research* (Vol. 2, pp. 206–229). White Plains, NY: Longman.

Bransford, J. D., Brown, A., & Cocking, R. R. (2000). *How people learn: Brain, mind experience and school.* Washington DC: National Academy Press.

Brookhart, S. M. (2003). Developing measurement theory for classroom purposes and uses. *Educational Measurement: Issues and Practices, 22,* 5–12.

Brookhart, S. M. (2006). *Formative assessment strategies for every classroom.* Alexandria, VA: Association for Supervision and Curriculum Development.

Brown-Chidsey, R., & Steege, M. W. (2005). *Response to intervention: Principles and strategies for effective practice.* New York: Guilford Press.

Burke, K. (2005). *How to assess authentic learning.* Thousand Oaks, CA: Corwin Press.

Burke, K. (2006). *From standards to rubrics in 6 steps.* Thousand Oaks, CA: Corwin Press.

Caldwell, J., & Leslie, L. (2004/2005). Does proficiency in middle school reading assure proficiency in high school reading? The possible role of think-alouds. *Journal of Adolescent and Adult Literacy, 47,* 324–335.

Caldwell, J., & Leslie, L. (2007). *The effects of thinking aloud in expository text on recall and comprehension.* Unpublished manuscript.

Caldwell, J. S. (2008). *Reading assessment: A primer for teachers and coaches* (2nd ed.). New York: Guilford Press.

Caldwell, J. S., & Leslie, L. (2005) *Intervention strategies to accompany informal reading inventory assessment: So what do I do now?* Boston: Allyn & Bacon.

Calfee, R., & Hiebert, E. (1991). Classroom assessment in reading. In R. Barr, M. L. Kamil, P. B. Moesenthat, & P. D. Pearson (Eds.), *Handbook of reading research* (Vol. 2, pp. 281–309). New York: Longman.

Calhoun, E. (2004). *Using data to assess your reading program.* Alexandria, VA: Association for Supervision and Curriculum Development.

Carlisle, J. F., & Rice, M. S. (2004). Assessment of reading comprehension. In C. A. Stone, E. R. Silliman, B. J. Ehren, & K. Apel (Eds.), *Handbook of language and literacy: Development and disorders* (pp. 521–540). New York: Guilford Press.

Chall, J. S., Bissex, G. L., Conrad, S. S., & Harris-Sharples, S. (1996). *Qualitative assessment of text difficulty.* Cambridge, MA: Brookline Books.

Chou-Hare, V., & Smith, D. C. (1982). Reading to remember: Studies of metacognitive reading skills in elementary school-aged children. *Journal of Educational Research, 75,* 157–164.

Chun, D. M., & Plass, J. L. (1997). Research on text comprehension in multimedia environments. *Language, Learning and Technology, 1,* 60–81.

Ciardiello, A. V. (1998). Did you ask a good question today? Alternative cognitive and metacognitive strategies. *Journal of Adolescent and Adult Literacy, 42,* 210–219.

Cizek, G. J. (2000). Pockets of resistance in the assessment revolution. *Educational Measurement: Issues and Practices, 19*(2), 16–24.

Cizek, G. J. (2005). High stakes testing: Contexts, characteristics, critiques, and consequences. In R. P. Phelps (Ed.), *Defending standardized testing* (pp. 23–54). Mahwah, NJ: Erlbaum.

Cizek, G. J., Fitzgerald, S. M., & Rachor, R. E. (1996). Teachers' assessment practices: Preparation, isolation and the kitchen sink. *Educational Assesment, 3,* 159–179.

Cooney, T., DiSpezio, M. A., Foots, B. K., Matamoros, A. L., Nyquist, K. B., Ostlund, K. L. (2000). *Scott Foresman science.* Glenview, IL: Scott Foresman.

Cote, N., Goldman, S. R., & Saul, E. U. (1998). Students making sense of informational text: Relations between processing and representation. *Discourse Processes, 25,* 1–53.

Crain-Thoreson, C., Lippman, M. Z., & McClendon-Magnuson, D. (1997). Windows of comprehension: Reading comprehension processes as revealed by two think-alouds. *Journal of Educational Psychology, 89,* 579–591.

Daneman, M. (1991). Individual differences in reading skills. In R. Barr, M. L. Kamil, P. B. Mosenthal, & P. D. Pearson (Eds.), *Handbook of reading research* (Vol. 2, pp. 512–538). White Plains, NY: Longman.

Davidson, J. W., Castillo, P., & Stoff, M. B. (2002). *The American nation.* Upper Saddle River, NJ: Pearson Education.

Davidson, M., & Myhre, O. (2000). Measuring reading at grade level. *Educational Leadership, 57,* 25–28.

Davis, F. B. (1944). Fundamental factors of comprehension of reading. *Psychometrika, 9,* 185–197.

Donahue, M. L., & Foster, S. K. (2004). Social cognition, conversation, and reading comprehension. In C. A. Stone, E. R. Silliman, B. J. Ehren, & K. Apel (Eds.), *Handbook of language and literacy* (pp. 363–379). New York: Guilford Press.

Duke, N. K. (2005). Comprehension of what for what: Comprehension as a nonunitary construct. In S. G. Paris & S. A. Stahl (Eds.), *Children's reading comprehension and assessment* (pp. 93–104). Mahwah, NJ: Erlbaum.

Farr, R. (1992). Putting it all together: Solving the reading assessment puzzle. *Reading Teacher, 46,* 26–37.

Farr, R. (1999). Putting it all together: Solving the reading assessment puzzle. In S. J. Barrentine (Ed.), *Reading assessment: Principles and practices for elementary teachers* (pp. 44–56). Newark. DE: International Reading Association.

Fountas, I., & Pinnell, G. S. (1996). *Guided reading: Good first teaching for all children.* Portsmouth, NH: Heinemann.

Francis, D. J., Fletcher, J. M., Catts, H. W., & Tomblin, J. B. (2005). Dimensions affecting the assessment of reading comprehension. In S. G. Paris & S. A. Stahl (Eds.), *Children's reading comprehension and assessment* (pp. 369–394). Mahwah, NJ: Erlbaum.

Fuchs, D., & Fuchs, L. S. (2006). Introduction to response to intervention: What, why and how valid is it? *Reading Research Quarterly, 41,* 93–99.

Fuchs, L. S., & Fuchs, D. (1999). Monitoring student progress toward the development of reading competence: A review of three forms of classroom-based assessment. *School Psychology Review, 28,* 659–672.

Fuchs, L. S., Fuchs, D., Hosp, M., & Jenkins, J. R. (2001). Oral reading fluency as an indicator of reading competence: A theoretical, empirical and historical analysis. *Scientific Studies of Reading, 5,* 293–256.

Gambrell, L. B., & Mazzoni, S. A. (1999). Principles of best practice: Finding the common ground. In L. B. Gambrell, L. M. Morrow, S. B. Neuman, & M. Pressley (Eds.), *Best practices in literacy instruction* (pp. 11–21). New York: Guilford Press.

Gersten, R., & Dimino, J. A. (2006). RTI (response to intervention): Rethinking special education for students with reading difficulties (yet again). *Reading Research Quarterly, 41,* 99–108.

Glickman-Bond, J. (2006). *Creating and using rubrics in today's classrooms: A practical guide.* Norwood, MA: Christopher-Gordon.

Goldman, S. G., & Rakestraw, J. A. (2000). Structural aspects of constructing meaning from text. In M. L. Kamil, P. B. Mosenthal, P. D. Pearson, & R. Barr (Eds.), *Handbook of reading research* (Vol. 3, pp. 311–336). White Plains, NY: Longman.

Goodman, D., & Hambleton, R. K. (2005). Some misconceptions about large-scale educational assessments. In R. P. Phelps (Ed.), *Defending standardized testing* (pp. 91–110). Mahwah, NJ: Erlbaum.

Goodrich, H. (1996–1997). Understanding rubrics. *Educational Leadership, 54,* 14–17.

Graesser, A. C., & Bertus, E. L. (1998). The construction of causal inferences while reading expository texts on science and technology. *Scientific Studies of Reading, 2,* 247–269.

Grasser, A., Golding, J. M., & Long, D. L. (1991). Narrative representation and comprehension. In R. Barr, M. L. Kamil, P. B. Mosenthal, and P. D. Pearson (Eds.), *Handbook of reading research* (Vol. 2, pp. 171–205). White Plains, NY: Longman.

Gunning, T. (2006) *An analysis of student performance on basic and higher level comprehension questions: An exploratory study.* Paper presented at the National Reading Conference, Los Angeles.

Harmon, J., Hedrick, W., & Fox, E. A. (2000). A content analysis of vocabulary instruction in social studies textbooks for grades 4–8. *Elementary School Journal, 100,* 253–271.

Harmon, J. M., Hedrick, W. B., Soares, L., & Gress, M. (2007). Assessing vocabulary: Examining knowledge about words and about word learning. In J. R. Paratore & R. L. McCormack (Eds.), *Classroom literacy assessment: Making sense of what students know and do* (pp. 135–153). New York: Guilford Press.

Hasbrouck, J. E., & Tindal, G. (1992). Curriculum-based oral reading fluency norms for students in grades 2 through 5. *Teaching Exceptional Children, 24,* 41–44.

Hasbrouck, J. E., & Tindal, G. (2006). Oral reading fluency norms: A valuable assessment tool for reading teachers. *Reading Teacher, 59,* 636–643.

Hetzner, A. (2007, April 18). Waukesha group suggests changes in grading. *Milwaukee Journal Sentinel,* Section 3B.

Hiebert, E. H., & Kamil, M. L. (Eds.). (2005). *Teaching and learning vocabulary: Bringing research to practice.* Mahwah, NJ: Erlbaum.

Hill, B. C., Ruptic, C., & Norwick, L. (1998). *Classroom based assessment.* Norwood, MA: Christopher-Gordon.

Hirsch, E. D., Jr. (1987). *Cultural literacy: What every American needs to know.* Boston: Houghton Mifflin.

Hirsch, E. D., Jr., Kett, J., & Trefil, J. (1998). *The dictionary of cultural literacy: What every American needs to know.* Boston: Houghton Mifflin.

Individuals with Disabilities Education Improvement Act (IDEA). (2004) *Federal Register, 71,* pp. 46539–46845. Retrieved from *www.ed.gov/policy/speced/guid/idea/idea2004.html.*

Jennings, J., Caldwell, J. S., & Lerner, J. (2006). *Reading problems: Assessment and teaching strategies.* Boston: Pearson Education.

Johnson, D. D. (2001). *Vocabulary in the elementary and middle school.* Boston: Allyn & Bacon.

Joint Committee on Testing Practices. (2004). *Code of fair testing practices in education.* Retrieved from *www.apa.org/science/fairtestcode.html.*

Kamil, M. J., & Hiebert, E. H. (2005). Teaching and learning vocabulary: Perspectives and persistent issues. In M. J. Kamil & E. H. Hiebert (Eds.), *Teaching and learning vocabulary: Bringing research to practice* (pp. 1–26). Mahwah, NJ: Erlbaum.

Kamil, M. L., Intrator, S. M., & Kim, H. S. (2000). The effects of other technologies on literacy and language learning. In M. L. Kamil, P. B. Mosenthal, P. D. Pearson, & R. Barr (Eds.), *Handbook of reading research* (Vol. 3, pp. 771–788). White Plains, NY: Longman.

Kintsch, E. (2005). Comprehension theory as a guide for the design of thoughtful questions. *Topics in Language Disorders, 25,* 51–64.

Kintsch, W. (1998). *Comprehension: A paradigm for cognition.* Cambridge, UK: Cambridge University Press.

Kintsch, W., & Kintsch, E. (2005). Comprehension. In S. G. Paris & S. A. Stahl (Eds.), *Children's reading comprehension and assessment* (pp. 71–92). Mahwah, NJ: Erlbaum.

Kohn, A. (2000). Burnt at the high stakes. *Journal of Teacher Education, 51,* 315–327.

Kohn, A. (2001). Fighting the test: A practical guide to rescuing our schools. *Phi Delta Kappan, 82*(5), 349–357).

LaBerge, D., & Samuels, S. M. (1974). Toward a theory of automatic information processing in reading. *Cognitive Psychology, 6,* 293–323.

Leslie, L., & Caldwell, J. (1989). The qualitative reading inventory: Issues in the development of a diagnostic reading test. In S. McCormick & J. Zutell (Eds.), *Cognitive and social perspectives for literacy: Research and instruction* (pp. 413–419). Chicago: National Reading Conference.

Leslie, L., & Caldwell, J. (2001). *Qualitative reading inventory—3.* New York: Addison Wesley Longman.

Leslie, L., & Caldwell, J. (2006). *Qualitative reading inventory—4.* Boston: Allyn & Bacon.

Lewandowski, L. J., & Martens, B. K. (1990). Selecting and evaluating standardized reading tests. *Journal of Reading, 33,* 384–388.

Lipson, M. Y. (1983). The influence of religious affiliation on children's memory for text information. *Reading Research Quarterly, 18,* 448–457.

Loxterman, J. A., Beck, L. L., & McKeown, M. G. (1994). The effects of thinking aloud during reading on students' comprehension of more or less coherent text. *Reading Research Quarterly, 29,* 353–368.

Manzo, K. K. (2003, October 8). Teachers picking up tools to map instructional practices. *Education Week, 23,* 8.

Marzano, R. J. (2000). *Transforming classroom grading.* Alexandria, VA: Association for Supervision and Curriculum Development.

Marzano, R. J. (2003). *What works in schools: Translating research into action.* Alexandria, VA: Association for Supervision and Curriculum Development.

Marzano, R. J., Kendall, J. S., & Gaddy, B. B. (1999). *Essential knowledge: The debate over what American students should know.* Aurora, CO: McREL.

Mayer, R. E., & Moreno, R. (1998). A split-attention effect in multimedia learning: Evidence for dual processing systems in working memory. *Journal of Educational Psychology, 90,* 312–320.

Mayer, R. E., & Wittrock, M. C. (2006). Problem solving. In P. A. Alexander & P. H. Winne (Eds.), *Handbook of educational psychology* (pp. 287–303). Mahwah, NJ: Erlbaum.

McCook, J. E. (2006). *The RTI guide: Developing and implementing a model in your schools.* Horsham, PA: LRP Publications.

McMillan, J. H. (2000). Fundamental assessment principles for teachers and school administrators. *Practical Assessment, Research and Evaluation, 7.* Retrieved from *PAREonline.net/getvn.asp?v=7&n=8.*

McMillan, J. H. (2003). Understanding and improving teachers' classroom assessment decision making: Implications for theory and practice. *Educational Measurement: Issues and Practice, 22*(4), 34–43.

McMillan, J. H., Myran, S., & Workman, D. (2002). Elementary teachers' classroom assessment and grading practices. *Journal of Educational Research, 95*(4), 203–213.

Meisels, S. J., & Piker, R. A. (2001). *An analysis of early literacy assessments used for instruction.* Retrieved from *www.ciera.org/library/reports/inquiry-2/2-013/2-013.html.*

Meloth, M., & Deering, P. (1994). Task talk and task awareness under different cooperative learning conditions. *American Education Research Journal, 31,* 138–165.

MetaMerics, Inc. (2001). *How is readability determined within the Lexile Framework for reading?* Durham, NC: MetaMetrics.

Meyer, B. J. F. (2003). Text coherence and readability. *Topics in Language Disorders, 23,* pp. 204–225. Retrieved from *www.topicsinlanguagedisorders.com.*

Meyer, B. J. F., & Rice, G. E. (1984). The structure of text. In P. D. Pearson, R. Barr, M. L. Kamil, & P. B. Mosenthal (Eds.), *Handbook of reading research* (Vol. 1, pp. 319–352). White Plains, NY: Longman.

Moreno, R., & Mayer, R. E. (2000). A learner-centered approach to multimedia explanations: Deriving instructional design principles from cognitive theory. *Interactive*

Multimedia Electronic Journal of Computer-Enhanced Learning. Retrieved from *imej.wfu.edu/articles/2000/2/05/index.asp.*

Myers, J. (1988). Diagnosis diagnosed: Twenty years after. *Professional School Psychology, 3,* 123–134.

Myers, J., & Lytle, S. (1986). Assessment of the learning process. *Exceptional Children, 53,* 113–144.

Myers, J., Lytle, S., Palladino, D., Devenpeck, G., & Green, M. (1990). Think-aloud protocol analysis: An investigation of reading comprehension strategies in fourth and fifth grade students. *Journal of Psychoeducational Assessment, 8,* 112–127.

Nagy, W. (2005). Why vocabulary instruction needs to be long-term and comprehensive. In M. J. Kamil & E. H. Hiebert (Eds.), *Teaching and learning vocabulary: Bringing research to practice* (pp. 27–44). Mahwah, NJ: Erlbaum.

National Reading Panel. (2000). *Report of the National Reading Panel teaching children to read: An evidence-based assessment of scientific-based literature on reading and its implications for reading instruction.* Washington, DC: National Institute of Child Health and Human Development.

National Research Council Committee on the Foundations of Assessment. (2001). *Knowing what students know: The science and design of educational assessment* (J. Pelligrino, N. Chudowsky, & R. Glaser, Eds.). Washington, DC: National Academy Press.

Nokes, J. D., & Dole, J. A. (2004). Helping adolescent readers through explicit strategy instruction. In T. L. Jetton & J. A. Dole (Eds.), *Adolescent literacy research and practice* (pp. 162–182). New York: Guilford Press.

Norlin, J. W. (2005). *NCLB and AYP: Consequences of failure.* Horsham, PA: LRP Publications.

Olshavsky, J. E. (1976). Reading as problem solving: An investigation of strategies. *Reading Research Quarterly, 4,* 654–674.

Olson, G. M., Duffy, S. A., & Mack, R. L. (1984). Thinking out loud as a method for studying real-time comprehension processes. In D. E. Kieras & M. A. Just (Eds.), *New methods in reading comprehension research* (pp. 245–278). Hillsdale, NJ: Erlbaum.

Olson, L. (1995, June 14). Cards on the table. *Education Week,* 23–28.

Oster, L. (2001). Using the think-aloud for reading instruction. *Reading Teacher, 55,* 64–74.

Paris, S. G., Carpenter, R. D., Paris, A. H., & Hamilton, E. E. (2005). In S. G. Paris & S. A. Stahl (Eds.), *Children's reading comprehension and assessment* (pp. 131–160). Mahwah, NJ: Erlbaum.

Paris, S. G., & Paris, A. H. (2001). Classroom applications of research on self-regulated learning. *Educational Psychologist, 36,* 89–101.

Pearson, P. D., & Hamm, D. N. (2005). The assessment of reading comprehension: A review of practices—past, present and future. In S. G. Paris & S. A. Stahl (Eds.), *Children's reading comprehension and assessment* (pp. 13–70). Mahwah, NJ: Erlbaum.

Pearson, P. D., Hansen, J., & Gordon, C. (1979). The effect of background knowledge on young children's comprehension of explicit and implicit information. *Journal of Reading Behavior, 11,* 201–209.

Pearson, P. D., Hiebert, E. H., & Kamil, M. (2007). Vocabulary assessment: What we know and what we need to learn. *Reading Research Quarterly, 42,* 282–297.

Pellegrino, J. W., Chudowsky, N., & Glaser, R. (Eds.). (2001). Knowing what students know: The science and design of educational assessment. Washington, DC: National Academy Press.

Phelps, R. P. (2005). The rich, robust research literature on testing's achievement benefits. In R. P. Phelps (Ed.), *Defending standardized testing* (pp. 55–90). Mahwah, NJ: Erlbaum.

Popham, W. J. (2001). *The truth about testing: An educator's call to action.* Alexandria, VA: Association for Supervision and Curriculum Development.

Popham, W. J. (2003). *Test better, teach better: The instructional role of assessment.* Alexandria, VA: Association for Supervision and Curriculum Development.

Pressley, M., & Afflerbach, P. (1995). *Verbal protocols of reading: The nature of constructively responsive reading.* Hillsdale, NJ: Erlbaum.

Pritchard, R. (1990). The evolution of instropective methodology and its implication for studying the reading process. *Reading Psychology, 11,* 1–13.

RAND Reading Study Group. (2002). *Reading for understanding: Toward an R & D program in reading comprehension.* Retrieved from *www.rand.org/publications/MR/ MR1465/.*

Raphael, T. E. (1982). Question-answering strategies for children. *Reading Teacher, 36,* 186–190.

Raphael, T. E. (1986). Teaching question–answer relationships, revisited. *Reading Teacher, 39,* 516–522.

Raphael, T., Highfield, K., & Au, K. (2006). *QAR now: Question answer relationships.* New York: Scholastic.

Rasinski, T. V. (2003). *The fluent reader: Oral reading strategies for building word recognition, fluency, and comprehension.* New York: Scholastic Professional Books.

Rasinski, T. V., Padak, N. D., Linek, W. L., & Sturdevant, E. (1994). Effects of fluency development on urban second graders. *Journal of Educational Research, 87,* 158–165.

Rasool, J. M., & Royer, J. M. (2001). Assessment of reading comprehension using the sentence verification technique: Evidence from narrative and descriptive texts. *Journal of Educational Research, 78,* 180–184.

Ravid, R. (2000). *Practical statistics for educators.* Lanham, MD: University Press of America.

Recht, D. R., & Leslie, L. (1988). The effects of prior knowledge on good and poor readers' memory for text. *Journal of Educational Psychology, 80,* 16–20.

Rosenshine, B., Meister, C., & Chapman, S. (1996). Teaching students to generate questions: A review of the intervention studies. *Review of Educational Research, 66,* 181–221

Royer, J. M. (2001). Developing reading and listening comprehension tests based on the sentence verification technique (SVT). *Journal of Adolescent and Adult Literacy, 45,* 30–41.

Royer, J. M., Abranovic, W. A., & Sinatra, G. (1987). Using entering reading performance as a predictor of course performance in college classes. *Journal of Educational Psychology, 79,* 19–26.

Royer, J. M., & Carlo, M. S. (1991). Assessing the language acquisition progress of limited-English proficient students: Problems and a new alternative. *Applied Measurement in Education, 4,* 85–113.

Royer, J. M., Greene, B. A., & Sinatra, G. M. (1987). The sentence verification technique: A practical procedure for testing comprehension. *Journal of Reading, 30,* 14–22.

Royer, J. M., Hastings, C. N., & Hook, C. (1979). A sentence verification technique for measuring reading comprehension. *Journal of Reading Behavior, 11,* 355–363.

Royer, J. M., Lynch, D. J., Hambleton, R. K., & Bulgareli, C. (1984). Using the sentence verification technique to assess the comprehension of technical text as a function of subject matter expertise. *American Education Research Journal, 21,* 839–869.

Sadowski, M., Goetz, E. T., & Fritz, J. B. (1993). Impact of concreteness on comprehensibility, interest, and memory for text: Implications for dual coding theory and text design. *Journal of Educational Psychology, 85,* 291–304.

Sarroub, L., & Pearson, P. D. (1998). Two steps forward, three steps back: The stormy history of reading comprehension assessment. *Clearing House, 72,* 97–105.

Schmoker, M. (1996). *Results: The key to continuous school improvement.* Alexandria, VA: Association for Supervision and Curriculum Development.

Schmoker, M. (2006). *Results now.* Alexandria, VA: Association for Supervision and Curriculum Development.

Schmoker, M., & Marzano, R. (1999). Realizing the promise of standards-based education. *Educational Leadership, 56*(6), 17–21.

Smith, J. K. (2003). Reconsidering reliability in classroom assessment and grading. *Educational Measurement, Issues and Practices, 22,* 26–33.

Smith, L. A. (2006). Think-aloud mysteries: Using structured, sentence-by-sentence text passages to teach comprehension strategies. *Reading Teacher, 59,* 764–773.

Smith, M. L., & Rottenburg, C. (1991). Unintended consequences of external testing in elementary schools. *Educational Measurement: Issues and Practices, 10,* 7–11.

Snow, C. E., Burns, M. S., & Griffin, P. (1998). *Preventing reading difficulties in young children.* Washington, DC: National Academy Press.

Solomon, P. G. (1998). *The curriculum bridge: From standards to actual classroom practice.* Thousand Oaks, CA: Corwin Press.

Southwest Educational Development Laboratory. (2007). *Reading assessment database.* Retrieved from *www.sedl.org/reading/rad/list.html.*

Stahl, S. A. (1986). Three principles of effective vocabulary instruction. *Journal of Reading, 29,* 662–668.

Stahl, S. A. (2005). Four problems with teaching word meanings (and what to do to make vocabulary an integral part of instruction). In E. H. Hiebert & M. J. Kamil (Eds.), *Teaching and learning vocabulary: Bringing research to practice* (pp. 95–115). Mahwah, NJ: Erlbaum.

Stahl, S. A., & Fairbanks, M. M. (1986). The effects of vocabulary instruction: A model-based meta-analysis. *Review of Educational Research, 56,* 72–110.

Stahl, S. A., & Heubach, K. (1993). *Changing reading instruction in second grade: A fluency-oriented program.* Athens: University of Georgia. National Reading Research Center.

Stahl, S. A., & Nagy, W. E. (2006). *Teaching word meanings.* Mahwah, NJ: Erlbaum.

Stanovich, K. E. (1986). Matthew effects in reading: Some consequences of individual differences in the acquisition of literacy. *Reading Research Quarterly, 21,* 360–407.

Sticht, T. G., & James, J. H. (1984). Listening and reading. In P. D. Pearson, R. Barr, M. L. Kamil, & P. B. Mosenthal (Eds.), *Handbook of reading research* (Vol. 1, pp. 293–318). White Plains, NY: Longman.

Taft, M. L., & Leslie, L. (1985). The effects of prior knowledge and oral reading accuracy on miscues and comprehension. *Journal of Reading Behavior, 17,* 163–179.

Taylor, B. M. (1982). Text structure and children's comprehension and memory for expository material. *Journal of Educational Psychology, 74,* 323–340.

Trabasso, T., & Magliano, J. P. (1996a). Conscious understanding during reading. *Discourse Processes, 21,* 255–287.

Trabasso, T., & Magliano, J. P. (1996b). How do children understand what they read and what can we do to help them? In M. Graves, P. van den Broek, & B. Taylor (Eds.), *The first R: A right of all children* (pp. 158–181). New York: Columbia University Press.

Trice, A. D. (2000). *A handbook of classroom assessment.* New York: Addison Wesley Longman.

U.S. Department of Education. (2005). *Testing: Frequently asked questions.* Retrieved from *www.ed.gov/print/nclb/accountability/ayp/testing-faq.html.*

Van den Broek, P., Kendeou, P., Kremer, K., Lynch, J., Butler, J., White, M. J., et al. (2005). Comprehension. In S. G. Paris & S. A. Stahl (Eds.), *Children's reading comprehension and assessment* (pp. 107–130). Mahwah, NJ: Erlbaum.

Wade, S. E., & Moje, E. B. (2000). The role of text in classroom learning. In M. L. Kamil, P. B. Mosenthal, P. D. Pearson, and R. Barr (Eds.), *Handbook of reading research* (Vol. 3, pp. 609–628). Mahwah, NJ: Erlbaum.

Wiggens, G. (1989). A true test: Toward more authentic and equitable assessment. *Phi Delta Kappan, 70,* 703–713.

Wiggens, G., & McTighe, J. (1998) *Understanding by design.* Alexandria, VA: Association for Supervision and Curriculum Development.

Wilhelm, J. D. (2001). *Improving comprehension with think-aloud strategies.* New York: Scholastic Professional Books.

Wilkinson, L. C., & Silliman, E. R. (2000). Classroom language and literacy learning, In M. L. Kamil, P. B. Mosenthal, P. D. Pearson, & R. Barr (Eds.), (Vol. 3, pp. 337–360). Mahwah, NJ: Erlbaum.

Winograd, P., & Arrington, H. J. (1999). Best practices in literacy assessment. In L. B. Gambrell, L. M. Morrow, S. B. Neuman, & M. Pressley (Eds.), *Best practices in literacy instruction* (pp. 210–244). New York: Guilford Press.

Wisconsin Department of Public Instruction. (1998). Wisconsin's model academic standards for social studies. Madison: Wisconsin Department of Public Instruction.

Wise, A. (2004, September 29). Teaching teams: A 21st-century paradigm for organizing America's schools. *Education Week, 24*(5), 23.

Wright, J. (2007). *RTI toolkit: A practical guide for schools.* Port Chester, NY: Dude Publishing.

Zakaluk, B. L., & Samuels, S. J. (1988). *Readability: Its past, present and future.* Newark, DE: International Reading Association.

Index